ACE

Aurally Coded English

SPELLING DICTIONARY

FOURTH EDITION

David Moseley

LDA

ACE INDEX

Index

Sound	N	O	P	Q	R	S	T	U	V	W	X	Y	Z	Word
a	21	—	22	24	24	25	28	29	29	30	—	30	30	ACTIVE CAT
e	45	45	46	47	48	50	52	53	53	54	54	55	55	HEALTHY ELEPHANT
i	81	81	82	83	84	87	90	91	91	92	—	—	93	BIG PIGLET
o	105	106	108	109	110	111	113	113	114	114	—	115	115	WATCHFUL DOG
u oo	127	127	128	128	129	130	133	134	136	136	—	136	—	DUCK AND WOODPECKER

Sound	N	O	P	Q	R	S	T	U	V	W	X	Y	Z	Word
ae	146	147	147	148	148	149	151	151	151	152	—	152	—	BABY SNAIL
ee	165	165	166	167	167	169	172	—	173	174	—	175	175	BREEDING EAGLE
ie	187	187	188	189	189	190	192	—	193	193	194	—	194	LIVELY LION
oe	202	203	204	206	206	207	208	208	208	209	—	209	209	LONELY GOAT
ue oo	218	218	219	219	220	221	222	223	223	223	—	224	224	SMOOTH NEWT

Sound	N	O	P	Q	R	S	T	U	V	W	X	Y	Z	Word
ar	232	—	233	233	233	234	235	—	235	—	—	235	235	BASKING SHARK
air	—	—	239	—	240	240	241	—	241	241	—	—	—	RARE BEAR
er	249	249	250	251	251	252	253	254	254	255	—	255	—	EARLY BIRD WITH WORM
or	263	264	265	266	266	267	268	268	268	269	—	269	—	WARLIKE HORSE
oi	273	273	274	274	274	275	275	—	275	—	—	—	—	JOYFUL OYSTER
ou	281	281	282	—	282	283	283	—	284	284	—	284	—	AN OWL SOUND

Acknowledgements

The author would like to thank all those who took part in the original field trials in England, Northern Ireland, Scotland and Wales. Special thanks are due to Bess Moseley for the animal drawings, to Gwyn Singleton for editorial and proofreading assistance and to George Macbride for help in meeting the pronunciation requirements of Scottish users. I am also grateful for many suggestions for improvement made by users of the *ACE Spelling Dictionary* since its first publication in 1986.

ACE Spelling Dictionary

ISBN-13: 978-1-85503-505-8

First edition © David Moseley and Catherine Nicol
Second edition © David Moseley
Third edition © David Moseley
Fourth edition © David Moseley 2011

Printed in the UK for LDA
Pintail Close, Victoria Business Park, Nottingham, NG4 2SG, UK

Contents

Introduction

How can you look up a word in a dictionary if you do not know how to spell it?

The *ACE Spelling Dictionary* is designed for writers of all ages who need to check spellings, and it is intended for use in educational settings and at home. The unique index always directs you to the page you need, taking away the frustration of hunting around in a conventional dictionary. After a little practice you will be able to find any word in just a few seconds, many times faster than in other dictionaries.

Another great advantage of using the ACE dictionary is that it actually improves your spelling. This is because the words are listed by vowel sound in alphabetical columns. This makes common spelling patterns stand out and draws attention to unusual features. Using the Index and choosing the correct syllable column on a page is itself a learning process, as you have to think about how a word sounds when spoken. This distinguishes the ACE dictionary from an electronic spelling checker, which forces the writer to attempt a spelling and then provides a long list of words from which little can be learned. Using the ACE dictionary is largely error free and many safety-nets are provided to take account of regional differences in pronunciation, indistinct speech and phonetically based guesswork.

The main concern of any writer, whatever their age, is communication. All too often difficulty with spelling gets in the way of expression and many people become frustrated to the point of giving up.

English spelling often appears illogical and does not obey simple rules. How to represent the vowel sounds ('singing-like' sounds like *aaaah* made with the mouth open) can be a real headache as you have to choose between two hundred ways of representing the eighteen vowel sounds of spoken English. This may lead to confusion and delay when looking up words in a standard dictionary.

The *ACE Spelling Dictionary* is aurally coded – it confronts the multitude of spelling patterns by grouping words according to the vowel sounds heard at or near the beginning of each word. In the *ACE Spelling Dictionary* the eighteen vowel sounds are reduced to sixteen by grouping together two related pairs.

To use the dictionary successfully you need to **LISTEN** for the first clear vowel sound and the initial letter, **LOOK UP** the word on the page shown on the index table and **LEARN** something about how the word is spelled. The process of choosing the correct column of words according to the number of spoken syllables is an important built-in aid to learning.

After reading this introduction you can practise finding words on your own, or with a teacher or helper. Learning to use the *ACE Spelling Dictionary* with a teacher or helper (see p. xi) includes four lessons that are suitable for use by individuals or in groups.

The Index is the key to the sixteen different sections of the dictionary. Once you have understood how it works, you should never again have to ask someone else how to spell a word that is in the ACE dictionary. Eventually you will be able to save time by going straight to the right vowel-sound section without using the Index at all.

The 20,000-word vocabulary contained in the *ACE Spelling Dictionary* is extensive, up to date and suitable for both formal and informal types of writing. While beginning writers will recognise most of the shorter words in the one- and two-syllable columns, older learners will find that specialised vocabulary for academic subjects is also included.

The *ACE Spelling Dictionary* consists of three main parts, each including five or six sections. All the words in a section have the same or nearly the same vowel sound.

The first five sections of words with 'short' vowel sounds are printed on pale blue paper. These vowel sounds are usually introduced at an early stage of phonic instruction:

Part 1

/a/ as in cat
/e/ as in elephant
/i/ as in pig
/o/ as in dog
/u/ as in duck and /oo/ as in woodpecker

Words containing vowel sounds that sound like or rhyme with letter names are printed on darker blue paper. These are 'long' vowel sounds:

Part 2

/ae/ as in snail
/ee/ as in eagle
/ie/ as in lion
/oe/ as in goat
/ue/ as in newt and /oo/ as in smooth

The last six sections are also printed on pale blue paper and include spellings with the letter 'r' and two double sounds. These sounds are often spoken in English as 'long' vowels (but not when the 'r' is rolled):

Part 3

/ar/ as in shark
/air/ as in bear
/er/ as in worm
/or/ as in horse
/oi/ as in oyster
/ou/ as in owl

The *ACE Spelling Dictionary* provides word meanings when two or more words sound the same or nearly the same. This allows you to choose the meaning you want. The options are usually nearby in the same column. The ACE dictionary is in fact the best resource there is for the study of such easily confused words, which are called *homonyms* (meaning 'same name').

Using the *ACE Spelling Dictionary* to look up spellings will make it easier to use other dictionaries for looking up meanings. The words within each section are arranged alphabetically, with subsections beginning with the same two letters (e.g. sc- sh- si- sk- sl- sm- sn- sp- sq- st- sw-) separated visually. Finding a word within a column makes use of exactly the same dictionary skills as finding a word in a dictionary that gives full definitions.

At the back of the book there is a section on improving spelling. The main focus is on much-needed words, especially those that are often misspelled. Personalised learning strategies for learning and correcting spellings are provided, as well as suggestions for studying spelling patterns. It is a good idea to write down unusual spellings in a personal spelling book, noting the 'tricky' part or parts and learning them by well-proven methods such as simultaneous oral spelling (naming the letters as you write them in chunks), 'look–say–cover–write–check' or visualisation with eyes closed. These and many more learning activities for use with the *ACE Spelling Dictionary* are also available in a separate publication, *ACE Spelling Activities* (Moseley and Singleton, 1993).

How to use the *ACE Spelling Dictionary* (self-help guide)

You need to understand the sixteen vowel sections of the Index and the clear vowel sounds they cover. To do this, open the dictionary at each of the sixteen sections in turn. You will see that each section has a different vowel sound symbol at the top right of each page. Read aloud a number of the shorter words in each section until you can recognise that they contain similar clear vowel sounds.

Make sure that you can say aloud the vowel sound symbols as listed on page viii and printed in blue at the top right-hand corner of each dictionary page. Outside the dictionary itself, slashes (e.g. /or/) are used to indicate sounds rather than letters.

To use the Index you have to do two things:
• Say the first clear vowel sound (the one that 'stands out').
• Name what you think is the first letter.

Reading across from the vowel sound and down from the first letter will take you to the page you need. Then you choose the correct column, according to the number of syllables in the word. Each column has one or more stars at the top showing the number of syllables. To begin with, say the word slowly and tap out the syllables at the same time. Try this rhyme if you need help:

* One tap for 'fun'	*** Three taps for 'stadium'
** And two for 'begun';	**** And four for 'gymnasium'.

If you want to find the word 'skyscraper' on page 190, for example, look in the column of three-syllable words. Words containing four or more syllables are on the right-hand side of each page. You will notice that every syllable contains a vowel sound.

The basic routine

To look up 'rhinoceros':

First	Say 'rhi' (say the first syllable really slowly)	Say /ie/ (say the vowel sound on its own)	Use the ACE Index (it's on pages ii and iii)
Second	Find /ie/ (as in lion) (the vowel sound /ie/ is next to the lion picture)	Find 'R' (from the alphabet across the top)	Go along from /ie/ and down from 'R' (you'll get to page 189)
Third	Find page 189 (in Part 2)	Open book in Part 2 (the darker blue pages)	Turn to page 189
Fourth	Tap out rhi-no-ce-ros (**** 4 syllables)	Go to the 4th column (**** 4 or more syllables)	**YOU'VE GOT IT!**

Neutral vowel sounds in the first syllable
(what the white boxes are for)

When using the ACE Index, go for a strong, clear vowel sound in the first or second syllable, one that really stands out. Neutral vowel sounds are not clear sounds and require very little effort to pronounce. They are not given a separate section in the ACE Index. So if you think that there is a neutral vowel in the first syllable of the word you want (e.g. annoy, prepare, observe, success), go for the vowel sound in the second syllable – in these words the sounds /oi/ /air/ /er/ and /e/.

The Scottish pronunciation of vowel sounds is much clearer than is usual in England, making virtually no use of neutral vowels. It is therefore important that Scottish users look up words according to the vowel sound in the syllable with the first strong beat.

Say you want to look up 'suspicious'. The vowel sound that stands out when you say the word is the /i/ sound in the second syllable, and you will find 'suspicious' in the /i/ section on page 88. However, if you were to go for the weaker sound in the first syllable, you would still find the word, on page 132, in the white 'neutral vowel' box. So, if you cannot see a word where you think it should be, see if it is in a white box. You will soon notice that the weak neutral vowels sound much the same as each other, rather like a quiet grunt or squeak.

Listen to the way you pronounce 'balloon', for example:

Say 'buh'	Say 'uh'	It's a neutral sound
(start to say the word)	(this sound is weak and unclear)	(it's not like the /a/ sound in 'cat')

To find 'balloon' in the dictionary, listen for the clear vowel sound (in the second syllable):

Say 'balloo'	Say /oo/	Then use the Index

In all the following words the strong beat (stress) is on the second syllable. You will probably succeed in finding the words if you try to identify the letters used for the first (neutral) vowel sound. However, it is easier to go by the first strong, clear vowel sound.

above	SHORT /u/	laboratory	SHORT /o/
advertisement	SOUND /er/	magician	SHORT /i/
appearance	LONG /ee/	manoeuvre	LONG /oo/
approach	LONG /oe/	observer	SOUND /er/
because	SHORT /o/	particular	SHORT /i/
before	SOUND /or/	performer	SOUND /or/
circumference	SHORT /u/	potatoes	LONG /ae/
collision	SHORT /i/	production	SHORT /u/
conductor	SHORT /u/	remain	LONG /ae/
confetti	SHORT /e/	remarkable	SOUND /ar/
despair	SOUND /air/	request	SHORT /e/
destroy	SOUND /oi/	reverse	SOUND /er/
discuss	SHORT /u/	surrender	SHORT /e/
emotional	LONG /oe/	surroundings	SOUND /ou/
enough	SHORT /u/	survivor	LONG /ie/
exhaust	SOUND /or/	towards	SOUND /or/
guitar	SOUND /ar/	trapeze	LONG /ee/
infectious	SHORT /e/	vocabulary	SHORT /a/

Learning to use the *ACE Spelling Dictionary* with a teacher or helper

Lesson 1 (counting syllables)

Aim: You need to be able to say how many syllables there are in any spoken word (up to four syllables). Counting syllables is a skill which is easier than counting phonemes and which can be built up from the age of 5. The 'Clap and Count' activity in *Letters and Sounds* (DES, 2007) is intended as an aid to both word recognition and spelling.

In one-to-one work a parent or friend should read out the words and say whether your responses are correct. A teacher can work with a group or whole class, asking for individual or group responses. The three stages below should be followed.

1 The teacher/helper (T/H) says a word slowly and taps out the syllables at the same time. You repeat the word and tap out the syllables. The T/H asks, 'How many taps?' This should be done with the following words, or with people's names.

play-ground	win-dow	ba-na-na	mud	un-for-tu-nate
Tap - Tap	Tap - Tap	Tap - Tap - Tap	Tap	Tap - Tap - Tap - Tap

Repeat more slowly if necessary, with the words in a different order.

2 The T/H says a word without tapping and asks you to repeat the word and tap it out. Each time the T/H asks, 'How many taps?' This is done with words from the following list until you tap out ten words correctly.

* * *	newspaper	* *	picture	*	paint	* * * *	television
* *	spider	*	mice	* *	monster	* * *	dinosaur
* *	postman	* *	burglar	* * *	acrobat	* * * *	politician
* *	pancake	* * *	margarine	* * * *	supermarket	* *	kitchen
*	crash	* * * *	helicopter	* *	rocket	* * *	motorbike

3 The T/H says a word and simply asks, 'How many syllables?' You carry on, taking words at random from the list below, until you achieve a success rate of 19/20.

* *	money	*	shop	* *	birthday	* *	present
* *	bedroom	*	door	* * *	wallpaper	*	stairs
* * *	holidays	*	weeks	* * *	underground	* * * *	underwater
* * *	crocodile	* * * *	alligator	*	shark	* *	danger
* * * *	caterpillar	*	moth	* * *	butterfly	*	eggs
* *	rabbit	* * * *	invisible	*	hat	* *	magic
*	win	* * *	manager	* *	football	* * * *	competition
* * * *	everybody	* *	children	* *	mother	* * *	grandfather
*	clock	* *	morning	* * *	afternoon	* * *	yesterday
* * * *	mysterious	* * *	horrible	* * *	beautiful	* * *	exciting

Lesson 2 (vowel sounds in Part 2)

Aims: You will correctly

a) identify long vowel sounds in words of one and two syllables

b) use the long vowel sounds part of the Index to find the page numbers for various words

c) look up words in the darker blue part of the dictionary.

1 Begin with listening and speaking activities only, starting with the long vowel animal names: **snail, eagle, lion, goat** and **newt**.

The T/H asks about a vowel sound in each of the five long vowel animal names. The expected answers are either 'yes' or 'no'; for example, 'Can you hear /ae/ in **snail**?' 'Can you hear /ee/ in **snail**? The vowel sounds can be made longer and louder if necessary. If you need further practice, your T/H may also ask you to identify these vowel sounds, giving a choice of three (e.g. 'What is the vowel sound in **snail**: /ae/, /ee/ or /ie/?)'. You will need to continue until you can correctly identify the sounds.

When you are confident and accurate with the animal names, you may move on to listening for long vowel sounds in other words, answering questions like 'Can you hear /ee/ in **fine**?' 'Can you hear /ae/ in **baby**?' Carry on until you can do this correctly with most words of one or two syllables.

It may also be helpful to play Odd Vowel Out with groups of four words. For example, your T/H asks which is the odd one out in:

• pail, sail, tail, tile
• cheap, choose, cheat, beach
• mice, dive, save, smile
• heap, slope, coach, slow
• stew, queue, duke, spoke.

You may then be asked to explain the difference between the two vowel sounds; for example, '**Tile** has an /ie/ sound, but the others have an /ae/ sound'.

2 Practise using the darker blue part of the Index to find page numbers. If working in a group each person should have an ACE dictionary to use (at least one between two) or else a copy of the Index from pages ii and iii. The T/H may like to make an OHT from *ACE Spelling Activities* (Moseley and Singleton, 1993) or display the Index on a whiteboard for class instruction.

Referring to the animal picture words, your T/H asks you to point first to the snail picture next to the letters 'ae' that stand for the sound /ae/. They then ask which letter 'snail' begins with and ask you to find the letter in the alphabet across the top of the page. You are then shown how to move one finger along the line of page numbers and another finger down, until they meet at a page number. **Snail** is on page 149. The same exercise is repeated with **eagle** (p. 157), **lion** (p. 185), **goat** (p. 199) and **newt** (p. 218). There is no reason why you should not look in the dictionary to find these words. In the case of **eagle** you will have to look in the second column.

You can then practise finding page numbers with some more animal words: **ape, beaver, bison, mule, poodle, reindeer, sheep, snake, tiger, whale**. This time you will need to listen for the vowel sound, find the correct sound symbol and confirm your choice with the animal picture. For example, what is the first vowel sound in **tiger**? It is /ie/, which you can also hear in **lion**.

Here are some more long vowel topic lists that you may use until you have mastered using the Index to find page numbers.

---

bacon, cake, cereal, cheese, doughnut, mousse, pie, steak, trifle, tuna

beans, beetroot, coleslaw, cucumber, leeks, maize, peanuts, peas, seaweed, swede

apricot, coconut, dates, grapefruit, lime, peach, pineapple, prunes, raisins, rhubarb

basin, bowl, knife, ladle, microwave, plate, scales, soap, teapot, toast

---

3 Now you are ready to look up words from the above lists or elsewhere in the darker blue part of the dictionary itself. After turning to the right page, say the word, tap out and count the syllables and then search down the appropriate column. If there is a homonym (e.g. leaks/leeks, stake/steak), check the meaning. Where the word is not given in plural form (e.g. prune), an 's' should be added. Note that in one case (swede) the target word is in a column that extends to three pages.

Lesson 3 (vowel sounds in Parts 1 and 2)

Aims: You will correctly

a) identify short vowel sounds in words of one and two syllables
b) use the short vowel sounds part of the Index to find the page numbers for various words
c) look up words in the first two parts of the dictionary.

1 Begin with listening and speaking activities only, starting with the short vowel animal names: **cat, elephant, pig, dog, duck** and **woodpecker**.

Your T/H asks about a vowel sound in each of the six short vowel animal names. The expected answers are either 'yes' or 'no'; for example, 'Can you hear /a/ in **cat**?' 'Can you hear /e/ in **pig**?' If you need further practice, your T/H may also ask you to identify these vowel sounds, giving a choice of three (e.g. 'What is the vowel sound in cat: /ae/, /a/ or /e/?') You will need to continue until you can correctly identify the sounds.

When you are confident and accurate with the animal names, you can move on to listening for short vowel sounds in other words, answering questions like 'Can you hear /a/ in **active**?' 'Can you hear /i/ in **big**?' Carry on until you can do this correctly with most words of one or two syllables.

It may also be helpful to play Odd Vowel Out with groups of four words. For example, your T/H asks which is the odd one out in:

• pat, fat, mat, pet
• nest, fist, chest, best
• giggle, wiggle, waggle, jiggle
• slope, stop, clock, stock
• shut, dust, shock, must
• look, book, cooker, cooler.

You may then be asked to explain the difference between the two vowel sounds; for example, '**Pet** has an /e/ sound, but the others have an /a/ sound.'

2 Practise using the first two parts of the Index to find page numbers, first for short and then for both short and long vowel words. If working in a group, each person should have an ACE dictionary to use (at least one between two) or else a copy of the Index from pages ii and iii. Teachers may like to make an OHT from *ACE Spelling Activities* or display the Index on a whiteboard for class instruction.

Referring to the animal picture words, your T/H asks you to point first to the cat picture next to the letter 'a' that stands for the sound /a/. They then ask which letter 'cat' begins with and ask you to find the letter in the alphabet across the top of the page. You will remember how to move one finger along the line of page numbers and another finger down, until they meet at the page number you want. **Cat** is on page 7. The same exercise is then repeated with **elephant** (p. 36), **pig** (p. 82), **dog** (p. 99), **duck** (p. 120) and **woodpecker** (p. 136). There is no reason why you should not look in the dictionary to find these words. In the cases of **elephant** and **woodpecker** you will have to look in the third column.

You can then practise finding page numbers with some more animal words: **camel, donkey, frog, hedgehog, kangaroo, leopard, monkey, pigeon, rabbit, rook**. This time you will need to listen for the vowel sound, find the correct sound symbol and confirm your choice with the animal picture. For example, what is the first vowel sound in **rabbit**? It is /a/, which you can also hear in **cat**.

Here are some more short vowel topic lists that you may use until you have mastered using the Index to find page numbers.

---

biscuit, bread, butter, chicken, chocolate, crisps, haddock, jam, popcorn, egg
broccoli, cabbage, cauliflower, celery, lettuce, mushroom, onion, pepper, pumpkin, spinach
apple, blackberry, cherry, damson, fig, lemon, melon, orange, plum, tangerine
bottle, brush, clock, fridge, matches, mirror, rack, scissors, sieve, whisk

---

After working with the short vowel part of the Index, you can practise finding the page numbers for both short and long vowel words from the following lists. If there is any confusion between short and long vowels, ask, for example, 'Is it short /a/ as in **cat**, or long /ae/ as in **snail**?' as appropriate.

---

black, blue, buff, crimson, gold, green, indigo, red, ruby, white
apron, boots, collar, dress, jeans, nightdress, shoes, sweater, tie, vest
bicycle, boat, glider, helicopter, motorcycle, scooter, submarine, train, van, yacht
bus, coach, cycle, ferry, hovercraft, liner, lorry, rocket, tricycle, truck
chewing, cooking, drinking, eating, helping, listening, nodding, sleeping, watching, writing
baker, bricklayer, cook, miner, optician, sailor, scientist, secretary, soldier, teacher

---

3 Now you are ready to look up words from the above lists or elsewhere in the first two parts of the dictionary. After turning to the right page, say the word, tap out and count the syllables and then search down the appropriate column. If there is a homonym (e.g. blue/blew, red/read), check the meaning. Where the word is not given in plural form (e.g. boot), an 's' should be added. Note that in some cases (apple, biscuit, bus, butter, crimson, drinking, fridge, indigo, matches, optician, orange, spinach, sweater) the target word is in a column that extends to two or more pages.

Lesson 4 (vowel sounds in Part 3)

Aims: You will correctly

a) identify vowel sounds in the third part of the dictionary, in words of one or two syllables

b) use the Index to find the page numbers for various words

c) look up words in all three parts of the dictionary.

1 Begin with listening and speaking activities only, starting with the animal names from the third part of the dictionary: **shark**, **bear**, **bird**, **horse**, **oyster** and **owl**.

Your T/H asks about a vowel sound in each of the six animal names. The expected answers are either 'yes' or 'no'; for example, 'Can you hear /ar/ in **shark**?' 'Can you hear /or/ in **owl**?' If you need further practice, your T/H may also ask you to identify these vowel sounds, giving a choice of three (e.g. 'What is the vowel sound in **shark**: /ar/, /ae/ or /or/?') You will need to continue until you can correctly identify the sounds.

When you are confident and accurate with the animal names, you can move on to listening for ACE part 3 vowel sounds in other words, answering questions like 'Can you hear /ar/ in **harmless**?' 'Can you hear /oi/ in **early**?' Carry on until you can do this correctly with most words of one or two syllables.

It may also be helpful to play Odd Vowel Out with groups of four words. For example, your T/H asks which is the odd one out in:

- car, fir, jar, tar
- stair, store, fair, chair
- farmer, nervous, person, service
- horse, north, south, score
- point, noise, choice, nice
- ground, grand, mountain, fountain.

You may then be asked to explain the difference between the two vowel sounds, for example, '**Fir** has an /er/ sound, but the others have an /ar/ sound.'

2 Practise using the third part of the Index to find page numbers, and then move on to all three parts. If working in a group, each person should have an ACE dictionary to use (at least one between two) or else a copy of the of the Index on pages ii and iii. The T/H may like to make an OHT from *ACE Spelling Activities* or display the Index on a whiteboard for class instruction.

Referring to the animal picture words, your T/H asks you to point first to the shark picture next to the letters 'ar', which stand for the sound /ar/. They then ask which letter 'shark' begins with and ask you to find the letter in the alphabet across the top of the page. You will remember how to move one finger along the line of page numbers and another finger down, until they meet at the page number you want. **Shark** is on page 234. The same exercise is then repeated with **rare** (p. 240), **worm** (p. 255), **warlike** (p. 269), **noisy** (p. 273) and **sound** (p. 283). There is no reason why you should not look in the dictionary to find these words. In the cases of **warlike** and **noisy** you will have to look in the second column.

You can then practise finding page numbers with some more animal words: **armadillo**, **cow**, **earthworm**, **hound**, **mouse**, **partridge**, **sardine**, **starfish**, **tortoise**. This time you will need to listen for the vowel sound, find the correct sound symbol and confirm your choice with the animal picture. For example, what is the first vowel sound in **partridge**? It is /ar/, which you can also hear in **shark**.

Here are some more topic lists that you may use until you have mastered using the Index to find page numbers.

burger, cornflakes, flour, lard, marmalade, oil, pork, prawn, sardine, trout
garlic, herbs, parsley, parsnips, pear, soya, sprouts, strawberry, turnip, walnut
boiler, carton, door, fork, jar, larder, margarine, starch, torch, towel

After working with the third part of the Index, you can practise finding the page numbers for words from any of the three parts, using the following lists. If there is any confusion between any pair of patterns, ask, for example, 'Is it /a/ or /ow/?' 'Is it /o/ or /ar/?' as appropriate.

aquamarine, brown, cream, ginger, grey, lilac, orange, pink, purple, rose, scarlet, silver, turquoise, violet, yellow

blouse, braces, coat, jacket, overalls, sandals, scarf, shorts, skirt, slippers, socks, sweater, tights, trainers, trousers

brushing, counting, cutting, ironing, learning, marking, painting, reading, serving, sewing, shaving, shopping, sweeping, swimming, working

actor, artist, dentist, diver, doctor, fisherman, hairdresser, joiner, journalist, musician, nurse, plumber, priest, tailor, warden

3 Now you are ready to look up words from the above lists or elsewhere in all three parts of the dictionary. Note that in some cases (aquamarine, cutting, slippers, sweeping, swimming) the target word is in a column which extends to two or more pages.

What you can achieve with ACE

As a learner:

- extend your vocabulary
- come to think well of yourself as a writer
- enjoy the processes of planning, writing, redrafting and proofreading
- never again have to ask how to spell a word
- spell correctly all the words you know, including homonyms ('sound-alikes')
- avoid confusing yourself by repeatedly misspelling certain words
- confidently use words that are hard to spell
- never limit the quantity and quality of what you write
- give priority to purpose, audience, communication and impact
- automatically improve rapid word recognition and spelling skills
- become familiar with common linguistic patterns and identify unusual spellings easily
- use the dictionary to search for words with rule-based features
- develop an interest in word derivations, patterns and families
- develop effective strategies for learning really hard spellings painlessly
- voluntarily study the words you want and need to learn
- improve alphabetical dictionary skills so you are more likely to use other dictionaries.

As a teacher/helper:

- use the ACE dictionary as a rich resource for phonic and linguistic instruction
- make spelling a positive experience as learners increasingly take responsibility for it
- develop personalised, paired and group learning approaches to word study
- meet and comfortably exceed all Key Stage spelling objectives
- have learners of all abilities proofread and correct their work from initial outline onwards
- see the quantity and quality of writing improve dramatically when the ACE dictionary is used daily
- ensure that learners can spell all specialist subject vocabulary up to A-level correctly.

A

*	**	***	***** **
act	aback	abacus es [abaci]	abnormally
*acts more than one	abbess es	abandon ed	abolition
act	abbey	abattoir	aboriginal
	abbot	abdomen	aborigine
add	abscess es	abnormal ly	absolutely
*adds does add	abseil	absentee	
*adze tool	absence	absolute	academic ally
	absent	abstraction	academy -ies
-aft	abstract		accentuate
		accident ally	accentuating
-alms	accent	accurate	accessory -ies
Alps	access es	acetate	accidental ly
	accessed	acquiesce d	accuracy
am	acid	acrobat	accurately
amp	acne	acronym	accusation
	acted	activate	acquiescence
an	acting	actively	acquisition
and	action	activist	acrobatic ally
*ant insect	active	actual ly	activity -ies
	actor	actuate	actuality -ies
apt	actress es		actually
	actual ly	adamant	acupuncture
as		adapter / adaptor	
ash es	adapt	additive	-adagio
-ask ed	added	addressee	adaptable
ass es	addend	adenoids	adaptation
	adder	adequate	adequacy
at	addict	adjective	adjectival ly
	adding	admirable	admirable
*-aunt relative	adept	admiral	admiration
	adult	adulthood	adolescence
*axe d chopping tool	-advance d	-advancement	adolescent
	advent	-advancing	advantageous
	adverb	-advantage	-advantaging
	adverse	-advantaged	adverbial ly
	advert	adversary -ies	adversary -ies
		advertise d	advertising
	affix es	advocate	advocacy
	Afghan		advocating
	-after	affluence	
		affluent	affirmation
	aggro	Africa	Afghanistan
	-aghast	African	
	agile	-aftermath	aggravation
		-afternoon	agitation
	alas	-afterwards	agoraphobia
	album		agoraphobic
	alcove	aggravate	agricultural ly
	algae	aggregate	agriculture
	Allah	agitate	
	alley	agonise d	alacrity
	alloy ed	ze	Albania
	ally -ies	agony -ies	☛
	allied		

for H . . .
see page 16 ▷

☛

albatross es
*albumen white of egg
*albumin protein
☛

for Scots: a -r
is on page 225 ▷

In these words you can hear the vowel sound a as in cat

A

**	***	**** ***
-almond	alchemy	alcoholic
alpha	alcohol	alcoholism
Alpine/alpine	algebra	algebraic ally
alto	alibi	Algeria
	alkali	algorithm
amass es	alkaline	alimentary
amassed	allegory -ies	allegation
amber	allergy -ies	allegorical ly
amble d	allocate d	allegory -ies
ambling	alphabet	allegretto
ambush es	Alsatian	alligator
ambushed	altitude	allocating
ampere	Alzheimer's	allocation
ample		alphabetical ly
amply	amalgam	alphanumeric
	amateur	altimeter
anchor	ambition	aluminium
anger ed	ambitious	
angle d	ambulance	amalgamate
*angler person who	amethyst	amalgamating
fishes with hook and	ammeter	amalgamation
line	amnesty -ies	ambassador
angling	ampersand	ambidextrous
angry -ier, -iest	amplify -ies	ambiguity -ies
anguish ed	amplified	ambiguous
ankle	amplitude	ambivalent
annexe d	amputate	ammunition
annual ly	amylase	amphibian
annum		amphibious
anode	anagram	amphitheatre
-answer ed	analogue	amplification
anthem	analyse d	amplifier
anthill	ze	
anthrax	analyst	anachronism
*antics strange	anarchy	anaerobic
behaviour	ancestor	anaesthesia/anesthesia
antique	ancestral	anaesthetic/anesthetic
*antiques very old	ancestry -ies	analogous
objects	anchorage	analogy -ies
antlers	andante	analysing
anvil	Anglican	zing
anxious	angora	analysis [analyses]
	angrier	analytic ally
aphid/aphis	angriest	anatomical ly
apple	angrily	anatomy -ies
aptly	*angular sharp-cornered	angiosperm
	animal	Anglo-Saxon
Arab	animate	animation
arid	aniseed	anniversary -ies
arrow ed	annual ly	annually
☛	anodise d	anonymity
	ze	antagonise d
	anorak	ze
	-answering	antagonism
	antarctic	antagonistic ally
	anteater	☛
	antelope	
	☛	

for H . . .
see page 16 ▷

for Scots: a -r
is on page 225 ▷

In these words you can hear the vowel sound **a** as in cat

A

* *

ashtray
-asking
aspect
asphalt
aspirin
asset
aster
asthma

athlete
atlas es
atoll
atom
attach es
attached
attack ed
attic
attract

-Auntie / Aunty

average d

*axes more than one
axe or axis
axing
*axis fixed or
imaginary line
axle

azure

impasse

* * *

antenna [antennae]
anthracite
anthropoid
antidote
antifreeze
antonym
anxiously

apathy
aperture
apparent
appetite
applicant
appliqué
apprehend
aptitude

aquatic
aqueduct
aqueous

Arabic
arable
arrogance
arrogant
arrowhead

asbestos
aspirin
assassin
assonance
asterisk
asteroid
astronaut
asymptote

athletic ally
athletics
Atlantic
atmosphere
attaché
attachment
attacker
attitude
attracted
attraction
attractive
attribute

avalanche
avant-garde
avarice
avenue
average d
averaging

axial ly
axiom

* * * * ** *

Antarctica
antecedent
anthology -ies
anthropologist
anthropology
antibiotic
antibody -ies
anticipate
anticipating
anticipation
anticyclone
antimony
antipathy -ies
antiquated
antiquity -ies
antiseptic ally
antisocial
antitoxin
anxiety -ies

apostolic ally
apparatus
apparently
apparition
appetising
applicable
application
apposition
apprehension

aquamarine

aristocracy -ies
aristocrat
aristocratic ally
arithmetically

asparagus
aspiration
assassinate
assassinating
assassination
astronomical ly
astrophysics

athletically
atmospheric ally

avaricious
averaging
avocado

axiomatic ally

for H . . .
see page 16

for Scots: a -r
is on page 225

In these words you can hear the vowel sound **a** as in **cat**

A

In these words the first letter 'a' is a neutral vowel.

*A*MAZING WORDS

abate	accumulating	adventure	allowable	appliance	assimilate
abating	accumulation	adventurous	allowance	applicable	assimilating
abbreviation	accumulator	adverbial ly	allude	apply -ies	assimilation
abeyance	accusative	adversity -ies	allusion	applied	assist
abide	accuse d	advertisement	alluvial	applying	assistance
abiding	accusing	advice	alluvium	appoint	assistant s
ability -ies	accustom ed	advisable	aloft	appointment	associate d
ablaze	acetylene	advise d	alone	appreciate	associating
aboard	achieve d	adviser	along side	appreciating	association
abode	achievement	advising	aloof	appreciative	associative
abolish es	achieving	advisory	aloud	apprentice d	assorted
abolished	acidic	Aegean	amaze d	apprenticeship	assortment
abominable	acidity	aesthetic ally	amazing	apprenticing	assume d
abominate	acknowledge d	afar	amenable	approach es	assuming
abominating	acknowledgement /	affair	amend ment	approached	assumption
abortion	acknowledgment	affect ed	amenity -ies	approaching	assurance
abound	acknowledging	affection	America n	appropriate ly	assure d
about	acoustic ally	affectionate ly	amid st	approval	assuring
above	acquaint ance	affiliate	amino	approve d	astern
abrasive	acquire d	affiliating	amiss	approximate ly	astigmatism
abreast	acquiring	affiliation	ammonia	approximating	astonish es
abroad	acquit ted	affirm ed	ammonium	approximation	astonished
abrupt ly	acquittal	affirmative ly	amoeba	aquarium	astonishment
abscond	acquitting	affix es	among st	Arabia	astound ed
absorb ed	acropolis	affixed	amount	arena	astounding
absorber	[acropoleis]	afflict	amuse d	arise	astray
absorption	across	affliction	amusement	[arose]	astrology
abstain ed	acrylic	afford	amusing	[arisen]	astronomer
absurd ity	acute	affront	anaemia / anemia	arising	astronomy
abundance	addicted	afloat	anaemic / anemic	arithmetic	asylum
abundant	addiction	afoot	anaesthetist /	aroma	atomic
abuse d	addictive	afraid	anesthetist	arose	atone d
abusing	addition al ly	afresh	anemone	around	atonement
abysmal ly	address es	again	anew	arouse d	atoning
abyss es	addressed	against	anneal ed	arousing	atrocious
accelerate	adhere d	agenda	annihilate	arrange d	atrocity -ies
accelerating	adhering	aggression	annihilating	arrangement	attain ed
acceleration	adhesive	aggressive	annihilation	arranging	attainment
accelerator	adieu	aggressor	announce d	array ed	attempt ed
accept able	adjacent	agility	announcement	arrest	attend ed
acceptance	adjoining	ago	announcer	arrival	attendance
accepting	adjourn ed	agog	announcing	arrive d	attendant s
accessibility	adjudicate	agree d	annoy ed	arriving	attention
accessible	adjudicating	agreeable	annoyance	ascend ing	attentive
accession	adjudication	agreement	annoying	ascension	attorney
accessory -ies	adjudicator	ahead	anoint	ascent	attribute d
acclaim ed	adjust er	ahoy!	anon	ascribe d	attributing
accommodate	adjustment	ajar	anonymous	ascribing	aurora
accommodating	administer ed	akin	another	ashamed	Australia
accommodation	administrate	alarm ed	apart	ashore	avail ed
accompaniment	administrating	alert	apartheid	aside	availability
accompany -ies	administration	alight	apartment	asleep	available
accompanied	administrator	align ed	apologetic ally	aspire d	availing
accomplice	admire d	alignment	apologise d	aspiring	avenge d
accomplish es	admiring	alike	apologising	assail ed	avenging
accomplished	admission	alive	apology -ies	assailant	avert
accomplishment	admit ted	allege d	apostle	assault	avoid ed
accord	admittance	allegedly	apostrophe	assemble d	avoidable
accordance	admitting	allegiance	appal led	assembling	await
according ly	ado	alleging	appalling	assembly -ies	awake d
accordion	adopt ion	allegro	appeal ed	assent	[awoke]
account	adorable	allergic	appear ed	assert	awaken ed
accountability	adore d	alliance	appearance	assertion	awaking
accountable	adoring	alliteration	append	assertive	award
accountancy	adorn ed	alliterative	appendicitis	assess es	aware ness
accountant	adrenalin	allot ted	appendix	assessed	away
accrue d	adrift	allotment	[appendices]	assessment	awhile
accruing	adsorption	allotting	applaud	assign ed	awoke n
accumulate	adultery	allow ed	applause	assignment	awry

4

B

*

backed
*bad not good
*bade did bid
badge
bagged
-balm
banned
*band strip of
  material / stripe /
  group
*bands more than one
  band
banged
banked
*banned forbidden
*banns announcement
  in church of plan to
  marry
bashes
bashed
*-basked enjoy
*Basque person living
  near the Pyrenees
batted
batches
-bathed

blacked
blagged
bland
blanked
-blast

-bra
brad
bragged
bran
-branches
-branched
brand
brash
-brasses
brat

* *

babbled
babbling
backbone
backcloth
background
backhand
backing
backlashes
backlog
backpacked
backstage
backstroke
back-up / backup
backward
backwards
backyard
badgered
badly
baffled
baffling
baggage
bagging
baggy -ier, -iest
bagpipes
balanced
ballad
ballast
*ballet dance
*balloted voting
-balmy
bamboo
-banal
bandaged
bandit
bandy -ies
bandied
banger
banging
bangle
banishes
banished
banjo es / s
banker
banking
bankrupt
banner
banning
banquet
baptised
  ze
Baptist
*baron lord
barracked
barracks
barraged
barrelled
*barren not fertile
barrowed

* * *

bachelor
backbencher
backstory -ies
backwardness
badminton
-Bahamas
balancing
balcony -ies
balloted
bamboozled
bamboozling
-banana
bandaging
bandwagon
Bangladesh
banishment
banister
bankruptcy -ies
baptising
  zing
baptism
barbaric ally
baritone
barraging
barrelling
barricade
barrier
barrister
-basketball
bathysphere
battalion
battery -ies
battlefield
battleground
battleship

blackberry -ies
blanketed

bombastic ally
bonanza
-Botswana

*-brassier more showy
*brassière bra
-bravado

* * * * *

bacterial
bacterium [bacteria]
ballerina
barbarically
barracuda
barricading

beatitude

bombastically
botanical

brutality

for Scots: a -r
is on page 226 ▷

In these words you can hear the vowel sound **a** as in **cat**

5

B

* *

basalt
-**basket**
-**basking**
-**bastard**
-**bathroom**
batik
***baton** short stick
batsman [batsmen]
***batted** did bat
***batten** board
batter
***battered** did batter
battery -ies
batting
battle d
battling

began
-**behalf**

bhangra

blackbird
blackboard
blacken ed
blackhead
blackmail ed
blackness
blackout
blacksmith
bladder
blagging
blanket ed
-**blast-off**

bracken
bracket
bradawl
braggart
bragging
bramble
-**branches**
brandish es
brandished
brandy -ies
brassière
-**brassy** -ier, -iest

for Scots: a -r
is on page 226 ▷

> **In these words the first letter 'a' is a neutral
> vowel. It sounds like the 'a' in 'astonish'.**
>
> | | |
> |---|---|
> | baboon | bazooka |
> | balloon ed | blancmange |
> | barometer | Brazil |
> | bazaar | |

In these words you can hear the vowel sound a as in cat

C

*

cab
*cache storage space
cadge d
-calf
-calm ed
-calve d
cam
camp ed
can ned
*cant insincere talk /
  sloping edge / tilt
*-can't cannot
cap ped
*cash money
cashes
cashed
*-cask barrel
*casque helmet
*-cast throw / mould /
  decide parts in a
  play / squint
-[cast]
*-caste social class
cat
catch es
[caught]

champ ed
*-chance lucky event /
  risk
-chanced
-chant
*-chants does chant /
  more than one chant
chap
chapped
chat ted
chav

clad
clam med
clamp ed
clan
clang ed
clank ed
clap ped
clash es
clashed
-clasp ed
-class es
-classed
☞

for Qu . . .
see page 24 ▷

* *

cabbage
cabin
*caching storing away
cackle d
cackling
cactus es [cacti]
*caddie person paid
  to carry golf clubs
*caddy -ies caddie /
  box to hold tea
  caddied
cadging
cafe / café
caffeine
*callous hard
*callus es hard growth
-calmly
camber ed
camel
camera
campaign ed
camper
*campers people in
  a camp
campfire
camphor
camping
*campus es college
  or university grounds
camshaft
canal
cancel led
cancer
*candid frank
*candied sugar-coated
candle
candy
canning
*cannon gun / stroke
  in billiards
cannoned
cannot
canny -ier, -iest
*canon musical round /
  rank in church / laws /
  list of works
canteen
*canter ed gentle gallop
*cantor leader of the
  singing
*canvas cloth
*canvass ed seek
  opinions and/or
  support
*canyon deep and
  narrow valley
☞

* * *

cabaret
cabinet
cadmium
calcium
calculate
calendar
calibrate
calibre
calico
callipers
calorie
camcorder
camembert
camera
cameraman [cameramen]
camouflage
campaigner
Canada
*canapé party nibble
cancelling
candidate
candlelight
candlestick
canister
cannabis
cannibal
*canopy -ies protective
  covering
capital
capturing
caramel
caravan
caribou
carolling
carriageway
carrier
carrion
carrycot
carrying
cascading
casserole d
castanets
-castaway
casually
casualty -ies
catalogue d
catalyst
catapult
cataract
category -ies
*catholic wide-ranging
*Catholic belonging
  to the Roman Catholic
  church
cavalier
cavalry
cavity -ies
☞

* * * * * * *

cafeteria
calamity -ies
calculation
calculating
calculator
calibrating
Cambodia
cameraman [cameramen]
camouflaging
cantankerous
cantilever ed
capacitor
capacity -ies
capitalise d
          ze
capitalising
          zing
capitalism
capitalist
cappuccino
captivity
Caribbean
caricature d
caricaturing
casually
casualty -ies
cataloguing
catalytic ally
catamaran
catastrophe
catastrophic ally
category -ies
caterpillar

championship
chandelier
characterisation
          zation
characterise d
          ze
characteristic ally
charioteer
charismatic ally
charitable
chrysanthemum

clarification
classically
classification
☞

for Scots: a -r
is on page 227 ▷

In these words you can hear the vowel sound a as in cat

7

C

*

crab
crack ed
-craft
crag
cram med
cramp ed
crank ed
crash es
crashed

* *

capping
capstan
capsule
captain ed
caption
captive
captor
capture d
carafe
*carat measure of
purity of gold
*caret insertion mark
carol led
carriage
*carrot vegetable
carry -ies
carried
cascade
cashew
cashier ed
*cashing turning into
cash
*-caster / castor
powdered sugar /
swivelling wheel
-casting
-castle
-castling
*-castor castor oil
casual ly
catching
catchment
cathode
*catholic wide-ranging
*Catholic belonging to
the Roman Catholic
church
catkin
cattle
catty -ier, -iest
cavern

chaffinch es
chalet
challenge d
champagne
-chancing
-chandler
channel led
chapel
chaplain
chapter
-charade
chasm
chassis

for Qu . . .
see page 24 ▷

* * *

ceramic

challenger
champion ed
-chancellor
chandelier
channelling
-chapati
character
chariot
charity -ies
chatterbox es

clarify -ies
clarified
clarinet
clarity
classical ly
classify -ies
classified

collapsing
combated / combatted
combating / combatting
-commander
-commandment
companion
compassion
contraction
contractor
contractual ly
contralto s
contraption

craftier
craftiest

kangaroo
-karate
Kazakhstan

-koala

* * * * *

collaborate
collaborating
collaboration
collapsible
companionship
comparative
comparatively
comparison
compassionate
compatible
congratulate
congratulating
congratulations
constabulary -ies
contaminate
contaminating
contamination
contractually

Karaoke

for Scots: a -r
is on page 227 ▷

In these words you can hear the vowel sound **a** as in **cat**

C

* *
chatroom
*chatted had a chat
chatter
*chattered talked
quickly and too much /
rattled
chatting
chatty -ier, -iest
*-chorale hymn tune

cladding
clamber ed
clamming
clammy -ier, -iest
clamour ed
clanger
clanking
clapper
clapping
claret
classic ally
-classmate
-classroom
clatter ed

collapse d
combat ed / ted
-command
compact
contract
-contrast
*-corral enclosure for
cattle and horses

In these words the first letter 'a' is a neutral vowel. It sounds like the 'a' in 'astonish'.		
cacao	capillary -ies	catarrh
cadet	capricious	cathedral
Canadian	career ed	chameleon
canary -ies	caress es	charisma
canoe d	caressed	
canoeing	casino s	

crackdown
cracker
crackle d
crackling
-craftsman [craftsmen]
-crafty -ier, -iest
craggy -ier, -iest
cramming
crankshaft
cranny -ies
crevasse

for Qu . . .
see page 24 ▷

for Scots: a -r
is on page 227 ▷

kebab

-khaki

-Koran / Qur'an

In these words you can hear the vowel sound a as in cat

D

*

dab bed
dad
-**daft**
-**dal/dhal**
*****dam** water-barrier /
mother of animal
*****dammed** held back by
a water-barrier
*****damn** swear word /
condemn
*****damned** cursed
damp ed
-**dance** d
dank
dash es
dashed

drab
*-**draft** rough plan /
selected group
drag ged
drank
*-**draught** current of
air / depth of ship
in water / piece in
game
-**draughts**

* *

dabbing
dabble d
dabbling
dachsund
daddy -ies
dagger
dally -ies
dallied
damage d
dampness
damsel
damson
-**dancer**
-**dancing**
dandruff
dandy -ies
dangle d
dangling
dapple d
dashboard
-**data**
dazzle d
dazzling

decamp ed
-**demand**
*****despatch** es send off
despatched
detach es
detached
detract

*****dispatch** es despatch /
message
dispatched
distract
divan

dragging
dragon
-**drama**
drastic ally
-**draughty** -ier, -iest

* * *

daffodil
dalmatian
damages
damaging
damnation

-**demanded**
-**demanding**
detachment

didactic
-**disaster**
-**disastrous**
dismantled
dismantling
distraction
distractor

dogmatic ally

dragonfly -ies
dramatic ally
dramatise d
ze
drastically

* * * * *

daddy-longlegs
dandelion

decapitate
declarative
defamatory

diagonal ly
dilapidated
dissatisfy -ies
dissatisfied
distractible

dogmatically

dramatically
dramatising
zing
drastically

*for Scots: a -r
is on page 228*

In these words you can hear the vowel sound **a** as in **cat**

E

*

**

elapse d

enact
encamp ed
-enchant
-enhance d
-entrance d

exact
exam
expand
expanse
extract

***

ecstatic ally

elaborate
elastic ally

embankment
embarrass es
embarrassed
emphatic ally

enamel led
enamour ed
-enchanting
-enhancing
entangle d
entangling
-entrancing

erratic ally

establish es
established

exactly
examine d
-example
expanded
expanding
expansion
expansive
extraction
extractor

*****

ecstatically

elaborate
elaborating
elaboration
elastically
elasticity

emancipate d
emancipating
emancipation
embarrassing
embarrassment
emphatically

enamelling

erratically

establishment

evacuate
evacuating
evacuation
evacuee
evaluate
evaluating
evaluation
evangelism
evangelist
evaporate
evaporating
evaporation

exacerbate
exaggerate
exaggerating
exaggeration
examination
examiner
examining
exasperate
exasperation
expandable
explanatory
extrapolate
extrapolating
extravagance
extravagant
extravaganza

for H . . .
see page 16 ▷

for I . . .
see page 17 ▷

for Scots: a -r
is on page 228 ▷

In these words you can hear the vowel sound **a** as in **cat**

11

F

*

fact
*facts more than one
fact
fad
fag ged
fan ned
fangs
-fast
*fat ter, test plump
*fax es machine for
sending copies
faxed

flag ged
flan
flange d
flank ed
flap ped
flash es
flashed
-flask
flat ted
flax

*franc French coin
-France
*frank plain and
honest
franked

*phat excellent

* *

fabric
-facade/façade
facet
facile
faction
factor
factory -ies
factual ly
faddy
fagging
faggots
fallow
family
famine
famish es
famished
fanbelt
fancy -ies
fancied
fanning
fascist
fashion ed
-fasten ed
-faster
-fastest
-father
-fathered
fathom ed
fatten ed
fattening
fatter
fattest
fatty -ier, -iest

finance d

flabby -ier, -iest
flagging
flagpole
flagship
flannel led
flapjack
flapper
flapping
flappy
flashback
flasher
flashing
flashy -ier, -iest
flatmate
*flatted made flat
flatten ed
flatter
*flattered did flatter
flattest
flatting

* * *

fabricate
fabulous
factorise d
ze
factory -ies
factual ly
faculty -ies
Fahrenheit
fallacy -ies
fallible
family -ies
fanatic ally
fanciful
fantasise d
ze
fantastic ally
fantasy -ies
fascinate
fascism
-fastener
-fatherly
fattening
fatuous

fiasco s
-finale
financial ly
financing

flamboyant
flannelling
flashforward
flattery -ies

fractional ly
fracturing
fragmented
franchising
frantically

* * * * *

fabricated
fabricating
fabrication
facsimile
factorising
zing
factually
fanatically
fanaticism
fantasising
zing
fantastically
fascinating
fascination
fashionable
fastidious
fatality -ies
-father-in-law

financially

flabbergasted

fractionally
fragmentation
frantically

philatelist

for th . . .
see page 28 ▷

for Scots: a -r
is on page 229 ▷

In these words you can hear the vowel sound a as in cat

F

* *
forbade / **forbad**

fraction
fracture d
fragile
fragment
franchise d
frankly
frantic ally

*for th . . .
see page 28* ▷

*for Scots: a -r
is on page 229* ▷

phantom

> **In these words the first letter 'a' is a neutral vowel. It sounds like the 'a' in 'astonish'.**
>
> facetious   familiar
> facilitate   familiarity
> facilitating   fatigue d
> facility -ies   flamingo es / s
> fallacious

In these words you can hear the vowel sound **a** as in cat

G

*

*gaff hook / pole to
support sail
*gaffe embarrassing
act
gag ged
gang
gap ped
gas es
gassed
gash es
gashed
-gasp ed

glad der, dest
-glance d
gland
-glass es

gnash es
gnashed
gnat

-gouache

grab bed
*-graft cause to grow
together / hard work
gram / gramme
gran
grand
-grant
graph ed
*graphed made a
graph
-grasp ed
-grass es
-grassed

* *

gabble d
gabbling
gadget
gagging
gaggle
-gala
gallant
*galleon ship
galley
*gallon measure
gallop ed
gallows
gambit
*gamble d risk
gambler
*gambling taking risks
*gambol led frisk
gamma
gammon
gander
gangling
gangplank
*gangsta member of
youth gang / type of
rap
*gangster member of
violent criminal gang
gangway
gannet
gantry -ies
gapping
garage d
garret
gasket
gassing
gastric
gasworks
gâteau
gather ed

-Ghana
-ghastly -ier, -iest

-giraffe

gladden ed
gladder
gladdest
gladly
glamour
-glancing
-glasses
-glassy -ier, -iest

-gouache

* * *

galaxy -ies
gallantry
gallery -ies
galvanise d
ze
*gambolling frisking
garrison
gathering

-Ghanaian

glacier
glamorous
glandular

gradual ly
graduate
gramophone
grandchildren
granddaughter
grandfather
grandiose
grandmother
grandparent
granular
graphical ly
-grasshopper
gratify -ies
gratified
gratitude
gravelling
gravitate
gravity

guarantee d

-gymkhana
gymnastics

* * * * *

galvanising
zing
gasometer
gastronomic

gelatinous

gladiator
gladiolus [gladioli]

gradually
graduation
grammatical ly
graphically
gravitation
gravitational

-Guatemala

for Scots: a -r
is on page 229

In these words you can hear the vowel sound a as in cat

G

* *

grabber
grabbing
gradual ly
grammar
grandad / **granddad**
grandchild
grandeur
grandma
grandpa
grandson
grandstand
granite
granny -ies
-granted
granule
graphic ally
graphite
grapple d
grappling
-grasping
-grassland
-grassroots / **grass-roots**
-grassy -ier, -iest
-gratis
gravel led

*for Scots: a -r
is on page 229* ▷

**In these words the first letter 'a' is a neutral
vowel. It sounds like the 'a' in 'astonish'.**

galena	gazump ed
galore	gradation
galoshes	graffiti
gazelle	gratuitous

H

*	**	***	****
hacked	habit	habitat	habitable
had	hacker	Halloween /	habitation
-half [halves]	haddock	Hallowe'en	handicapping
-halve d	hadn't	hamburger	
ham med	haggard	handicap ped	
hand	haggis	handicraft	
hang	haggle d	handiwork	
[hung]	haggling	handkerchief s	
hanged	-half-time / halftime	handlebar	
has	-halfway	handwriting	
hash es	hallo	handwritten	
hashed	-halving	handyman	
hat	hamlet	hangover	
hatch es	hammer ed	haphazard	
hatched	hamming	happening	
hath	hammock	happier	
have	hamper ed	happiest	
[had]	hamster	happily	
	hamstring	happiness	
	[hamstrung]	harassment	
	handbag	haricot	
	handbook	haversack	
	handbrake	-Hawaii	
	handcuff ed	-Hawaiian	
	handed	hazardous	
	handful		
	handgun	heptathlon	
	handle d		
	handler		
	handling		
	*handmade / hand-made		
	made by hand		
	*handmaid servant		
	handout / hand-out		
	handshake		
	*handsome fine-looking		
	handspring		
	handy -ier, -iest		
	*hangar shed for planes		
	*hanger coat hanger		
	hanging		
	hanky -ies		
	*hansom cab		
	happen ed		
	happy -ier, -iest		
	harass ed		
	harrow ed		
	hasn't		
	hassle d		
	hassling		
	hatchback		
	hatchet		
	hatching		
	hatter		
	haven't		
	having		
	havoc		
	hazard		

> **Here the first 'a' is spoken as a neutral sound.**
> habitually   hallucination

for Scots: a -r
is on page 230 ▷

16

In these words you can hear the vowel sound **a** as in **cat**

I

*

* *

impasse

intact

-Iran
-Iraq

Islam

* * *

imagine d
imbalance
impasto

inhabit ed

-Iraqi

Islamic

Italian
italic

* * * * **

imaginary
imagination
imaginative
imagining
immaculate
-impassable
implacable
impractical

inaccuracy -ies
inaccurate
inadequate ly
infallibility
infallible
infatuate d
infatuation
inflammable
inflammatory
inhabitant
inhabited
inhabiting
insanitary
insanity
intractable
intransitive
invaluable

irrational ly

italicise d
ze
italicising
zing

for E . . .
see page 11

In these words you can hear the vowel sound a as in cat

17

J

SHORT VOWEL a

*

jab bed
jack ed
*jam fruit boiled with sugar / crush / block
jammed
*jamb side post of door or window
jazz es
jazzed

* *

-giraffe

gymnast

jabber ed
jabbing
jackal
jackdaw
jacket
jack-knife d
jackpot
jagged
jamjar
jamming
jampot
jangle d
jangling
Japan
jasper

* * *

-gymkhana
  gymnastics

jaguar
jamboree
Japanese
javelin

* * * *

gelatinous

January

for dr . . .
see page 10

for Scots: a -r
is on page 230

> **In these words the first letter 'a' is a neutral vowel. It sounds like the 'a' in 'astonish'.**
>
> Jacuzzi s   Jamaica   Jamaican

K

*

knack
*knap chip off

*nap short sleep / take a snooze

for C . . .
see page 7

for Qu . . .
see page 24

* *

kebab

-khaki

knacker ed
knapsack

-Koran / Qur'an

* * *

kangaroo
-karate
  Kazakhstan

-koala

* * * *

Karaoke

> **Here the 'a' is neutral.**
>
> kaleidoscope

In these words you can hear the vowel sound a as in cat

L

*	**	***	****
lab	lacking	Labrador	labradoodle
lack ed	lacquer ed	labyrinth	lamentable
*lacks does lack	ladder ed	lacerate	laminated
lad	lagging	laminate	laminating
lag ged	lambing	Lancashire	laryngitis
lamb ed	lamp-post	landlady -ies	laterally
lamp	lampshade	landowner	lavatory -ies
-lance d	-lancing	landscaping	
land	landed	lariat	legality -ies
*lap thighs of seated	landfill	-lasagne	
person / once round	landing	lateral ly	
a track / splash	landlord	latitude	
gently / drink by	landmark	Latvia	
using tongue / be	landscape	-laughable	
placed together	landslide	lavatory -ies	
or overlapping	language	lavender	
*Lapp native of	languid	lavishing	
Lapland	languish es	laxative	
*Lapps more than	languished		
one Lapp	languor	-legato	
*laps more than one	lanky -ier, -iest		
lap	lantern		
*lapse d slip / end	Lapland		
through disuse	lapping		
lash es	lapsing		
lashed	laptop		
lass es	lapwing		
-last	larynx		
latch es	lasso s / es		
latched	-lasted		
-laugh ed	-lastly		
*lax slack	-lather ed		
	Latin		
	latte		
	latter		
	lattice d		
	-laughter		
	-lava		
	lavish es		
	lavished		
	-llama		

for Scots: a -r is on page 231 ▷

In these words the first letter 'a' is a neutral vowel. It sounds like the 'a' in 'astonish'.

laboratory -ies	lagoon
laborious ly	lament
laconic ally	lapel

M

*

-ma
ma'am
mac
mad der, dest
mall
man [men]
man ned
manse
Manx
map ped
mash es
mashed
-mask ed
mass es
*massed crowded
*-mast pole
*mat small rug
match es
matched
maths
*matt not shiny

* *

macho
mackerel
*madam English form
of address
*madame French form
of address
madden ed
maddening
madder
maddest
madness
maggot
magic ally
magma
*magnate wealthy
businessman
*magnet iron which
attracts iron
magpie
malice
mallard
mallet
malware
-mama
mammal
mammoth
manage d
mandate
*mandrel spindle
*mandrill baboon
mangle d
mangling
mango es / s
manhood
manic ally
mankind
*manna food
*manner way
mannered
manning
*manor landed estate
mansion
*mantel frame round
fire
*mantle cloak
manual ly
mapping
marriage
married
marrow
marry -ies
married
mascot
massage d
masseur
masseuse
*massif highlands
*massive huge

* * *

-macabre
mackerel
mackintosh
maddening
mademoiselle
madrigal
mafia
magazine
magical ly
magistrate
magnetic ally
magnetise d
ze
magnify -ies
magnified
magnitude
majesty -ies
-Malawi
malleable
management
manager
managing
mandolin
manganese
manically
manicure d
manifest
manifold
*mannequin model
*mannikin dwarf
manpower
manslaughter
mantelpiece
manual ly
manuscript
marathon
marigold
mariner
marital
maritime
mascara
masculine
masochist
masquerade
massacre d
massacring
massaging
-masterful ly
-masterly
-masterpiece
-mastery
mastodon
masturbate
matador
matinée
maximise d
maximum

* * * * * *

macaroni
Madagascar
magically
magnanimous
magnesium
magnetically
magnetising
zing
magnetism
magnification
magnificent
magnolia
maladjusted
malleable
malnutrition
mammalian
manageable
manageress es
managerial
mandatory
manically
manicuring
manicurist
manifestation
manifesto
mannerism
manometer
manually
manufacture d
manufacturer
manufacturing
marijuana
marionette
masculinity
masochism
masochistic ally
massacring
-masterfully
masturbating
masturbation
mathematical ly
mathematician
mathematics
matrimonial
matrimony
maturation

mechanical ly
menagerie
metabolism

miraculous ly

for Scots: a -r
is on page 232

20

In these words you can hear the vowel sound a as in cat

M

* *
-**master** ed
mastiff
matches
matching
***matted** twisted in
a thick mass
matter
***mattered** did matter
matting
mattress es
maxim

meringue

-**mirage**

-**morale**
-**moustache** d

* * *
meander ed
mechanic ally
medallion

Mohammed
molasses

* * * *
morality

In these words the first letter 'a' is a neutral
vowel. It sounds like the 'a' in 'astonish'.

machine d	malaria	marauder
machinery	Malaya	marauding
machining	Malaysia	marina
machinist	malevolent	maroon ed
Madeira	malicious	material ly
magician	malignant	materialism
mahogany	manipulate	materialist ic
majestic ally	manipulation	mature d
Majorca	manoeuvre d	maturity
majority -ies	manure d	

*for Scots: a -r
is on page 232* ▷ ▷

N

*
gnash es
gnashed
gnat

knack
***knap** chip off

naff
nag ged
nan
***nap** ped take a snooze

* *
knapsack
knacker ed

nagging
nana
nanny -ies
napkin
napping
nappy -ies
narrow ed
-**nasty** -ier, -iest
national
natural
-**Nazi**

* * *
narrative
narrowly
-**nastier**
-**nastiest**
national ly
nationalise d
    ze
nationalist
natural ly
naturalise d
    ze
naturalist
navigate
-**Nazism**

nomadic
nostalgia
nostalgic ally

* * * * * *
nationalise d
    ze
nationalising
    zing
nationalism
nationalist ic ally
nationality -ies
nationally
naturalisation
    zation
naturalise d
    ze
naturalising
    zing
naturalist
naturally
navigable
navigating
navigation
navigator

normality
nostalgically

In these words the first letter 'a' is a neutral
vowel. It sounds like the 'a' in 'astonish'.

narrate	narrator
narrating	nasturtium
narration	nativity -ies

*for Scots: a -r
is on page 232* ▷

In these words you can hear the vowel sound **a** as in **cat**

P

*

*fat plump

pack
*packed tightly filled
*pact agreement
pad ded
pal
-palm ed
pan ned
pang
pant
pants
-pass es
*-passed went by
*-past time that has
  passed / beyond
pat ted
patch es
patched
-path

*phat excellent

plaid
plait
plan ned
plank ed
-plant
plaque

pram
-prance d
prank

-psalm

* *

package d
packer
packet
packing
padded
padding
paddle d
paddling
paddock
paddy -ies
padlock ed
pageant
palace
*palate taste
*palette board for
  mixing colours
*pallet mattress / tool
pally -ier, -iest
pampas
pamper ed
pamphlet
panache
pancake
*panda animal
*pander ed encourage
  by bad example or
  taste
panel led
panic
panicked
panning
pansy -ies
panther
panties
pantry -ies
-papa
para
parish -es
parrot
parry -ies
parried
passage
-passing
passion
passive
-passport
-password
pasta
*pastel crayon /
  soft colour
*pastille sweet
-pastime
-pasture d
pasty -ies

* * *

pacifist
packaging
-Pakistan
Palestine
pancreas
panelling
panicking
pantograph
pantomime
paprika
parable
parachute
paradigm
paradise
paradox es
paraffin
paragraph ed
parakeet
parallel ed
paralyse d
       ze
paramount
paranoid
parapet
paraphrase
parasite
parasol
paratroop
parity
parody -ies
passageway
passenger
-passers-by
passionate
passively
-Passover
-pasteurise d
       ze
-pastoral ly
-pasturing
patio
patriot
patronage
patronise d
       ze

pentathlon

pianist
piano s
-piranha

* * * * * *

-Pakistani
palaeontologist /
paleontologist
palaeontology /
paleontology
Palestinian
panacea
pandemonium
panorama
paparazzo [paparazzi]
papier-mâché
parabola
paracetamol
parachuting
paradoxical ly
paraglider
paragliding
parallelogram
Paralympic
paralysing
       zing
paralysis [paralyses]
paralytic
paramecium
parameter
paranoia
paraphernalia
parasitic al ly
paratrooper
passionately
-pasteurising
       zing
-pastorally
pathological ly
patriotic ally
patriotism
patronising
       zing

philanthropist
philanthropy
philatelist
philately

pianoforte
-pistachio s

planetary

polarity -ies
potassium

for Scots: a -r
is on page 233

22   In these words you can hear the vowel sound **a** as in **cat**

P

* *

patchwork
patchy -ier, -iest
patent
-pathway
*patted did pat
patter
*pattered did patter
pattern ed
patting
patty -ies

perhaps

phantom

pianist
piano s
pince-nez

placard
placid
planet
plankton
planner
planning
-planted
-planter
-planting
plasma
-plaster ed
plastic
plateau
platen
platform
platter

*practice action
*practise d do or act /
 repeat for improvement
-prancing

* * *

planetary
-plantation
-plasterboard
plasticine
platinum
platitude
platypus es

practical ly
practising
pragmatic ally
protractor

-pyjamas

* * * * *

practicable
practically
practitioner
pragmatically
pragmatism
preparatory

for Scots: a -r
is on page 233 ▷

In these words the first letter 'a' is a neutral vowel. It sounds like the 'a' in 'astonish'.

Pacific	parishioner
pagoda	pathetic ally
palatial ly	pathology
papyrus es [papyri]	patrol led
parade	patrolling
parading	pavilion
parental	placebo s
parenthesis	platoon
[parentheses]	

In these words you can hear the vowel sound **a** as in **cat**

23

Q

*

quack ed

* *

quagmire
quango s
-**Qur'an** / **Koran**

* * *

quackery

* * * *

R

*

***rack** ed stretch to the
limits / framework
with bars / cogged bar
-**raft**
rag ged
ram med
ramp
ran
-**ranch** es
rang
rank ed
***rap** knock / speech
music
***rapped** knocked /
performed rap
***rapt** entranced
rash es
-**rasp** ed
rat ted

***wrack** seaweed
***wrap** cover by
winding or folding
***wrapped** covered

* *

rabbi
***rabbit** animal
***racket** racquet / din /
dishonest way of
making money
***racquet** bat with
strings
radish es
raffle d
-**rafter**
ragged
ragging
rally -ies
rallied
ramble d
rambler
rambling
ramming
rampage d
rampant
rampart
rancid
random
ranking
ransack ed
ransom ed
rapid
***rapper** rap artist
***rapping** knocking /
performing rap
rapport
rapture
***rarebit** cheese
on toast
-**rascal** ly
rasher
-**raspberry** -ies
ratchet
-**rather**
ration ed
ratted
ratting
rattle d
rattling
ratty -ier, -iest
ravage d

* * *

rabbited
rabbiting
radical ly
raffia
Ramadan
rampaging
ramshackle
randomise d
ze
randomly
rapidly
-**rascally**
-**raspberry** -ies
ratify -ies
ratified
rational ly
rationale
rattlesnake
ravaging
ravenous

reaction
reactor
refraction
refractive
regatta

rhapsody -ies

romancing
romantic ally

* * * * * *

radicalism
radically
randomising
zing
Rastafarian
ratification
rationalisation
zation
rationalise d
ze
rationalising
zing
rationality
rationally
ravioli

reactionary -ies
reality -ies
retaliate
retaliating
retaliation

romantically

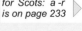

for Scots: a -r
is on page 233

In these words you can hear the vowel sound a as in cat

R

* *

react
refract
relax es
relaxed

for Scots: a -r
is on page 233 ▷

romance d

wrangle d
wrangling
*wrapper protective
covering
*wrapping covering

In these words the first letter 'a' is neutral.

raccoon / racoon
rapidity
ravine

S

*	* *	* * *	* * * * * *
-psalm	chalet	ceramic	chandelier
	champagne		
*sac pouch	-charade	chandelier	sabotaging
*sack large bag /	chassis		sacrificial ly
plunder / dismiss		sabotage d	sacrificing
from a job	sabbath	saboteur	salivary
sacked	*sachet small soft bag	saccharin / saccharine	salmonella
*sacks more than one	sadden ed	sacrament	salutary
sack / does sack	sadder	sacrifice d	salutation
*sacs pouches	saddest	-safari	sanatorium s [sanatoria]
sad der, dest	saddle d	-Sahara	sanctuary -ies
sag ged	saddling	-salami	sanitary
sand	sadly	salaried	sanitation
sang	sadness	salary -ies	satisfaction
sank	-saga	salutary	satisfactorily
sap ped	sagging	salvaging	satisfactory
sash es	salad	salvation	satisfying
sat	salmon	sanctify -ies	saturated
*sax saxophone	salon	sanctified	saturating
	salsa	sanctity	saturation
scab	salvage d	sanctuary -ies	
scalp ed	samba	sandpaper	Scandinavia
scam	-sample d	sandpiper	-scenario s
scamp	-sampler	sanitary	
scan	-sampling	sanity	semantically
*scanned did scan	sanction	Santa Claus	
*scant hardly enough	sandal led	satanic	-Somalia
scrap ped	sandbag	satellite	
scratch es	sandbank	satisfy -ies	spasmodically
scratched	sander	satisfied	spectacular ly
	sandstone	saturate	sporadically
shack	sandwich es	Saturday	
-shaft	sandwiched	savaging	
shag	sandy -ier, -iest	savanna	
shall	Santa	saveloy	for Scots: a -r
sham med	sapling	saxophone	is on page 234 ▷
shank	sapphire		
shrank	sapping		
	sapwood		

for Scots: a -r
is on page 234 ▷

In these words you can hear the vowel sound a as in cat

25

S

*	**	***	**** **
slab bed	*sashay glide forward	scaffolding	standardisation
slack ed	at an angle	scandalous	zation
slam med	satchel	scantiest	standardising
slang	satin	scavenging	zing
-slant	satire		statically
slap ped	sat-nav	semantic ally	statistician
slash es	Saturn	semantics	statutory
slashed	savage d		strangulation
slat	Saxon	-sonata	stratification
		-soprano s	
smack ed	scabbard		substantially
smash es	scabby -ier, -iest	sparrowhawk	
smashed	scaffold	spasmodic ally	syllabically
	scallop ed	spatula	syllabification
snack	scalpel	sporadic ally	syllabify -ies
snag ged	scamper ed		syllabified
snap ped	scandal	-staccato	
snatch es	scanner	staggering	
snatched	scanning	stalactite	
	scanty -ier, -iest	stalagmite	
spam med	scatter ed	stamina	
span ned	scavenge d	stampeding	
spank ed	scrabble	standardise d	
spat	scrabbling	ze	
splash es	scraggy -ier, -iest	statically	
splashed	scramble d	statuesque	
sprang	scrambling	stratagem	
sprat	scrapbook	strategy -ies	
	scrapping	stratify -ies	
stab bed	scrappy -ier, -iest	stratified	
stack ed	scrapyard	stratosphere	
-staff ed	scratchy -ier, -iest		
stag		substantial ly	
stamp ed	shabby -ier, -iest	substantive	
-stance	shadow ed	subtracting	
stand	shaggy -ier, -iest	subtraction	
[stood]	shallow	-sultana	
stank	shambles	-surpassing	
strand	shamming		
strap ped	shampoo ed	syllabic ally	
	shamrock		
-suave	shandy -ies		
	shanty -ies		
swag	shatter ed		
swam	shrapnel		
swank ed			
	-slalom		
	slamming		
	-slander ed		
	slapping		
	smasher		
	smashing		

for Scots: a -r
is on page 234

In these words you can hear the vowel sound **a** as in **cat**

S

* *

snagging
snapping
snappy -ier, -iest
snapshot
spammer
spamming
Spaniard
spaniel
Spanish
spanner
spanning
sparrow
spasm
spastic
splashdown

stabbing
stagger ed
stagnant
stallion
stammer ed
stampede
standard
stand-by
standing
standpoint
standstill
stand-up
stanza
static ally
statue
stature
statute
straggle d
straggling
stranded
strangle d
strangling
strapping
-stratum [strata]

subtract
-surpass es
-surpassed

for Scots: a -r
is on page 234 ▷

swagger ed

> **In these words the first letter 'a' is a neutral vowel. It sounds like the 'a' in 'astonish'.**
>
> | | | |
> |---|---|---|
> | sadistic ally | saluting | stabiliity |
> | salinity | samosa | statistic al ly |
> | saliva | satirical ly | statistics |
> | saloon | savoy | strategic ally |
> | salute | spaghetti | |

In these words you can hear the vowel sound a as in cat

27

T

*

tab
tack
*tacked did tack
*tacks more than
    one tack
*tact skill in putting
    things to people
tag ged
tan ned
tank
tap ped
-task
*tax es money taken
    by government
taxed

than
thank ed
thanks
that
thatch es
thatched
that's
*thrash es beat
thrashed
*thresh es beat corn
threshed

track
*tracked did track
*tract pamphlet
tram
tramp ed
-trance
trap ped
trash es
trashed

twang ed

* *

tabby -ies
tableau
tablet
tabloid
tacit
tackle d
tackling
tacky -ier, -iest
tactful ly
tactic s
tactile
tactless
tadpole
tagging
talcum
talent
tally -ies
tallied
talon
tamper ed
tampon
tandem
tangent
tangle d
tangling
tango s
tangoed
tankard
tanker
tanner
tanning
tantrum
tappet
tapping
tariff
tassel led
tattered
tavern
taxi s
taxman [taxmen]

thankful ly
thank-you
that'd
that'll

timbre

tracksuit
traction
tractor
traffic
trafficked
tragic ally
trample d
trampling
tramway

* * *

tabulate
tactfully
tactical ly
taffeta
talented
tambourine
tangerine
tangible
tantalise d
    ze
tapestry -ies
taxable
taxation
taxpayer

thankfully
thematic ally

-tiara

tobacco s
-tomato es

trafficker
trafficking
tragedy -ies
tragically
trampoline d
tranquilly
transaction
transcendent
transcribing
transcription
transferring
transformer
transfusion
transistor
transition
transitive
transitory
translating
translation
translator
translucent
transmission
transmitted
transmitter
transmitting
transparent
transpiring
transposing
transversal
transvestite
trapezoid
traveller
travelling
traversing

* * * * * *

tabulating
tabulation
tabulator
tachometer
tactically
tantalising
    zing
Tanzania
tapioca
tarantula
Tasmania

theatrical ly
thematically

tobacconist
totality

trafficator
tragically
trajectory -ies
trampolining
tranquilliser
    zer
tranquillity
transatlantic
transcendental
transferable
transformation
transistorise d
    ze
transitional ly
transitory
transmutation
transparency -ies
transpiration
transportation
transubstantiation

tyrannical ly
tyrannosaurus es
[tyrannosauri]

*for Scots: a -r
is on page 235* ▷

In these words you can hear the vowel sound **a** as in **cat**

T

* *
tranquilly
***transact** make a deal
transcribed
***transect** cut across
transept
transferred
transfixes
transfixed
transformed
transit
translate
transmitted
transpired
transplant
transport
transposed
transverse
trapdoor
trapper
trapping
travelled
traveller
travelling
traversed

> **In these words the first letter 'a' is neutral.**
>
> tattoo ed   trajectory -ies
> trachea   trapeze
> tradition   trapezium s [trapezia]
> traditional ly

for Scots: a -r is on page 235 ▷

U

*   * *   * * *   * * * * *
                                                             Uganda   **unanimous**ly
                                                             unhappy -ier, -iest   **unhappily**
                                                                                unhappiness

V

*   * *   * * *   * * * * *
valved   **vaccine**   **vaccinate**   **vaccination**
van   **vacuum** ed   **vacillate**   **vacillating**
-**vase**   **valiant**   **vacuole**   **vacillation**
-**vast**   **valid**   **vagabond**   **validation**
vat   **valley**   **vaginal**   **valuable**
               valour   **valentine**   **valuation**
               valued   **valiant**   **vandalism**
               vampire   **validate**
               vandal   **valium**   **vernacular**
               vanishes   **valuable**
               vanished   **valuing**   **vocabulary** -ies
               vanquishes   **vandalise** d   **volcanically**
               vanquished   ze
               -**vantage**   **vanity** -ies   **vulgarity** -ies
               -**vastly**   **vaseline**
               -**vastness**   **Vatican**

> **Here the first 'a' is a neutral vowel.**
>
> vacate
> vacating
> vacation
> vagina
> validity
> vanilla
> variety -ies

veranda/ verandah

-**vibrato**

volcanic ally

for Scots: a -r is on page 235 ▷

In these words you can hear the vowel sound **a** as in **cat**

W

*

*rack ed stretch to the
limits / framework with
bars / cogged bar
*rap knock / speech
music
*rapped knocked /
performed rap
*rapt entranced

wag ged
*wax ed grow larger
or stronger / plastic
substance

whack ed
*whacks more than
one whack

*wrack seaweed
*wrap cover by winding
or folding
*wrapped covered
-wrath

* *

*rapping knocking /
performing rap

wacky -ier, -iest
wagging
waggle d
wagon
wagtail

withstand
[withstood]

wrangle d
wrangling
wrapper
*wrapping covering

* * *

Y

*

yank ed
yap ped

* *

yapping

* * *

* * * *

for Scots: a -r
is on page 235 ▷

Z

*

zap ped

* *

zapping

* * *

Zambia

-Zimbabwe

* * * *

30

In these words you can hear the vowel sound a as in cat

A

*

* *

* * *

* * * * * *

abreast

acceptance
accepting
accession

accelerate
accelerating
acceleration
accelerator
acceptable
accessibility
accessible
accessory -ies
acetylene

*accept take
something offered

adventure

address es
addressed
adept

aesthetic ally

affected
affection

*affect alter
afresh

adrenalin
adventurous

again
against

agenda
aggression
aggressive
aggressor

aesthetically

ahead

affectionate
affectionately

alleging
allegro
already

allege d

amend

allegedly

amendment

America
American

annexe d
any

annexing
anyhow
anymore
anyone
anything
anyway
anywhere

anemone
anybody

append

arrest

appendicitis
apprenticeship
apprenticing

ascend
*ascent climb
*assent agree
assess es
assessed

appendix -ces
apprentice d

authentically

ascending
ascension
assemble d
assembling
assembly -ies
assessment

attempt
attend

avenge d

attempted
*attendance those
present / rate of
attending
attendant
*attendants servants
attended
attention
attentive

*effect result / bring
about

*except not including

authentic ally

for Scots: e -r
is on page 242

avenging

In these words you can hear the vowel sound e as in elephant

B

*

beck
bed ded
beg ged
belch es
belched
*bell instrument
*belle beauty
belt
bench es
bend
[bent]
best
bet ted
[bet]

bled
blend
bless es
blessed
[blest]

*bread food
*breadth width
breast
*breath air passing
in and out of lungs
*bred produced
young / reared

* *

beckon ed
bedclothes
bedding
bedrock
bedroom
bedside
bedtime
befell
befriend
beggar
begging
behead
beheld
Belgian
Belgium
bellow ed
belly -ies
benchmark ed
bending
benzene
bereft
*beret flat, round cap
*berry -ies fruit
beset
[beset]
betted
better
betting
bevel led
beverage

blessed
blessing

breakfast
breastbone
breathless
brethren

*bury -ies place deep
down
buried

* * *

Belarus
benefit ed
besetting
bestseller
bevelling
beverage

breathalyse d
ze
breathtaking

burial

* * * * *

beneficial ly
beneficiary -ies
benefited
benefiting
benevolent

breathalyser
zer
breathalysing
zing

Here the first letter 'e' has a short 'i' sound.

BEHAVING WORDS

became	belong ed
because	belonging s
become	beloved
[became]	below
[become]	bemuse d
becoming	bemusing
befall	beneath
[befell]	benign
[befallen]	bereave d
before	bereavement
beforehand	beseech es
begin	beseeched
[began]	[besought]
[begun]	beside
beginner	besides
beginning	besiege d
behalf	besieging
behave d	besotted
behaving	bestow ed
behaviour	betray ed
behavioural	betrayal
behind	between
behold	betwixt
[beheld]	beware
belated ly	bewilder ed
belief	bewilderment
believe d	bewitch es
believer	bewitched
believing	beyond

---

for Scots: e -r
is on page 243 ▷

In these words you can hear the vowel sound e as in elephant

C

*

*cell unit
Celt
*cent money /
  hundred
*cents money

*check ed stop / test
chef
*cheque order to bank
chess
chest

cleanse d
clef
cleft
clench es
clenched

crèche / creche
crêpe / crepe
crept
cress es
crest

*Czech Czechoslovakian

kelp
kept
ketch es

*scent perfume / smell
*scents more than one
  scent

*sell exchange for money
*sense understandable
  pattern
*sent made to go

for Qu . . .
see page 47 ▷

* *

cadet
caress es
caressed
cassette

*cellar underground
  storage room
cello s
Celtic
cement
*censer pan for
  burning incense
*censor judge of what
  may not be published
*census es official count
centaur
central ly
centre
centring
*cession giving up
  ownership

checking
checklist
chemist
cherish es
cherished
cherry -ies
chestnut

cleansing
clever

collect
commence d
compel led
compress es
compressed
condemn ed
condense d
confess es
confessed
connect
consent
contempt
contend
content
contest
correct
courgette

credit ed
crescent
crevice
☛

* * *

celebrate
celery
celestial
cellophane
cellular
celluloid
cellulose
Celsius
cemetery -ies
censorship
centigrade
centipede
centrally
century -ies
cerebral
cerebrum

chemical ly
chemistry

cleanliness
clerical

collecting
collection
collective ly
collector
commencing
compelling
complexion
compression
compressor
concentric
conception
conceptual ly
concession
condenser
condensing
confession
confessor
confetti
congested
congestion
conjecture d
connected
connecting
connection
connector
consensus es
contention
contestant
convection
convector
convention
corrected
correction
correctly
☛

* * * * * *

celebrated
celebrating
celebration
celebrity -ies
celestial
centenary -ies
centimetre
centrifugal ly
centurion
cerebellum
ceremonial ly
ceremony -ies

chemically
cholesterol

collectively
commemorate
commemoration
competitive
competitiveness
competitor
complexity -ies
conceptually
confectioner
confectionery
confessional
congenital ly
conjecturing
consecutive
contemporary -ies
contemptible
contemptuous
conventional ly
cosmetically

credibility
crematorium s
[crematoria]

Czechoslovakia

kinetically

for Scots: e -r
is on page 244 ▷

In these words you can hear the vowel sound e as in elephant

C

SHORT VOWEL **e**

✳ ✳

Kelvin / kelvin
kennel
kestrel
ketchup
kettle

*seller person who sells
*senses means of gaining
information
*sensor detecting device
*session meeting / period

for Qu . . .
see page 47 ▷

✳ ✳ ✳

cosmetic ally
cosmetics

credential
credible
credited
creditor
crescendo s

kinetic ally

**Here the first letter 'e'
has a short 'i' sound.**

cremate   cremation
cremating   crevasse

for Scots: e -r
is on page 244 ▷

D

✳

dead
deaf
dealt
death
debt
deck ed
den
*dense closely packed /
stupid
dent
*dents more than one
dent
depth
desk

dread ed
dreamt
dredge d
dregs
drench es
drenched
dress
dressed

dwell ed
[dwelt]

✳ ✳

deaden ed
deadline
deadlock ed
deadly -ier, -iest
deafen ed
deafer
deafest
deathly
debit ed
debris
debtor
debut / début
decade
deckchair
defect
defence
defend
deflect
delta
deluge d
demo s
denim
Denmark
dental
dentist
depend
depot
depress es
depressed
descant
descend
*descent way down
desert
desktop
desperate
despot
detect
detest
devil led
dexterous / dextrous
☞

✳ ✳ ✳

deafening
debited
December
deception
deceptive
decimal
decorate
dedicate
defective
defector
defendant
defender
defensive
deference
deficit
definite
deflection
delegate
delicate
deluging
democrat
demonstrate
denigrate
density -ies
*dependant person
who depends
*dependants people
who depend
depended
*dependence reliance
*dependent relying /
hanging
depending
depression
depressive
deputy -ies
derelict
☞

✳ ✳ ✳ ✳ ✳ ✳

decimetre
declaration
decorated
decoration
decorative
decorator
dedicated
dedication
defamation
deferential ly
definitely
definition
degradation
delegation
delicacy -ies
delicatessen
deliquescent
delphinium
democratic ally
demographic ally
demolition
demonstrating
demonstration
denigrating
dependable
dependency -ies
deposition
deprivation
derivation
desiccated
desiccation
designated
designating
desolation
☞

for Scots: e -r
is on page 245 ▷

In these words you can hear the vowel sound **e** as in **elephant**

D

* *

digest
direct
dispense d
dissect
*dissent disagreement
distress es
distressed

dreaded
dreadful ly
dredger
dredging
dresser
dressing

dweller
dwelling

* * *

*descendant offspring
descended
*descendent moving down
designate
desolate
desperate ly
destiny -ies
destitute
detection
detective
detector
detention
*deterrence prevention by causing fear
deterrent
*deterrents more than one deterrent
detonate
detriment
devastate
develop ed

digestion
dilemma
dimension
directed
direction
directive
directly
director
discredit ed
discretion
dishevelled
dispelling
dispenser
dispensing
displeasure
dissension
dissenter
distressing

domestic ally

dreadfully

dyslexic / dyslectic

* * * * * *

desperately
desperation
despotism
destination
detectable
detonating
detonator
detrimental
devastated
devastating
devastation
developer
developing
development
developmental ly

digestible
directory -ies
discredited
discrepancy -ies
disseminate
dissemination

domestically
domesticate

dyslexia

Here the first letter 'e' has a short 'i' sound.

D*E*LIGHTFUL WORDS

debate
debating
decamp ed
decay ed
decease d
deceit ful ly
deceive d
deceiving
decide
deciding
deciduous
decipher ed
decision
decisive
declare d
declaring
decline d
declining
decree d
decry -ies
decried
deduce d
deducing
deduct ion
deductive
defeat ed
defer red
deferring
defiance
defiant
deficiency -ies
deficient
define d
defining
deform ed
defy -ies
defied

degree
delay ed
delete
deleting
deletion
deliberate ly
delicious
delight ed
delightful ly
delirious
deliver ed
deliverance
delivery -ies
delusion
demand ed
demanding
demean ed
demise
demob bed
democracy -ies
demolish es
demolished
demonstrative
denial
denomination
denominator
denote
denoting
denounce d
denouncing
denunciation
deny -ies
denied
depart ure
department
deplete
deploy ed

deployment
deport
deposit ed
depositing
depreciate
depreciating
depreciation
deprive d
depriving
derail ed
derailment
derivative
derive d
deriving
derogatory
describe d
describing
description
descriptive
desert ed
deserve d
deserving
design ed
designer
desirable
desire d
desiring
despair ed
despatch es
despatched
despise d
despising
despite
despondency
despondent
dessert
destroy ed

destroyer
destruction
destructive
detach es
detached
detain ed
deter red
detergent

deteriorate
deteriorating
deterioration
determination
determine d
determining
deterring
detract

device
devise d
devising
devoid
devote d
devotion
devour ed
devout

for Scots: e -r is on page 245 ▷

In these words you can hear the vowel sound *e* as in elephant

E

*	**	***	**** ****
ebb ed	*accept take something offered	aesthetic ally	aesthetically
edge d		anyhow	anybody
	*affect alter	anymore	
egg ed		anyone	eccentrically
	any	anything	economic
elf [elves]		anyway	economical ly
elm	**echo** ed	anywhere	economics
else	**eczema**		ecstatically
		ebony	ecumenical ly
end	**eddy** -ies		
	eddied	**eccentric** ally	editorial ly
etch es	**edging**	**ecstasy** -ies	educated
etched	**edit** ed	**ecstatic** ally	educating
		Ecuador	education
	*effect result / bring about	eczema	educational ly
			educator
	effort	edible	Edwardian
		edifice	
	ego	edited	effectively
		editor	effectiveness
	eject	educate	effervescence
			effervescent
	elbow ed	**effective**	effervescing
	elder	**effervesce** d	efficacy -ies
	eldest	**effigy** -ies	
	elect	**effortless**	egoism / egotism
	elsewhere		egoistic / egotistic
		egoist / egotist	
	embed ded		electoral ly
	ember	**ejector**	electorate
	emblem		electrical ly
	empire	**elderly**	electrician
	empress es	**election**	electricity
	empty -ies	**elector**	electrocute
	emptied	**electric** ally	electrocution
		electrode	electrolyse d
	enclave	**electron**	ze
	ending	**elegance**	electrolysing
	endless	**elegant**	zing
	engine	**element**	electrolysis
	ensign	**elephant**	electrolyte
	entail ed	**elevate**	electrolytic ally
	enter ed	**eleven** th	electromagnetic ally
	enthral led	**eloquence**	electronic ally
	entrails	**eloquent**	electronics
	entrance		electrostatic ally
	entrench es	**embargo** es	elementary
	entrenched	embargoed	elevated
	entry -ies	**embassy** -ies	elevation
	envoy	**embedded**	eligible
	envy -ies	**embellish** es	elocution
	envied	embellished	☞
	enzyme	**embezzle** d	
		embryo s	
	epic	**emerald**	
	☞	**emery** ☞	

See also E
on page 65 ▷

for H . . .
see page 40 ▷

for I . . .
see page 41 ▷

for Scots: e -r
is on page 245 ▷

In these words you can hear the vowel sound e as in elephant

E

* *

erect
errand
error

escort
esquire
essay
essence

etching
ethics
ethnic ally

event
ever
every

excel led
*except not including
*excerpt selected
passage
excess es
excise
exempt
exhale d
exhort
exile d
exit
expect
expel led
expense
expert
exploit
export
express es
expressed
extend
extent
extra
extract

* * *

emigrant
emigrate
eminence
eminent
empathy
emperor
emphasis [emphases]
emphasise d
    ze
emphatic ally
emptiness

endeavour ed
endocrine
enemy -ies
energy -ies
engineer ed
entering
enterprise
entertain ed
enthralling
entity -ies
*envelop ed surround
*envelope letter holder
envious

epilogue
episode
epitaph
epithet

equinox es
equity

erection

escalate
escapade
Eskimo s
esplanade
espresso / expresso
essential ly
estimate
estuary -ies

etcetera
ethical ly
ethnical ly
etiquette

eventual
evergreen
everyday
everyone
everything
everywhere
evidence
evident
☞

* * * * * * *

embarkation
embryonic ally
emigration
emissary -ies
emphatically
empirical ly

energetic ally
engineering
entertainer
entertainment
enveloping
enviable

epicyclic ally
epidemic ally
epilepsy
epileptic ally

equatorial
equilibrium
equitable

escalator
especially
essentially
estimated
estimating
estimation

etcetera
ethically
ethnically
etymological ly
etymology

eventually
everlasting
everybody
evidently

excavating
excavation
excellency -ies
exceptional ly
excitation
exclamation
executing
execution
executioner
executive
exemplary
☞

See also E
on page 65 ▷

for H . . .
see page 40 ▷

for I . . .
see page 41 ▷

for Scots: e -r
is on page 245 ▷

In these words you can hear the vowel sound e as in elephant

E

Here the first letter 'e' has a short 'i' sound.

E XCITING WORDS

ecclesiastical ly
eclipse d
eclipsing
ecologist
ecology
edition
efficient
Egyptian
elaborate
elaborating
elaboration
elapse d
elastic ally
elasticity
elated
elation
elicit ed
eliciting
eliminate
eliminating
elimination
Elizabethan
ellipse
elliptical ly
elope d
eloping
elucidate
elude
eluding
elusive
emancipate
emancipation
embankment
embark ed
embarrass es
embarrassed
embarrassing
embarrassment
embroider ed
embroidery
emerge d
emergence
emergency -ies
emerging
emission
emit ted
emitting
emotion
emotional ly
emotive
empirical ly
employ ed
employee
employer
employment
empower ed
emulsion ed
enable d
enabling
enact
enamel led
enamelling
enamour ed
encamp ed
encase d
encasing
enchant ing
encircle d
encircling
enclose d
enclosing

enclosure
encounter ed
encourage d
encouragement
encouraging
encroach es
encroached
encyclopedia
endanger ed
endear ed
endearment
endorse d
endorsing
endow ed
endurance
endure d
enduring
enfold
enforce d
enforcement
enforcing
engage d
engagement
engaging
engrave d
engraving
engross es
engrossed
engulf ed
enhance d
enhancing
enjoy ed
enjoying
enjoyment
enlarge d
enlarging
enlighten ed
enlist
enormous ly
enough
enquire d
enquiring
enquiry -ies
enrage d
enraging
enrich es
enriched
enrol led
enrolment
enslave d
enslaving
ensure d
ensuring
entangle d
entangling
enthusiasm
enthusiast
enthusiatic ally
entire ly
entitle d
entitlement
entitling
entrancing
entrust
enumerate
enumerating
environment al ly
environmentalism
environmentalist
envisage d
envisaging

epitome
equality
equate
equation
equator
equip ped
equipment
equipping
equivalence
equivalent
erase d
eraser
erasing
erode
eroding
erosion
erotic ally
erratic ally
erroneous ly
erupt ed
eruption
escape d
escaping
escarpment
establish es
established
establishment
estate
esteem ed
estrange d
eternal ly
evacuate
evacuating
evacuation
evacuee
evade
evading
evaluate
evaluating
evaluation
evaporate
evaporating
evaporation
evasion
evasive
evict
evoke d
evoking
evolve d
evolving
exacerbate
exact ly
exaggerate
exaggerating
exaggeration
exalt
exam ination
examine d
examining
example
exceed
exceeding ly
exchange d
exchanging
excitable
excite d
excitedly
excitement
exciting
exclaim ed
exclude

* * *

excavate
excellence
excellent
excelling
exception
excessive
exchequer
execute
exemption
*exercise practice / use
*exercise d take
exercise / use
exhaling
exodus es
*exorcise d cast out devil
expectant
expected
expelling
expensive
expertise
exporter
expressing
expression
expressive
expresso / espresso
exquisite
extended
extending
extension
extensive
external ly
extravert / extrovert

* * * * * *

exhibition
exhortation
expectancy -ies
expectantly
expectation
expedition
expeditious
expendable
expenditure
experiential ly
experiment
experimental ly
experimentation
experimenter
explanation
exploitation
exploration
exponential ly
exposition
expressionism
externally
extraversion /
extroversion
extremity -ies
exultation

for Scots: e -r
is on page 245 ▷

See also E
on page 65 ▷

for H . . .
see page 40 ▷

for I . . .
see page 41 ▷

excluding
exclusion
exclusive ly
excrete
excreting
excretion
excruciating
excursion
excuse d
excusing
exert ion
exhaust ed
exhaustion
exhibit ed
exhibiting
exhilarating
exist ed
existence
exorbitant
exotic ally
expand ed
expandable
expanding

expanse
expansion
expansive
expedient
experience d
experiencing
expire d
explain ed
explanatory
explicit
explode
exploding
exploratory
explore d
explorer
exploring
explosion
explosive
exponent
expose d
exposing
exposure
expulsion

exquisite
exterior
exterminate
extermination
external ly
extinct ion
extinguish ed
extinguisher
extract ion
extractor
extraneous
extraordinarily
extraordinary
extrapolate
extrapolating
extravagance
extravagant
extravaganza
extreme ly
extremist
extrusion
exuberance
exuberant

In these words you can hear the vowel sound **e** as in elephant

F

*

fed
fell
*felled cut down
*felt did feel / type of
cloth
fen
fence d
fend
fetch es
fetched
fête

fleck ed
fled
flesh ed
flex es
flexed

French
fresh
fret ted
friend

phlegm

for th . . .
see page 52

* *

feather
fellow
fencing
fennel
ferment
ferret ed
ferry -ies
ferried
fester ed
festive
*feta cheese
*fetter ed chain

fledgeling / fledgling
Flemish

foretell
[foretold]
forget
[forgot]
[forgotten]
forwent / forewent

freckles
Frenchman [Frenchmen]
frenzy -ies
frenzied
fretful ly
fretting
friendly
friendship

pheasant

* * *

February
federal ly
fellowship
feminine
feminist
ferreted
ferreting
festival

flexible
fluorescence
fluorescent

forensic
forever
forgetful ly
forgetting

Frenchwoman
[Frenchwomen]
frenetic ally
freshwater
fretfully
friendliness

phonetic ally

* * * * *

February
federally
federation
femininity
feminism
festivity -ies

fidelity

flexibility
fluorescence
fluorescent

forgetfully
forgetfulness
forget-me-not

frenetically

phonetically

for Scots: e -r
is on page 246

Here the first letter 'e' has a short 'i' sound.

ferocious   ferocity

G

*

*gel semi-solid mixture
gem
get
[got]

glen

guess es
*guessed did guess
*guest person invited

*jell set as a jelly
jest
jet ted

The 'e' is neutralised.

geranium
gregarious
guerilla / guerrilla

---

* *

gazelle

gender
general ly
generous
gentile
gentle
gently
gesture d
getting

ghetto es / s

jealous
jelly -ies
jellied
jemmy -ies
jester
jetted
jetty -ies

* * *

gelatine / gelatin
general ly
generalise d
ze
generate
generic
generous
genetic ally
gentleman [gentlemen]
gentleness
genuine
gestation
gesturing
getaway

jealousy -ies
jellyfish
jeopardy
jettison ed

* * * * * *

generalisation
zation
generalise d
ze
generalising
zing
generally
generation
generator
generosity
genetically
genuinely
geriatric
gesticulate

for Scots: e -r
is on page 246

In these words you can hear the vowel sound **e** as in elephant

H

*

head
health
hedge d
held
hell
helm
help ed
hem med
hemp
hen
hence

* *

headache
head-dress /
headdress es
headed
header
heading
headlamp
headland
headlight
headline d
headlong
headphones
headscarf -ves
headstrong
heady -ier, -iest
healthcare
healthy -ier, -iest
heather
heaven
heavy -ier, -iest
heckle d
heckling
hectare
hectic ally
hedgehog
hedgerow
hedging
hefty -ier, -iest
heifer
hello
helmet ed
helper
helpful ly
helping
helpless
helpline
hemming
henceforth
herald
*heron large bird
*Herren title for
German men
herring
herself

himself

* * *

haematite / hematite
haemorrhage /
hemorrhage d

headier
headiest
headlining
headmaster
headmistress es
headquarters
headteacher
headwaters
healthier
healthiest
healthily
heavenly
heavier
heaviest
heavily
heaviness
heavyweight
hectically
heftier
heftiest
helical ly
heliport
helmeted
helpfully
helplessly
helplessness
hemisphere
heptathlon
heraldry
heresy -ies
heretic
heritage
*heroin drug
*heroine female hero
hesitant
hesitate
hexagon

horrendous

hysterics

* * * * **

hectically
helically
helicopter
helter-skelter
hepatitis
hereditary
heredity
heretical ly
heroism
hesitantly
hesitation
heterogeneous
heterosexual
hexagonal ly

hysterical ly

for Scots: e -r is on page 247

> **Here the first letter 'e' has a short 'i' sound.**
>
> heroic   heroically

In these words you can hear the vowel sound *e* as in elephant

I

*	* *	* * *	* * * * * *
	immense	immensely	identifier
	impel led	impeller	identity -ies
	impress es	impelling	
	impressed	impending	illegible
		impregnate	
	incense d	impression	immeasurable
	indent	impressive	immensity
	inept		impeccable
	infect	incensing	impeccably
	inject	incentive	impediment
	inspect	inception	impenetrable
	instead	incessant	imperative
	intend	indebted	impetuous
	*intense extreme	indented	impregnable
	intent	indenture d	impregnating
	*intents purposes	infection	impressionable
	invent	infectious	impressionism
	invest	inflection	impressionist
		ingestion	
	itself	inherent	incredible
		inherit ed	incredibly
		injection	indefinitely
		inspection	inedible
		inspector	ineptitude
		intensely	inevitable
		intensive	inevitably
		intention	inflexible
		intestine	inflexibly
		invention	inheritance
		inventive	inherited
		inventor	inheriting
		investment	insecticide
		investor	insensitive
			integrity
			intelligence
			intelligent
			intelligible
			intelligibly
			intensify -ies
			intensified
			intensity -ies
			intentional ly
			interrogate
			interrogation
			investigate
			investigating
			investigation
			investigator
			irregular
			irregularity -ies
			irrelevance
			irrelevant
			irreparable
			irreparably

for E . . .
see page 36

for Scots: e -r
is on page 247

In these words you can hear the vowel sound *e* as in elephant

J

*

*gel semi-solid mixture
gem

*__jell__ set as a jelly
__jest__
__jet__ted

* *

gender
general ly
generous
gentile
gentle
gently
gesture d

__jealous__
__jelly__ -ies
jellied
__jemmy__ -ies
__jester__
__jetted__
__jetty__ -ies

for dr . . .
see page 34

* * *

gelatine / gelatin
general ly
generalise d
　　　ze
generate
generic
generous
genetic ally
gentleman
[gentlemen]
gentleness
genuine
gestation
gesturing

__jealousy__ -ies
__jellyfish__
__jeopardy__
__jettison__ ed

* * * * * *

generalisation
　　　　zation
generalise d
　　　　ze
generalising
　　　　zing
generally
generation
generator
generosity
genetically
geriatric
gesticulate

for Scots: e -r
is on page 248

K

*

__kelp__
__kept__
__ketch__ es

__knelt__

for C . . .
see page 33

for Qu . . .
see page 47

* *

__Kelvin / kelvin__
__kennel__
__Kenya__
__kestrel__
__ketchup__
__kettle__

* * *

__kinetic__ ally

* * * * *

__kinetically__

for Scots: e -r
is on page 248

In these words you can hear the vowel sound e as in elephant

L

*

*lead metal
*leant did lean
 leaped / leapt
*led showed / shown
 the way
 ledge
 left
 leg ged
 lend
*[lent] did lend
 length
 lens es
*Lent the 40 days
 before Easter
 less
 lest
 let
 [let]
 let's

* *

lament
lapel

leather ed
lectern
lecture d
ledger
left-hand
left-wing
legend
leggings
leisure d
lemon
lender
lending
lengthen ed
lengthy -ier, -iest
lentil
leopard
leper
*lessen ed make less
lesser
*lesson period of
instruction
letter ed
letting
lettuce
*levee embankment /
quay
level led
*levy -ies charge /
collect
levied

* * *

Lebanese
Lebanon
lecturer
lecturing
legacy -ies
legendary
legislate
lemonade
leprechaun
leprosy
lesbian
lessening
lethargy
letterbox es
lettering
levelling
lexical
lexicon

libretto [libretti]
lieutenant

* * * *

legendary
legislation
legislative
legislator
legislature
levitation

longevity

for Scots: e -r
is on page 248 ▷

Here the first letter 'e' has a short 'i' sound.	
legality -ies	legitimate
legato	lethargic
legitimacy	

In these words you can hear the vowel sound e as in elephant

M

*	**	***	**** ***
meant	many	majestic ally	majestically
melt			malevolent
[molten]	meadow	measurement	
men	measure d	measuring	measurable
mend	*medal award /	mechanise d	mechanising
mesh es	memento	ze	zing
meshed	*meddle d interfere	meddlesome	mechanism
mess es	*meddler person who	medical ly	mechanistic ally
messed	interferes	medicine	medically
met	meddling	meditate	medication
	medicine	megabyte	medieval
	*medlar fruit	megaphone	meditating
	medley	megaton	meditation
	mellow ed	melody -ies	Mediterranean
	melon	membership	melancholy
	melted	memento es / s	Melanesia
	melting	memorable	melanoma
	member	memorably	memorable
	membrane	memorise d	memorably
	memo	ze	memorandum
	memoirs	memory -ies	memorising
	menace d	meniscus es [menisci]	zing
	mental ly	menopause	meningitis
	mention ed	menstruate d	menopausal
	mentor	mentally	menstruating
	menu	merited	menstruation
	merit ed	meriting	mentality -ies
	merry -ier, -iest	merrily	mesmerising
	message	merriment	zing
	*messes more than one	mesmerise d	metabolic
	mess / does mess	ze	metabolism
	Messieurs	messaging	metallurgy
	*Messrs plural of 'Mr'	messenger	metamorphic
	messy -ier, -iest	metalwork	metamorphosis -es
	*metal mineral	metaphor	Methodism
	substance	Methodist	methodological ly
	metalled	metrical ly	methodology -ies
	method	metricate	methylated
	metric ally	metronome	metrically
	*mettle courage	Mexican	metricating
		Mexico	metrication
	misdealt		metropolitan
	misled	momentum	
	misspell ed		millennium s [millennia]
	[misspelt]		
	misspend		molecular
	[misspent]		

Here the first letter 'e' has a short 'i' sound.

mechanic ally	meridian
medicinal ly	methodical ly
melodic al ly	meticulous
melodious	metropolis es
memorial	mnemonic

for Scots: e -r
is on page 249 ▷

In these words you can hear the vowel sound **e** as in e**le**phant

N

*	**	***	*****
knelt	necklace	nebula	necessarily
	nectar	nebulous	necessary
neck ed	neglect	necessary	necessity -ies
nest	nephew	nectarine	neglectfully
net ted	nestle d	negative	negligible
next	nestling	neglectful ly	nepotism
	netball	negligence	nevertheless
	nether	negligent	
	netted	Netherlands	numerical ly
	netting	networking	
	nettle d		
	netware	November	
	network ed		
	never	numeric al	
	Noel		

Here the first letter 'e' has a short 'i' sound.	
negate	negotiating
negation	negotiation
negotiable	negotiator
negotiate	

O

*	**	***	*****
	object	already	authentically
	obsess es		
	obsessed	authentically	objectionable
			objectively
	offence	objection	objectivity
	offend	objective	obscenity -ies
		obsession	obsessional ly
		obsessive	
	oppress es		ostensible
	oppressed	offender	ostensibly
		offensive	
		oppression	
		oppressive	
		oppressor	

for Scots: e -r is on page 249 ▷

for Scots: e -r is on page 249 ▷

In these words you can hear the vowel sound **e** as in elephant

P

*

peck ed
peg ged
pelt
pen ned
pence
pest
pet ted

phlegm

pledge d

press es
pressed

* *

peasant
pebble
*pedal foot lever
pedalled
*peddle d carry and
try to sell
peddler
peddling
pegboard
pegging
pellet
pelvic
pelvis
penance
pencil led
pendant
pending
penguin
penknife
pennant
*penne pasta
penning
*penny -ies old coin
pension ed
pepper ed
peptic
percent / per cent
perfect
peril
perish es
perished
perplex es
perplexed
pester ed
pestle
petal led
*petrel sea-bird
*petrol fuel
petting
petty -ier, -iest

pheasant

pleasant
pleasure
pledging
plenty

possess es
possessed

* * *

parental
pathetic ally

pedalling
pedalo s
pedestal
pedigree
pelican
penalty -ies
pendulum
penetrate
penniless
pensioner
pentagon
pentathlon
peppermint
percentage
perception
perceptive
perceptual ly
peregrine
perfection
perilous
periscope
perpetual ly
perplexing
perspective
pessimist
pesticide
petrify -ies
petrified
petticoat

phonetic ally

pleasantly
plentiful ly
plethora

possession
possessive
potential ly

*precedence priority
precedent
*precedents previous
examples
precipice
predator
predatory
predicate
preferably
preference
pregnancy -ies
prejudice d

* * * * * *

parenthesis
[parentheses]
pathetically

pedestrian
penetrating
penetration
penicillin
*peninsula land
almost surrounded
by water
*peninsular of or like
a peninsula
perceptible
perceptually
perennial ly
perfectionist
perishable
peristalsis
perpetually
pessimism
pessimistic ally

phonetically

pleasurable
plentifully

potentially

predatory
preferably
preferential ly
premiership
preparation
preposition
prepositional ly
Presbyterian
presentable
presentation
preservation
presidency -ies
presidential ly
professional ly
professionalism
progressively
propensity -ies
prophetically

pterodactyl

*for Scots: e -r
is on page 250*

In these words you can hear the vowel sound e as in elephant

P

**

precious
preface
preference
pregnant
prelude
premier
premise /premiss
***presence** being
present
present
***presents** gifts
pressing
pressure d
prestige
presto
pretence
pretend
prevent
profess es
professed
progress es
progressed
project
propel led
prospect
protect
protest

***

premature
premier
premiership
premises
presented
presenting
presently
president
pressuring
prestigious
pretended
pretentious
prevalence
prevalent
prevention
preventive
procession
profession
professor
progression
progressive
projectile
projection
projector
propeller
propelling
prophetic ally
prospective
prospector
prospectus es
protected
protection
protective
protector

for Scots: e -r
is on page 250 ▷

The first letter 'e' in these words is a neutral short vowel. It is pronounced like the 'i' in 'pig'.

PH*E*NOMENAL WORDS

peculiar	petroleum	precipitation	preferring	preserving
peculiarity -ies	phenomenal ly	precise ly	preliminary -ies	preside
peninsula	phenomenon	precision	prepared	presiding
peninsular	[phenomena]	preclude	preparing	presumably
perimeter	precaution	precocious	prescribe d	presume d
peripheral ly	precede d	predict able	prescribing	presuming
periphery -ies	preceding	prediction	prescription	presumptuous
peroxide	precipitate	predominant ly	preservative	prevail ed
petition ed	precipitating	prefer red	preserve d	prevailing

Q

*

quell ed
quench es
quenched
quest

**

quelling
question ed
quintet

***

***questioner** person
    who asks
***questionnaire** set
    of questions

****

questionable

In these words you can hear the vowel sound e as in elephant

R

*

***read** looked at and understood
realm
***red** colour
ref
rend
[rent]
rent
***rest** repose / ones left over
***retch** es try to vomit
retched
***rev** rotation per minute
***Rev** the Reverend
***rex / Rex** king

wreck ed
***wrecks** does smash / more than one wreck
wren
wrench es
wrenched
***wrest** seize
***wretch** unhappy creature

* *

ready -ier, -iest
rebel led
recess es
recessed
reckless
reckon ed
record
rector
rectum
redden ed
redder
reddest
reddish
redhead
redskin
redwood
reference d
reflect
refresh es
refreshed
refuge
refuse
reggae
regret ted
reject
relent
relic
relish es
relished
remnant
render ed
renege d
rental
repel led
repent
repress es
repressed
reptile
request
rescue
resent
resin
respect
respite
rested
restful
resting
restless
revel led
revenge d
reverence
***reverend** deserving respect
***Reverend** title
***reverent** feeling or showing reverence

rosette

* * *

readier
readiest
readily
readiness
rebelling
rebellion
rebellious
reception
receptive
receptor
recession
recessive
recipe
recognise d ze
recollect
recommend
reconcile d
rectangle
rectify -ies
rectified
rectory -ies
redemption
referee
reference d
referencing
reflected
reflection
reflector
reflexive
reformer
refreshment
refugee
regiment
register ed
registrar
registry -ies
regretful ly
regretted
regretting
regular
regulate
rejection
relative
relegate
relentless
relevance
relevant
remedy -ies
remedied
remember ed
remembrance
reminisce d
Renaissance
rendition
reneging
renovate d

* * * * *

receptacle
receptionist
recitation
recitative
recognisable zable
recognising zing
recognition
recollection
recommendation
reconciliation
reconciling
recreation
recreational
rectangular
rectifier
rectifying
referencing
referendum s
[referenda]
reformation
regimental ly
registration
regretfully
regularity -ies
regularly
regulating
regulation
regulator
regulatory
relatively
relativity
relegating
relegation
remembering
reminiscence
reminiscent
reminiscing
renovated
renovating
renovation
repertory -ies
repetition
repetitive
replication
representation
representative
represented
representing
reputable
reputation

for Scots: e -r is on page 251 ▷

In these words you can hear the vowel sound **e** as in e**l**e**phant**

R

SHORT VOWEL e

* *
wreckage
wrestle d
wrestler
wrestling
wretched

Here the first letter 'e' has a short 'i' sound.

R**E** FRESHING WORDS

rebound
rebuke d
recall ed
recede d
receding
receipt
receive d
receiver
receiving
recipient
reciprocal ly
reciprocate
recital
recite
reciting
reclaim ed
recline d
reclining
recoil ed
record ed
recorder
recording
recount
recourse
recover ed
recovery -ies
recruit ment
recuperate
recur red
recurrence
recurrent
recurring
reduce d
reducing
reduction
redundancy -ies
redundant
refer red
referral
referring
refine d
refinery -ies
refining
reform ed
refract ion
refractive
refrain ed
refrigerator
refund
refusal
refuse d
refute
refuting
regain ed
regard ed

regardless
regatta
rehearsal
rehearse d
rejoice d
rejoicing
rejoin ed
relate d
relating
relation
relationship
relax es
relaxed
release d
releasing
reliability
reliable
reliance
relief
relieve d
relieving
religion
religious
relinquish es
relinquished
reluctance
reluctant ly
rely -ies
relied
remain ed
remainder
remaining
remark ed
remarkable
remind ed
reminder
remote
removable /
removeable
removal
remove d
removing
remuneration
renew ed
renewal
renown ed
repair ed
repay
[repaid]
repeal ed
repeat ed
repeating
replace d
replacement
replacing
reply -ies

replied
report ed
reporter
repose d
reposing
reprieve d
reprisal
reproach es
reproached
republic an
repudiate
repudiating
repulsive
repute
require d
requirement
requiring
research es
researched
researcher
reserve d
reserving
resign ed
resist ance
resistor
resolve d
resolving
resort
resource d
resourceful
resources
resourcing
respire d
respond
response
responsibility -ies
responsible
responsive
restore d
restoring
restrain ed
restraint
restrict ion
restrictive
result ed
resultant
resulting
resume d
resuscitate
resuscitating
resuscitation
retain ed
retard ed
retire d
retirement
retiring

* * *
repartee
repellent
repelling
repentance
repertoire
repertory -ies
replica
represent
repression
repressive
requiem
rescuing
resemblance
resemble d
resembling
resentful ly
resentment
reservoir
*residence house
resident
*residents occupiers
residue
resolute
resonance
resonant
respectful ly
respective
restaurant
résumé
retention
retentive
retina
retrograde
revelling
revelry -ies
revenging
revenue
reverence
*reverend deserving
respect
*Reverend title
*reverent feeling or
showing reverence
reversal

rhetoric

* * * * * *
resentfully
reservation
residential
resignation
resolution
respectable
respectfully
respectively
respiration
respiratory
restoration
resurrection
retribution
retrospective
retroviral
retrovirus
revelation
revolution
revolutionary -ies

*for Scots: e -r
is on page 251* ▷

---

retort	reverberating	revive d
retreat	reversal	reviving
retrieval	reverse d	revolt
retrieve d	reversible	revolve d
retrieving	reversing	revolver
return ed	review ed	revolving
returnable	revise d	revue
returning	revising	revulsion
reveal ed	revision	reward
reverberate	revival	

In these words you can hear the vowel sound e as in elephant

S

*
*cell unit
Celt
*cent money / hundred
*cents money

chef

said
says

*__scent__ perfume / smell
*__scents__ more than one
scent

sect
*__sects__ religious groups
self
*__sell__ exchange for
money
[sold]
send
[sent]
*__sense__ understandable
pattern
sensed
*__sent__ made to go
set
[set]
*__sex__ es male / female
sexed

shed
[shed]
shelf [shelves]
shell ed
shelved
shred ded

sketch es
sketched

sledge d
slept

smell ed
[smelt]

speck
sped
spell ed
[spelt]
spend
[spent]
spread
[spread]
☞

* *
*__cellar__ underground
storage room
Celtic
cement
*__censer__ pan for burning
incense
*__censor__ judge of what
may not be published
*__census__ es official count
centaur
central ly
centre d
centring
*__cession__ giving up
ownership

sceptic
sceptre d
schedule d

second
section
sector
segment
seldom
select
selfish
*__seller__ person who
sells
semblance
senate
sending
señor es
*__senses__ means of
gaining information
sensing
*__sensor__ detector
sensual ly
sentence d
sentry -ies
sepal
separate
septic
*__session__ meeting /
period
setback
setted
settee
setter
setting
settle d
settler
settling
set-up
seven th
sever ed
several
☞

* * *
celebrate
celery
celestial
cellophane
cellular
celluloid
cellulose
Celsius
cemetery -ies
censorship
centigrade
centipede
centrally
century -ies
cerebral
cerebrum

sceptical ly
scheduling

secateurs
secession
secondary -ies
second-hand /
secondhand
secondly
secretary -ies
secular
sedative
sediment
segregate
selected
selecting
selection
selective
selector
sellotape
semibreve
seminar
senator
señora s
sensation
sensible
sensibly
sensitive
sensory
sensual ly
sensuous
sentencing
sentiment
sentinel
separate
September
sepulchre
sequential ly
serenade
sesame
settlement
☞

* * * * * *
celebrated
celebrating
celebration
celebrity -ies
celestial
centenary -ies
centimetre
centrifugal ly
centurion
cerebellum
ceremonial ly
ceremony -ies

scepticism

secondary -ies
secretarial
secretary -ies
sedimentary
segmentation
segregating
segregation
selectively
self-reliant
self-sufficient
semicircle
semicircular
semicolon
semiconductor
semi-detached
semi-final
semiquaver
semolina
señorita
sensational ly
sensibility -ies
sensitivity -ies
sentimental ly
separated
separately
separating
separation
separatism
separatist
sequentially
serenading
serenity
seventieth
severity
sexuality
sexually
☞

for Scots: e -r
is on page 252 ▷

50

In these words you can hear the vowel sound e as in elephant

S

*

squelch es
squelched

stealth
stem med
stench es
*step pace / stage
*steppe dry, treeless
plain
stepped
stet
strength
stress es
stressed
stretch es
stretched

sweat
swell
[swollen]
swept

* *

sexist
sextet
sexual ly
sexy -ier, -iest

shedding
shellfish
shelter ed
shelving
shepherd
sheriff
sherry -ies
shredded
shredder
shredding

sketchy -ier, -iest

sledging
slender

smelter

special ly
speckle d
spectre
spectrum [spectra]
speller
spelling
spending
splendid
splendour
spreading
spreadsheet

steady -ies
steadied
stealthy -ier, -iest
stellar
stemming
stencil led
stepping
sterile
steroid
strengthen ed
stretcher

subject
subtend
success es
suggest
suppress es
suppressed
suspect
suspend
suspense

sweater

* * *

seventeen th
seventy -ies
several
severance
sexism
sexual ly

skeleton

spaghetti
specialise d
ze
specialist
specially
specify -ies
specified
specimen
spectacle
spectacles
spectator
speculate
spherical ly

steadily
steadiness
stealthier
stealthiest
stencilling
stepbrother
stepdaughter
stepfather
stepmother
stepsister
stereo s
sterilise d
ze
stethoscope
strenuous

subjected
subjection
subjective
successful ly
succession
successive
successor
suggested
suggesting
suggestion
suggestive
suppression
surrender ed
suspected
suspension

symmetric al
synthetic ally
systemic ally

* * * * * * *

sincerity

specialisation
zation
specialising
zing
speciality -ies
specification
spectacular ly
speculating
speculation
speculative
spherically

stegosaurus es
[stegosauri]
stereophonic ally
stereoscopic ally
stereotype
stereotypical ly
sterilising
zing

successfully
suggestible
susceptibility -ies
susceptible

symmetrical ly
synthetically
systemically

Here the first letter 'e' has a short 'i' sound.

scenario s
seclude d
secrete
secreting
secretion
secure d
securing
security -ies
seduce d
seducing
seduction
seductive
semantic ally
semantics
sequoia
severe ly
specific ally

---

for Scots: e -r
is on page 252

In these words you can hear the vowel sound **e** as in elephant

T

*

tell
[told]
tempt
ten th
tend
*tense form of verb /
stretched tight
tensed
tent
tenth
*tents more than one
tent
test
text

Thames
theft
them
then
thence
thread ed
threat

tread
[trod]
[trodden]
trek ked
trench es
trend

twelfth
twelve

* *

technique
techno
teddy -ies
telling
telly -ies
temper ed
tempest
template
temple
tempo s
tenant
tender ed
tendon
tendril
*tenner ten pound
note
tennis
tenon ed
*tenor male voice
tensing
tension
tepid
terrace d
terrain
terror
tested
testing
testis [testes]
tether ed
textbook
textile
textual
texture d

themselves
threadbare
threaded
threaten ed
threshold

treadle
treasure d
treble d
trebling
trekking
trellis ed
tremble d
trembling
tremor
trendy -ier, -iest
trestle

twenty -ies

* * *

technical ly
technician
tectonic
telecom
telegram
telegraph ed
telephone d
telescope d
televise d
temperament
temperate
temperature
temporary
temptation
tenancy -ies
tendency -ies
tenderness
tenement
tentacle
tentative
tenuous
terracing
terrapin
terrible
terribly
terrier
terrify -ies
terrified
territory -ies
terrorise d
ze
terrorist
tessellate
testament
testicle
testify -ies
testified
tetanus
textual ly

therapist
therapy -ies

together
torrential ly

treacherous
treachery -ies
treasurer
treasury -ies
tremendous

twentieth

* * * * * * *

pterodactyl

technically
technological ly
technology -ies
telecommunications
telegraphy
telepathic ally
telepathy
telephoning
telephonist
telephoto
telescoping
televising
television
temperamental ly
temperature
temporarily
temporary
tentatively
terrarium
terrestrial ly
terrifying
territorial ly
territory -ies
terrorising
zing
terrorism
tessellating
tessellation
testimonial
testimony -ies
tetrahedron
textually

therapeutic ally

torrentially

trajectory -ies
tremendously

for Scots: e -r is on page 253 ▷

Here the first letter 'e' has a short 'i' sound.

terrific ally   thematic ally   thesaurus es [thesauri]

In these words you can hear the vowel sound *e* as in elephant

U

*

* *
unless

* * *
unhelpful

* * * *
unspecified

V

*	* *	* * *	* * * * * * *
Venn	vector	vegetable	vasectomy -ies
vent	Velcro	venison	
vest	velvet	venomous	vegeburger
vet ted	vending	ventilate	vegetable
vex es	vendor	ventricle	vegetarian
vexed	vengeance	venturing	vegetarianism
!31-55_p10.dpd	venom	verify -ies	vegetation
	venture d	verified	Venezuela
	venue	veteran	ventilating
	very		ventilation
	vessel		ventilator
	vested		ventriloquist
	vestry -ies		verification
	veteran		veterinary
	vetted		
	vetting		

for Scots: e -r
is on page 254 ▷

In these words the first 'e' is a neutral vowel.

velocity -ies   Venetian   veranda / verandah

In these words you can hear the vwel sound *e* as in elephant

W

*

*rest repose / ones left over
*retch es try to vomit retched
*rex / Rex king

wealth
web bed
wed ded
[wed]
wedge d
weft
*weld join metal by heat
well
*welled gushed
Welsh
wench es
went
wept
west
*wet ted, ter, test make wet / not dry [wet]

whelk
whelp ed
when
whence
*whet ted sharpen

wreck ed
*wrecks does smash / more than one wreck
wren
wrench es
wrenched
*wrest seize
*wretch es unhappy creature

* *

waistcoat

wealthy -ier, -iest
weapon
*weather conditions outside / endure
weathered
webbing
webcam
webcast
webpage
website
wedded
wedding
wedging
Wednesday
welcome d
welfare
well-known
well-off
Welshman [Welshmen]
western
westward / westwards
*wether neutered ram
wetsuit
*wetted made wet
wetter
wettest
*wetting making wet

*whether if
*whetted sharpened
*whetting sharpening

wreckage
wrestle d
wrestler
wrestling
wretched

* * *

weathercock
weathering
weatherman
[weathermen]
weathervane
webmaster
welcoming
wellbeing
wellington
westerly
West Indies

whenever

* * * *

weatherwoman
[weatherwomen]

for Scots: e -r is on page 255

X

*

* *

X-ray ed

* * *

* * * * *

xenophobia
xenophobic

In these words you can hear the vowel sound **e** as in elephant

Y

SHORT VOWEL e

*
yeah
yell ed
yelp ed
yen
yep
yes
yet

* *
yelling
yellow
Yemen

yourself
yourselves

* * *
yesterday

* * * *
yellowhammer

*for Scots: e -r
is on page 255* ▷

Z

*
Zen
zest

* *
zealot
zealous
zebra
zenith
zephyr

* * *

* * * * *
xenophobia
xenophobic

A

*

* *

abyss es

acquit ted

admit ted
adrift

affix es
affixed
afflict

akin

amid
amidst
amiss

assist

* * *

abysmal ly

acidic
acquittal
acquitted
acquitting
acrylic

addicted
addiction
addictive
addition
admission
admittance
admitted
admitting

affliction

ambition
ambitious

arisen

*assistance help
assistant
*assistants helpers

attribute

* * * *

ability -ies
abysmally

acidity

additional ly
administer ed
administrate
administrating
administration
administrator

affiliate
affiliating
affiliation

agility

alliteration
alliterative

anticipate
anticipating
anticipation

applicable

arithmetic

assimilate
assimilating
assimilation
astigmatism

attributed
attributing
atypical ly

auxiliary -ies

for Scots: i -r
is on page 242 ▷

In these words you can hear the vowel sound i as in pig

B

*	* *	* * *	* * * * *
*been past form of 'be'	became	becoming	beatitude
	because	befallen	behavioural
	become	beforehand	belatedly
bib	[became]	beginner	belligerent
bid	[become]	beginning	benevolent
[bade]	befall	behaving	bewilderment
[bid]	[befell]	behaviour	
[bidden]	[befallen]	believing	bibliography -ies
big	before	belonging	binocular
bill	befriend	belongings	binoculars
*billed did bill	begin	beloved	
*bin container	[began]	bemusing	Bolivia
binge	[begun]	bereavement	
bit	behalf	besetting	brilliantly
bitch es	behave d	besieging	
bitched	behead	besotted	businesswoman
	beheld	bewilder ed	[businesswomen]
blink ed	behind		
bliss	behold	biblical	
blitz ed	[beheld]	bickering	
	belief	bikini	
brick ed	believe d	bilberry -ies	
bridge d	belong ed	bishopric	
brim med	beloved	bitterly	
bring	below	bitterness	
[brought]	bemuse d		
brink	beneath	blissfully	
brisk	benign		
	bereave d	bricklayer	
*build construct	[bereft]	bricklaying	
[built]	beseech es	brigadier	
	beseeched	brilliance	
	[besought]	brilliant ly	
	beset		
	[beset]	busier	
	beside	busiest	
	besides	busily	
	besiege d	businessman	
	besought	[businessmen]	
	bestow ed		
	betray ed		
	between		
	betwixt		
	beware		
	bewitch es		
	bewitched		
	beyond		

for Scots: i -r
is on page 243

In these words you can hear the vowel sound i as in pig   **57**

B

* *

bicker ed
bidden
bidder
bidding
bigger
biggest
bilious
billiards
billion
billow ed
binging
bingo
biscuit
bishop
***bitten** past form of
'bite'
bitter
***bittern** bird
bizarre

blinkered
blinkers
blissful ly
blister ed
blizzard

Brazil
breeches
brickwork
bridging
brigade
brilliance
brilliant
brimming
bringing
briskly
bristle d
bristling
***Britain** country
British
***Briton** British person
brittle

builder
building
business
busy -ies
busied
busy -ier, -iest

*for Scots: i -r
is on page 243* ▷

In these words you can hear the vowel sound i as in pig

C

*

chick
chid
chill ed
chimp
chin
chink
chintz
chip ped

cinch es

click ed
cliff
cling
[clung]
clink ed
clip ped

crib bed
cringe d
crisp
crypt

cyst

kick ed
kid ded
kids
kill ed
kiln
kilt
kin
king
kink ed
kiss ed
kit ted
kith

* *

cement

chicken ed
chicklit
chickpea
chidden
chiffchaff
chiffon
chilblain
children
*Chile country
*chilli hot spice
*chilly -ier, -iest cold
chimney
chipboard
chipmunk
chipping
chisel led
christen ed
christening
Christian
Christmas

cigar
cinder
cirrus [cirri]
cistern
citrus
city -ies
civic
civil ly

clinic ally
clipper
clipping

commit ted
conflict
conscript
consist
convict
convince d

create
cremate
cribbing
cricket
crimson
crinkle d
crinkly
cripple d
crippling
crisscross ed
critic ally
critique
crystal

* * *

capricious

celestial
ceramic

charisma
chickenpox
chicory
chimpanzee
chiselling
chivalrous
chivalry
christening
chrysalis

cigarette
*cilia more than one
cilium
ciliary
cilium [cilia]
cinema
cinnamon
citizen
civilian
civilise d
ze
civilly

clickable
clinical ly
clinician
clitoris

cognition
collision
commission ed
commitment
committed
committee
committing
condition ed
conscription
consider ed
consistent
consisting
constriction
continual ly
continue d
contribute
conviction
convincing

* * * * *

calligraphy
capillary -ies
captivity

celebrity -ies
celestial
certificate

Christianity
chrysanthemum

ciliary
citizenship
civilian
civilisation
zation
civilising
zing

clinically

commissioner
conditional ly
conditioner
configuration
coniferous
considerable
considerate
consideration
consistency -ies
consistently
conspicuous
conspiracy -ies
conspirator
constituency -ies
constituent
contingency -ies
continual ly
continuance
continuation
continuing
continuous ly
continuum
contributed
contributing
contributor

for Qu . . .
see page 83 ▷

for Scots: i -r ▷
is on page 244

In these words you can hear the vowel sound i as in pig

59

C

**

cuisine

***cygnet** young swan
***cymbals** discs to
clash
cynic
cystic

kebab

kick-off
kidded
kidding
kidnap ped
kidney
killer
killing
kindle d
kindling
kingdom
king-size
kinky -ier, -iest
kinship
kipper
kissing
kitchen
kitted
kitten
kitting

***signet** seal / ring

***symbols** signs

***

created
creating
creation
creative
creator
cremating
cremation
crescendo s
cricketer
criminal ly
crinoline
critical ly
criticise d
    ze
crystalline
crystallise d
    ze

cylinder
cynical ly
Cypriot
cystitis

kidnapper
kidnapping
kilobyte
kilogram
kimono s
kinetic ally
kingfisher

***sillier** more silly

**** *

creativity
criminally
criminology
critically
criticising
    zing
criticism
crystallisation
      zation
crystallising
     zing

curricular
curriculum [curricula]

cylindrical
cynically
cynicism

kilometre
kindergarten
kinetically

for Qu . . .
see page 83 ▷

for Scots: i -r
is on page 244 ▷

In these words you can hear the vowel sound i as in pig

D

*

did
dig ged
[dug]
dim med
din
ding
dip ped
disc / disk
dish es
dished
ditch es
ditched

drift
drill ed
drink
[drank]
[drunk]
drip ped

**

debate
decamp ed
decay ed
decease d
deceit
deceive d
decide
declare d
decline d
decrease d
decree d
decry -ies
decried
deduce d
deduct
defeat
defect
defence
defend
define d
deflect
deform ed
defy -ies
defied
degree
delay ed
delete
delight
demand
demean ed
demise
demob bed
denote
denounce d
deny -ies
denied
depart
depend
depict
deplete
deploy ed
deport
depress es
depressed
deprive d
derail ed
derive d
descend
*descent way down
describe d
*desert leave
deserve d
design ed
desire d
despair ed
*despatch es send off
despatched
☜

***

deceitful ly
deceiving
December
deception
deceptive
deciding
decipher ed
decision
decisive
declaring
declining
decreasing
deducing
deduction
deductive
defeated
defective
defector
defendant
defender
defensive
defiance
defiant
deficient
defining
deflection
deleting
deletion
deliberate
delicious
delighted
delightful ly
delinquent
deliver ed
delusion
demanded
demeanour
demolish es
demolished
denial
denoting
denouncing
department
departure
*dependant person
who depends
*dependants people
who depend
depended
*dependence reliance
*dependent relying /
hanging
depending
deployment
☜

* * * * **

decapitate
decapitating
deceitfully
deciduous
deficiency -ies
deliberate
deliberately
deliberating
delightfully
delinquency
delirious
deliverance
delivery -ies
democracy -ies
demonstrative
demoralise d
ze
demoralising
zing
denomination
denominator
denunciation
dependable
dependency -ies
deposited
depositing
depreciate
depreciating
depreciation
derivative
desirable
despicable
detectable
deteriorate
deteriorating
deterioration
determination
determining
developer
developing
development

dictatorial ly
dictatorship
dictionary -ies
differential
differentiate
differentiating
differentiation
differently
difficulty -ies
☜

*for Scots: i -r
is on page 245* ▷

In these words you can hear the vowel sound i as in pig

61

D

**

despise d
despite
*dessert sweet dish
destroy ed
detach es
detached
detain ed
detect
deter red
detest
detract
*device gadget / plan
*devise d invent /
work out
devoid
devote
devour ed

dickey / dicky
dictate
diction
didn't
differ ed
difference
different
diffuse d
digest
digger
digging
digit
dimmer
dimming
dimple d
*dinghy -ies small boat
*dingy -ier, -iest dull
dinner
diphthong
dipper
dipping
dipstick
direct
disarm ed
discard
discern ed
discharge d
disclose d
disco s
discount
discourse
*discreet careful not
to embarrass
*discrete separate
*discus es [disci] heavy
disc to throw in games
*discuss es debate
*discussed debated
disdain ed
↙

***

deposit ed
depression
depressive
depriving
deriving
descendant
descended
describing
description
descriptive
deserted
deserving
designer
desiring
despising
destroyer
destruction
destructive
detachment
detection
detective
detector
detention
detergent
determine d
*deterrence prevention
by causing fear
deterrent
*deterrents more than
one deterrent
deterring
develop ed
devoted
devotion

dictating
dictation
dictator
dictionary -ies
difference
different
differently
difficult
diffusing
diffusion
digestion
digital ly
dignify -ies
dignified
dignity -ies
dilemma
diligence
diligent
dimension
diminish es
diminished
↙

**** **

digestible
digitally
dilapidated
diphtheria
diplodocus es
diplomacy
diplomatic ally
directory -ies
disability -ies
disablement
disadvantage d
disagreeable
disagreement
disappearance
disappointment
disapproval
disapproving
disarmament
disassemble d
disciplinarian
disciplinary
discouraging
discovery -ies
discredited
discrepancy -ies
discriminate
discriminating
discrimination
disgracefully
dishonesty
dishonourable
disinfectant
disintegrate
disintegrating
disloyally
disloyalty
disobedience
disobedient
disorganise d
ze
disposition
disproportionate ly
disqualify -ies
disqualified
dissatisfaction
dissatisfy -ies
dissatisfied
disseminate
dissertation
dissimilar
dissolution
↙

for Scots: i -r
is on page 245 ▷

In these words you can hear the vowel sound i as in pig

D

**

disease d
disgrace d
disguise d
*disgust strong dislike
dishcloth
dishes
dislike d
dislodge d
disloyal ly
dismal ly
dismay ed
dismiss ed
dismount
disown ed
*dispatch es despatch /
message
dispatched
dispel led
dispense d
disperse d
displace d
display ed
displease d
dispose d
disprove d
[disproven]
dispute
disrupt
dissect
*dissent disagreement
dissolve d
*distal farthest from
point of attachment
distance d
distant
distaste
*distil led make pure
distinct
distort
distract
distraught
distress es
distressed
district
distrust
disturb ed
disused
dither ed
ditto
divan
diverge d
diverse
divert
divide
divine d
divorce d
dizzy -ier, -iest

***

diploma
diplomat
directed
direction
directive
directly
director
disable d
disabling
disagree d
disappear ed
disappoint
disapprove d
disaster
disastrous
disbelief
discharging
disciple
discipline d
disclosure
discomfort
discontent
discordant
discothèque
discourage d
discover ed
discredit ed
discretion
discussing
discussion
disgraceful ly
disgracing
disgruntle d
disgruntling
disgusting
dishearten ed
dishevelled
dishonest
dishwasher
disinfect
disliking
dislodging
disloyal ly
disloyalty
dismally
dismantle d
dismantling
dismissal
dismissing
dismissive
disobey ed
disorder ed
dispelling
dispenser
dispensing
dispersing

* * * * * *

distillation
distinguishable
distractible
distributing
distribution
distributive
distributor
diversification
diversify -ies
diversified
diversity
divinity -ies
divisibility
divisible
divisional

dysentery
dyslexia

for Scots: i -r
is on page 245 ▷

In these words you can hear the vowel sound i as in pig

63

D

**

dribble d
dribbling
drifted
driftwood
drinker
drinking
dripping
driven
drizzle d
drizzling

dwindle d
dwindling

***

displacement
displacing
displeasing
displeasure
disposal
disposing
disproven
disproving
disputing
disregard
disrespect
disruption
disruptive
dissension
dissenter
*dissidence disagreeing
with those in power
dissident
*dissidents protesters
dissolving
distancing
distasteful
distillate
distilling
distinction
distinctive
distinctly
distinguish es
distinguished
distortion
distraction
distractor
distressing
distribute
disturbance
disturbing
divided
dividend
dividers
dividing
division
divisor
divorcee
divorcing
dizziness

dynasty -ies
dysentery
dyslexic / dyslectic
dystrophy -ies

*for Scots: i -r
is on page 245* ▷

In these words you can hear the vowel sound **i** as in **pig**

E

*

**

*accept take something
offered

*affect alter

éclair
eclipse d

*effect result / bring
about

eject

elapse d
elect
élite
ellipse
elope d
elude

embark ed
embed ded
embrace d
embroil ed
emerge d
emit ted
employ ed
empower ed

enact
encamp ed
encase d
enchant
enclose d
encroach es
encroached
endear ed
endorse d
endow ed
endure d
enfold
enforce d
engage d
England
English
engrave d
engross es
engrossed
engulf ed
enhance d
enjoy ed
enlarge d
enlist
enough
enquire / inquire d

for H . . .
see page 71 ▷

for I . . .
see page 72 ▷

***

eccentric ally
eclipsing

edition

effective
efficient

Egyptian

ejector

elaborate
elastic ally
election
electors
electric ally
electrode
electron
eleven th
*elicit ed draw out
élitist
eloping
eluding
*elusive hard to find

embankment
embargo es
embargoed
embarrass es
embarrassed
embedded
embedding
embellish es
embellished
embezzle d
embody -ies
embodied
embracing
embroider ed
emergence
emerging
emission
emitted
emitting
emotion
emotive
emphatic ally
employee
employer
employment
empower ed
emulsion ed

enable d
enabling
enamel led
enamour ed

**** *****

eccentrically
ecclesiastical ly
ecology
economy -ies

effectively
effectiveness
efficiency
efficiently

elaborate
elaboration
elastically
elasticity
electoral ly
electorate
electrical ly
electrician
electricity
electrocute
electrolyse d
          ze
electrolysis
electrolyte
electrolytic ally
electromagnetic ally
electronic ally
elicited
eliciting
eliminate
eliminating
elimination
élitism
Elizabethan
elliptical ly
elucidate

emancipate d
emancipating
emancipation
embarrassing
embarrassment
embroidery
emergency -ies
emotional ly
emphatically
empirical ly

In these words you can hear the vowel sound i as in pig

65

E

* *

enrage d
enrich es
enriched
enrol led
enslave d
*ensure d make certain
entail ed
entire
entrance d
entrench es
entrenched
entrust / intrust

equate
equip ped

erase d
erect
erode
erupt

escape d
escort
estate
esteem ed
estrange d

evade
event
evict
evoke d
evolve d

exact
exalt
exam
exceed
excel led
*except not including
excess es
exchange d
excite
exclaim ed
exclude
excrete
excuse d
exempt
exert
exhaust
exhort
exist

* * *

encasing
enchanting
encircle d
encircling
enclosing
enclosure
encounter ed
encourage d
endanger ed
endearment
endeavour ed
endorsing
endurance
enduring
enforcement
enforcing
engagement
engaging
Englishman
[Englishmen]
engraving
enhancing
enigma
enjoying
enjoyment
enlarging
enlighten ed
enormous
enquiring / inquiring
enquiry / inquiry -ies
enraging
enrolling
enrolment
enslaving
*ensuring making
certain
entangle d
entangling
entirely
entitle d
entrancing
envelop ed
envisage d

equation
equator
equipment
equipping

eraser
erasing
erection
eroding
erosion
erotic ally
erratic ally
erupted
eruption

* * * * * * *

enamelling
encouragement
encyclopedia
Englishwoman
[Englishwomen]
enormously
enthusiasm
enthusiast
enthusiastic ally
entitlement
enumerate
enumerating
enveloping
environment
environmental ly
environmentalism
environmentalist
envisaging

epitome

equality
equivalence
equivalent

erotically
erratically
erroneous ly

esophagus / oesophagus
esophagus es [esophagi]
especially
essentially
establishment

etcetera
eternally

evacuate
evacuation
evacuee
evaluate
evaluation
evangelism
evangelist
evaporate
evaporation
eventually

exacerbate
exaggerate
exaggeration
examination

for H . . .
see page 71

for I . . .
see page 72

In these words you can hear the vowel sound **i** as in pig

E

* *

expand
expanse
expect
expel led
expense
expire d
explain ed
explode
exploit
explore d
expose d
express es
expressed
extend
extent
extinct
extract
extreme
exult

*inshore near the shore
*insure d protect against
loss

* * *

escaping
escarpment
essential ly
establish es
established

etcetera
eternal ly

evading
evasion
eventual ly
evoking
evolving

exactly
examine d
example
excellent
excelling
exception
excessive
exchanging
exchequer
excited
excitement
exciting
excluding
exclusion
exclusive
excreting
excretion
excursion
excusing
exemption
exertion
exhausted
exhaustion
exhibit ed
existed
existence
exotic ally
expanded
expanding
expansion
expansive
expectant
expected
expelling
expensive
explaining
explicit
exploding
explorer
exploring
explosion
explosive

* * * * * * *

exceedingly
exceptional ly
excitedly
exclamation
exclusively
excruciating
executive
exemplary
exhibited
exhibiting
exhilarating
exorbitant
exotically
expandable
expectantly
expediency
expedient
expenditure
experience d
experiencing
experiential ly
experiment
experimental ly
explanatory
exploratory
exterior
exterminate
externally
extinguisher
extraordinarily
extraordinary
extraneous
extrapolate
extravagance
extravagant
extravaganza
exuberance
exuberant

for H . . .
see page 71

for I . . .
see page 72

In these words you can hear the vowel sound i as in pig

67

E

* * *
exponent
exposing
exposure
expressing
expression
expressive
expulsion
exquisite
extended
extending
extension
extensive
external ly
extinction
extinguish es
extinguished
extraction
extractor
extremely
extremist
extrusion

for H . . .
see page 71 ▷

for I . . .
see page 72 ▷

*illicit illegal
*illusive deceptive

*insuring protecting
against loss

F

*	* *	* * *	* * * * * *
fib bed	fibbing	familiar	facilitate
fifth	fiction		facilitating
fig	fiddle d	ferocious	facility -ies
fill ed	fiddler		familiarity
film ed	fiddling	*fiancé man engaged	fastidious
filth	fiddly	to be married	
*fin what fish use	fidget ed	*fiancée woman	ferocity
to swim and balance	fifteen th	engaged to be married	fertility
finch es	fifty -ies	fiasco s	
*Finn citizen of Finland	figure d	fictional	fidelity
finned	filler	fictitious	figurative
fiord / fjord	fillet	fidgeted	financially
*fish es creature(s)	filling	fidgeting	financier
with tail and fins	filly -ies	fidgety	
fished	*filter ed pass through	fiesta	frenetically
fist	filthy -ier, -iest	fiftieth	frivolity
fit ted	finance d	filament	
fix es	finger ed	filthiest	phenomenal ly
fixed	*finish es end	filtration	phenomenon
fizz es	finished	☞	[phenomena]
fizzed	Finland		☞
☞	*Finnish language		
	spoken by Finns / of		

for th . . .
see page 90 ▷

or from Finland
☞

for Scots: i -r
is on page 246 ▷

In these words you can hear the vowel sound **i** as in pig

F

*

flick ed
flinch es
fling
[flung]
flint
flip ped
flit ted

fridge
frill ed
fringe d
frisk ed

*phish ed attempt
internet fraud

* *

fiord / fjord
fiscal
***fisher** person who
fishes
fishes
***fishing** trying to catch
fish
fission
***fissure** d crack
fistful
fitful ly
fitness
fitted
fitting
fixture
fizzle d
fizzy -ier, -iest

flicker ed
flimsy -ier, -iest
flippant
flipper
flipping
flitted
flitting

forbid
[forbade / forbad]
[forbidden]
forgive
[forgave]
[forgiven]

friction
frigate
frigid
Frisbee
fritter ed
frizzy -ier, -iest

fulfil led

*philtre love-potion
*phishing attempting
internet fraud
physics
physique

* * *

finale
financial ly
fingernail
fingerprint
fingertip
finicky -ier, -iest
finishing
fisherman [fishermen]
fishery -ies
fishmonger
fitfully
fixation

flamingo es / s

forbidden
forbidding
forgiven
forgiveness
forgiving

frenetic ally
frivolous
fruition

fulfilling
fulfilment

physically
physician
physicist

* * * * * * *

philatelist
philosopher
philosophical ly
philosophy -ies
physically
physiological ly
physiology
physiotherapist
physiotherapy

for th . . .
see page 90 ▷

for Scots: i -r
is on page 246 ▷

In these words you can hear the vowel sound i as in pig

G

*

gift
gig
*gild paint with gold
[gilt]
*gilled having gills
gills
*gilt gilded
gin
gist
give
[gave]
[given]

glib
glimpse d
glint

grid
*grill ed cook by
direct heat /
bars for cooking /
food so cooked
*grille protecting set
of bars in door or
window
grim
grin ned
grip ped
grit ted

*guild association
*guilt responsibility
for doing wrong

gym

jib bed
jig ged
jilt
*jinks lively behaviour
*jinx es cause bad luck
jinxed

* *

giggle d
giggling
gilded
*gilder person who
gilds
gimlet
gimmick
ginger ed
gingham
gipsy / gypsy -ies
giraffe
given
giver
giving

glimmer ed
glimpsing
glisten ed
glitter ed

grenade
griddle
gridlock ed
griffin / gryphon
grimace d
grimly
grinning
gripping
*grisly -ier, iest horrible
gristle
gritting
gritty -ier, iest
grizzle d
grizzling
*grizzly -ier, iest grey /
bear

*guilder old Dutch coin
guilty -ier, -iest
*guinea twenty one
old shillings
*Guinea West African
country
guitar

gymnast
gymslip
gypsy / gipsy -ies

jibbing
jiffy
jigging
jiggle d
jigsaw
jihad
jingle d
jingling

* * *

genetic ally

gibberish
Gibraltar
gigabyte
gingerbread
gingerly

glycerine

*gorilla ape

grimacing

*guerrilla / guerilla
agent of political
violence
guillemot
guillotine d
guiltily
guinea-pig
guitarist

gymkhana
gymnastics
gymnosperm

* * * * *

gelatinous
genetically
geography -ies
geology
geometry -ies
geranium

gregarious

guillotining

gymnasium s [gymnasia]

*for Scots: i -r
is on page 246* ▷

In these words you can hear the vowel sound *i* as in pig

H

*
hid
hill
hilt
***him** that male
individual
hinge d
hint
hip
his
hiss ed
hit
[hit]
hitch es
hitched

***hymn** song with
verses sung in church

* *
hiccup ped
hidden
hijab
hillside
hilltop
himself
hinder ed
hindrance
Hindu
hip-hop
hippy -ies
hissing
hither
hitting

hymnal

* * *
habitual ly

heroic ally

hiccupping
hickory
hideous
historic ally
history -ies
hitherto

holistic ally
horrific ally

hypnosis
hypnotic ally
hypnotise d
            ze
hypocrite
hysterics

* * * * **
habitually

hereditary
heredity
heroically

higgledy-piggledy
hilarious
Himalayas
Hinduism
hippopotamus es
[hippopotami]
historian
historical ly

holistically
horrifically
hostility -ies

hypnotically
hypnotising
            zing
hypnotism
hypocrisy
hypocritical ly
hysteria
hysterical ly

I

*	* *	* * *	* * * * · * * *
if	*ensure d make certain	*allusion reference	**idiomatic** ally
			idiotic ally
ill	**igloo**	*elicit ed draw out	
	ignite	*elusive hard to find	**iguanodon**
imp	**ignore** d	*ensuring making certain	
			illegally
*in not outside	**illness** es	**idiom**	**illegible**
inch es		**idiot**	**illiterate**
inched	**image** d		**illogical** ly
ink	**immense**	**igneous**	**illuminate**
*inn small hotel	**immerse** d	**ignition**	**illumination**
	immune	**ignorance**	**illustrating**
is	**impact**	**ignorant**	**illustration**
	impair ed	**ignoring**	**illustrative**
it	**impart**		**illustrator**
itch es	**impasse**	*ileum part of	**illustrious**
itched	**impede** d	intestine	
*its belonging to it	**impel** led	*ilium [ilia] part of	**imaginary**
*it's it is	**impinge** d	hip-bone	**imagination**
	implore d	**illegal** ly	**imaginative**
	imply -ies	*illicit illegal	**imagining**
	implied	*illusion false belief or	**imitating**
	import	appearance	**imitation**
	impose d	*illusive deceptive	**immaculate**
	impress es	**illustrate**	**immeasurable**
	impressed		**immediate** ly
	imprint	**imagery**	**immensity**
	improve d	**imagine** d	**immigration**
	impulse	**imaging**	**immortality**
	impure	**imbalance**	**immortally**
		imitate	**immovable**
	inbox es	**immature**	**immunisation**
	incense d	**immediate**	zation
	incest	**immensely**	**immunising**
	*incite encourage	**immersing**	zing
	strong feeling or	**immersion**	**immunity**
	action	**immigrant**	**impartially**
	incline d	**immigrate**	**impassable**
	include	**imminent**	**impatiently**
	income	**immobile**	**impeccable**
	increase d	**immoral** ly	**impediment**
	incur red	**immortal** ly	**impenetrable**
	indeed	**immunise** d	**imperative**
	indent	ze	**imperceptible**
	in-depth	**impartial** ly	**imperial** ly
	index es [indices]	**impasto**	**imperialism**
	indexed	**impatience**	**impermeable**
	indict	**impatient**	**impersonal**
	indie	**impeachment**	**impersonate**
	indoor	**impeding**	**impersonation**
	indoors	**impeller**	**impertinent**
	induce d	**impelling**	**impervious**
	indulge d	**imperfect**	**impetuous**
	inept	**impetus** es	
	inert	**implement**	
		implicate	
		implicit	
		imploring	

for E . . .
see page 65

for H . . .
see page 71

for Scots: i -r
is on page 247

72 In these words you can hear the vowel sound i as in pig

I

**

infant
infect
infer red
infirm
inflame d
inflate
inflict
influx es
inform ed
infringe d
ingot
inhale d
inject
injure d
inland
in-law
inlet
inmate
innate
inner
innings
input
inquest
inquire / enquire d
insane
inscribe d
insect
insert
*inshore near the
shore
inside
*insight understanding
insist
inspect
inspire d
instal led / install ed
*instance example
instant
*instants moments
instead
instinct
instruct
insult
*insure d protect
against loss
intact
intake
intend
*intense very strong
intent
*intents purposes
inter red
interest
into
intrigue d
intrude
intrust / entrust

for E . . .
see page 65

for H . . .
see page 71

***

impolite
importance
important
imposing
impotence
impotent
impregnate
impression
impressive
imprison ed
impromptu s
improper
improvement
improving
improvise d
impudence
impudent
impulsive

incarnate
incensing
incentive
incessant
*incidence rate of
happening
incident
*incidents events
incision
incisor
inciting
inclining
included
including
inclusion
inclusive
incoming
incomplete
incorrect
increasing
incurring
indebted
indecent
indented
indenture d
India
Indian
indicate
indictment
indifferent
indignant
indigo
indirect
indiscreet
indistinct

for Scots: i -r
is on page 247

* * * * **

implacable
implementation
implication
impossibility
impossible
impoverish ed
impractical
impregnable
impregnating
impressionable
impressionism
impressionist
imprisonment
improvisation
improvising
impunity
impurity -ies

inability
inaccessible
inaccuracy -ies
inaccurate
inadequate ly
inadvertent ly
inappropriate
inattentive
inaudible
inaugural
inauguration
incapable
incidental ly
inclination
incognito
incompatible
incomprehensible
inconceivable
incongruity -ies
incongruous
inconsistent
inconvenience
inconvenient
incorporate d
incorporating
increasingly
incredible
incredibly
incubation
incubator
incurable
indecisive
indefensible
indefinite ly
independence
independent
indestructible
indeterminate

In these words you can hear the vowel sound i as in pig

73

I

* *

invade
invent
inverse
invert
invest
invite
invoice d
invoke d
involve d
inward
inwards

Iran
Iraq

Islam
isn't
Israel
issue d
isthmus es [isthmi]

itself

* * *

inducing
induction
inductive
indulgence
indulgent
indulging
industry -ies
inertia
infamous
infancy
infantile
infantry
infection
infectious
inference
inferring
infinite
inflaming
inflating
inflation
inflection
influence d
informal ly
informant
informer
infrared / infra-red
infrequent
infringement
ingenious
inhabit ed
inhaler
inhaling
inherent
inherit ed
inhibit
inhuman
initial led
injection
injuring
injury -ies
injustice
innermost
innkeeper
*innocence freedom
from guilt
innocent
*innocents people who
have done no wrong
innovate
inquiring / enquiring
inquiry / enquiry -ies
inscribing
inscription

* * * * * * *

indicated
indicating
indication
indicator
indifferent
indigenous
indigestible
indigestion
indignation
indiscretion
indiscriminate ly
indispensable
individual ly
individualism
individuality
indivisible
Indonesia
industrial ly
industrialisation
        zation
industrialise d
        ze
industrialist
industrious
inedible
ineffective ly
ineffectual ly
inefficiency -ies
inefficient ly
ineptitude
inequality -ies
inevitable
inevitably
inexpensive ly
inexperienced
infatuate d
infatuation
inferior
inferiority
infinitely
infinitive
infinity
infirmary -ies
inflammable
inflammation
inflammatory
inflationary
inflexible
influential ly
influenza
informally
information
informative
infrastructure
infuriate
infuriating

for E . . .
see page 65

for H . . .
see page 71

for Scots: i -r
is on page 247

In these words you can hear the vowel sound i as in pig

I

* * *

insecure
insertion
insider
insipid
insisted
insistence
insofar
insolence
insolent
inspection
inspector
inspiring
installing
instalment /
installment
instantly
instinctive
institute
instruction
instructive
instructor
instrument
insulate
insulin
insulting
insurance
*insuring protecting
against loss
integer
integral
integrate
intensely
intensive
intention
interact
intercept
interchange
intercourse
interested
interesting
interface
interfere d
interim
interlock ed
interlude
internal ly
internet
interpret ed
interrupt
intersect
intersperse d
interval
intervene d
interview ed

for Scots: i -r
is on page 247

* * * * * *

ingenious
ingenuity
ingredient
inhabitant
inhabited
inhabiting
inheritance
inherited
inheriting
inhibition
inhospitable
iniquity
initialling
initially
initiate
initiating
initiative
injurious
innovation
innovative
innumerable
inoculate
inoculation
inorganic ally
inquisition
inquisitive
insanitary
insanity
inscrutable
insecticide
insensitive
insidious ly
insignificant
insoluble
insomnia
inspiration
installation
instantaneous
institution al
instrumental ly
insufficient ly
insulating
insulation
insulator
insuperable
integrating
integration
integrity
intellectual ly
intelligence
intelligent
intensify -ies
intensified
intensity -ies
intentional ly

for E . . .
see page 65

for H . . .
see page 71

In these words you can hear the vowel sound i as in pig

I

* * *

intestine
intimate
intranet
intricate
intriguing
intrinsic ally
introduce d
introvert
intruder
intruding
intrusion
intrusive
Inuit
inundate
invaded
invader
invading
invalid
invasion
invention
inventive
inventor
inventory -ies
inversely
inversion
inverted
investment
investor
invited
invoicing
invoking
involvement
involving
inwardly

Iraqi
irrigate
irritate

Islamic
Israel
Israeli
issuing

Italian
italic
Italy

* * * * **

interaction
interactive
interception
interchangeable
interested
interesting ly
interference
interfering
interior
intermediate
interminable
intermission
intermittent
internally
international ly
interpolate
interpolating
interpretation
interpreted
interpreter
interpreting
interrogate
interrogating
interrogation
interrogative
interrupted
interruption
intersection
interspersing
intervening
intervention
interwoven
intestinal ly
intimacy -ies
intimidate
intimidating
intolerable
intolerance
intonation
intoxicate
intoxicating
intoxication
intransitive
intravenous
intrinsically
introducing
introduction
introductory
introversion
intuition
intuitive
inundating
inundation
invaluable
invariably
☞

for E . . .
see page 65

for H . . .
see page 71

for Scots: i -r
is on page 247

In these words you can hear the vowel sound i as in pig

I

SHORT VOWEL **i**

* * * * * *

inventory -ies
invertebrate
investigate
investigating
investigation
investigator
invincible
invisible
invitation
involuntarily

Iranian
irrational ly
irregular
irregularity -ies
irrelevance
irrelevant
irreparable
irresistible
irrespective ly
irresponsible
irrigating
irrigation
irritability
irritable
irritating
irritation

italicise d
     ze
italicising
     zing
iteration
itinerant
itinerary

oesophagus es [oesophagi]

for E . . .
see page 65

for H . . .
see page 71

for Scots: i -r
is on page 247

J

*	* *	* * *	* * * * *
gin	ginger ed	genetic ally	gelatinous
gist	gipsy / gypsy -ies		genetically
	giraffe	gibberish	geography -ies
gym		Gibraltar	geology
	gymnast	gingerbread	geometry -ies
jib bed	gymslip	gingerly	geranium
jig ged	gypsy / gipsy -ies		
jilt		gymkhana	gymnasium s [gymnasia]
*__jinks__ lively behaviour	**jibbing**	gymnastics	
*__jinx__ es cause bad luck	**jiffy**	gymnosperm	**judicially**
jinxed	**jigging**		**judiciary** -ies
	jiggle d	**judicial** ly	**judiciously**
	jigsaw	**judicious**	
	jihad		
	jingle d		
	jingling		

for dr . . .
see page 61

In these words you can hear the vowel sound i as in pig

K

*	**	***	* * * * **
kick ed	kebab	kidnapper	kilometre
kid ded		kidnapping	kinaesthetic ally
kids	kick-off	kilobyte	kindergarten
kill ed	kidded	kilogram	
kiln	kidding	kimono s	knickerbocker
kilt	kidnap ped	kinetic	
kin	kidney	kingfisher	
king	killer		
kink ed	killing		
kiss ed	kindle d		
kit ted	kindling		
kith	kingdom		
	king-size		
*knit ted loop together	kinky -ier, -iest		
with needles	kinship		
[knit]	kipper		
	kissing		
*nit egg of louse / nitwit	kitchen		
	kitted		
	kitten		
	kitting		

for C . . .
see page 59

knickers
knitted

for Qu . . .
see page 83

knitting

for Scots: i -r
is on page 248

In these words you can hear the vowel sound i as in pig

L

*	**	***	* * * * **
lick ed	liberal ly	legato	legitimacy
lid	Libya	lethargic	legitimate
lift	lichen		
*limb part of body / branch	*licker creature that licks	liberal ly	liberalism
*limn draw the outline	licorice / liquorice	liberate	liberally
limp ed	lifted	liberty -ies	liberation
link ed	lifting	libretto [libretti]	limitation
*links connections / golf course	lift-off	Libya	linguistically
lip	lily -ies	licorice / liquorice	linoleum
lisp ed	limit ed	ligament	liquidating
list	limpet	limited	liquidation
lit	linen	limiting	liquidity
live d	linger ed	lineage	listeria
	linguist	linear	literacy
lynch es	linkage	linguistic ally	literally
lynched	linking	linguistics	literary
*lynx es animal	linseed	liniment	literature
	lintel	liquefy -ies	Lithuania
	lipid	liquefied	litigation
	lipstick	liquidate	
	liquid	listener	logistical ly
	*liquor alcoholic drink	listening	
	listed	literal ly	lyrically
	listen ed	literate	
	listener	literature	
	listening	lithium	
	listing	lithosphere	
	listless	liturgy -ies	
	litmus es	liverish	
	litter ed	livery -ies	
	little		
	liver	logistic ally	
	livid		
	living	lyrical ly	
	lizard		
	lyric ally		
	lyrics		

M

*	**	***	***** *
midge	miaow	magician	manipulate
midst	mickey	malicious	manipulation
*mil measuring unit	midday / mid-day	malignant	
milk ed	middle		mechanical ly
*mill building equipped	midfield	meander ed	medicinal ly
for grinding or	midget	mechanic ally	melodically
manufacturing / move	midnight	medallion	melodious
in a confused mass	midpoint	melodic ally	memorial
milled	midway	melodious	menagerie
*mince cut into small	midwife	memento es / s	meridian
pieces	mildew ed	meniscus es [menisci]	methodical ly
minced	milkman [milkmen]		meticulous
mink	miller	middle-class	metropolis es
mint	millet	midfielder	
*mints more than one	million	midsummer	military
mint	mimic ked	militant	millennium s [millennia]
Miss	mineral	military	millilitre
miss es	mingle d	militia	millimetre
*missed did miss	mingling	milligram	millionairess es
*mist thin fog	minim	milliner	mineralogy
mitt	minnow	millionaire	minestrone
mix es	minstrel	millipede	minimising
mixed	minute	mimicking	zing
	mirage	mimicry	ministerial
myth	mirror ed	mineral	minority -ies
	mischief	miniature	miraculous ly
	misdeal	minibus es	misbehaviour
	[misdealt]	minimal ly	miscellaneous
	mishap	minimise d	miserable
	misjudge d	ze	misogynist
	mislay	minimum s [minima]	misogyny
	[mislaid]	minister ed	missionary -ies
	mislead	ministry -ies	misunderstand
	[misled]	Minorca	[misunderstood]
	missile	minuend	misunderstanding
	missing	miracle	mitigating
	mission	mischievous	
	misspell ed	miserable	mobility
	[misspelt]	misery -ies	
	misspend	misfortune	mysterious ly
	[misspent]	misgivings	mysticism
	mistake	misjudging	mythology -ies
	[mistook]	misleading	myxomatosis
	[mistaken]	missionary -ies	
	mistress es	mistaken	
	mistrust	mistaking	
	misuse d	mistletoe	
	mitten	misusing	
	mixture	mitigate	
	Monsieur [Messieurs]	mnemonic	
	Mr	myriad	
	Mrs	mystery -ies	
		mystical	
	*mystic deeply hidden /	mystify -ies	
	spiritual explorer	mystified	
	*mystique air of secrecy	mythical	

for Scots: i -r
is on page 249

80

In these words you can hear the vowel sound i as in pig

N

*

*knitted loop together
with needles
[knit]

nib
nil
nip ped
***nit** egg of louse /
nitwit

nymph

**

knickers
knitted
knitting

negate
neglect

nibble d
nibbling
nickel
nickname
nimble
nimbus es [nimbi]
nipping
nipple
nitwit

* * *

mnemonic

negating
negation
neglectful ly

nutrition
nutritious

* * * * *

knickerbocker

narcissus es [narcissi]
nativity -ies

necessity -ies
neglectfully
negotiable
negotiate
negotiating
negotiation
negotiator

Nicaragua

nutritional
nutritionist

O

*

**

omit ted

outbid
[outbid]
[outbidden]

* * *

official ly

Olympic

omission
omitted
omitting

opinion

* * * * **

auxiliary -ies

obituary -ies
obligatory
obliterate
obliterating
oblivion
oblivious
obsidian

oesophagus / **esophagus**
oesophagus es
[oesophagi]

officially

original ly
originality
originate
originating

In these words you can hear the vowel sound i as in pig

P

*

*fish es creature(s)
with tail and fins

*phish ed attempt
internet fraud

pick ed
pig ged
pill
pin ned
pinch es
pinched
pink ed
pip ped
piss ed
pit ted
pitch es
pitched
pith

prick ed
*prince son of king
print
*prints more than
one print

* *

*filter ed pass through
*fishing trying to catch
fish

permit ted
persist

*philtre love-potion
*phishing attempting
internet fraud
physics
physique

pianist
piano s
picket
picking
pickle d
pickling
pickup
picky -ier, -iest
picnic
*picture painting,
drawing or photo
pictured
*pidgin mixture of
two languages
*pigeon bird
pigging
piglet
pigment
pigtail
pilchard
pilgrim
pillar
pillow ed
pimple d
pincers
pinpoint
ping-pong
pinion
pinning
pipit
pipping
pissing
*pistil part of flower
*pistol small handgun
piston
*pitcher large jug
pitchfork
pitching
piteous
pitfall
pitta / pita
pitting
pity -ies
pitied

* * *

Pacific
pavilion

peculiar
permission
permitted
permitting
pernicious ly
persistence
persistent ly
petition ed

Philippines
physical ly
physician
physicist

pianist
piano s
piccolo s
pictogram
pictograph
picturesque
pilgrimage
pinafore
pincushion
pinnacle
piranha
pirouette d
piteous
pitiful ly
pivoted
pivoting

position ed

precaution
preceded
preceding
precisely
precision
precocious
prediction
preferring
preparing
prescription
presented
presenting
prestigious
presumptuous
pretended
pretentious
prettier
prettiest
prevailing
prevention
preventive

* * * * * * *

parishioner
participant
participate
participating
participation
particular ly

peculiar ly
peculiarity -ies
pedestrian
*peninsula land
almost surrounded
by water
*peninsular of / like a
peninsula
perimeter
peripheral ly
periphery -ies
permissible
perniciously
persistently
petroleum

phenomenal ly
phenomenon
[phenomena]
philatelist
philosopher
philosophical ly
philosophy -ies
physically
physiological ly
physiology
physiotherapist
physiotherapy

pianoforte
pictorial ly
pirouetting
pistachio s
pitifully
pituitary

political ly
polyphony

precipitate
precipitating
precipitation
predictable
predominant ly
preliminary -ies
preoccupation

In these words you can hear the vowel sound i as in pig

P

**

pivot ed
pixel
pixie
pizza

precede
precise
preclude
predict
prefer red
prepare d
prescribe d
present
preserve d
preside
presume d
pretence
pretend
pretty -ier, -iest
prevail ed
prevent
prickle d
prickly
primrose
princess es
printed
printer
printing
prism
prison
prisoner
pristine
privet
privy

pygmy -ies

***

primitive
*principal chief
principally
*principle rule for action
principled
prisoner
privacy
privilege d
prodigious
proficient
prohibit ed
prolific ally
provincial
provision
provisions

pyjamas
pyramid
Pyrenees
pyrites

* * * * *

prerogative
presentable
presumably
presumptuous
principally
proficiency -ies
prohibited
prohibiting
prohibitive
proliferate
proliferating
proliferation
prolifically
provisional ly
proximity

publicity

Q

*

quick
quid
quill
quilt
quin
quince
quip ped
quit ted
[quit]
quiz zed

**

quibble d
quibbling
quicker
quickest
quickly
quinine
quintet
quipping
quitted
quitting
quiver ed

***

quicksilver
quintuplet
quizmaster

* * * *

for Scots: i -r
is on page 251 ▷

In these words you can hear the vowel sound i as in pig

R

*	**	***	* * * * **
*real genuine	react	reaction	rapidity
	really	reactor	
rib bed	rebel led	reagent	reactionary -ies
rich es	rebound	realise d	realising
rid ded	rebuke d	ze	zing
[rid]	recall ed	realism	realism
ridge d	receipt	rebelling	realistic ally
rift	receive d	rebellion	reality -ies
rig ged	recess es	rebellious	receptacle
*rill small stream	recessed	rebuking	receptionist
rim med	recite	receding	recipient
*ring ed circle	reclaim ed	receiver	reciprocal ly
*ring sound	recoil ed	receiving	reciprocate
[rang]	record	reception	reciprocating
[rung]	recount	receptive	recovery -ies
rink	recruit	receptor	recuperate
rinse d	recur red	recession	redundancy -ies
rip ped	redeem ed	recessive	refinery -ies
risk ed	reduce d	recital	refrigerate
	refer red	reciting	refrigerating
*wring twist	refine d	recorded	refrigeration
[wrung]	reflect	recorder	refrigerator
wrist	reform ed	recording	regretfully
writ	refract	recover ed	relationship
	refrain ed	recruitment	reliability
	refresh es	recurrence	reliable
	refreshed	recurrent	reluctantly
	refund	recurring	remarkable
	refuse d	redemption	remembering
	regain ed	reducing	removable /
	regard	reduction	removeable
	regret ted	redundant	remuneration
	rehearse d	referral	repetitive
	reject	referring	republican
	rejoice d	refining	repudiate
	rejoin ed	reflected	repudiating
	relate	reflection	resentfully
	relax es	reflector	resilience
	relaxed	reflexive	resilient
	release d	reformer	respectable
	relent	refraction	respectfully
	relief	refreshment	respectively
	relieve d	refusal	responsibility -ies
	rely -ies	refusing	responsible
	relied	regarded	resuscitate
	remain ed	regarding	resuscitating
	remark ed	regardless	resuscitation
	remind	regatta	retaliate
	remote	regretful ly	retaliating
	remove d	regretted	retaliation
	renege d	regretting	returnable
	renew ed	rehearsal	reverberate
	renown ed	rehearsing	reversible
	repaid	rejection	
	repair ed	rejoicing	
	repay		
	[repaid]		

In these words you can hear the vowel sound i as in pig

R

* *

repeal ed
repeat
repel led
repent
replace d
reply -ies
replied
report
repose d
repress es
repressed
reprieve d
reproach es
reproached
repute
request
require d
research es
researched
resent
reserve d
resign ed
resist
resolve d
resort
resource d
respect
respire d
respond
response
restore d
restrain ed
restraint
restrict
result
resume d
retain ed
retard
retire d
retort
retreat
retrieve d
return ed
reveal ed
revenge d
reverse d
review ed
revise d
revive d
revolt
revolve d
reward

rhythm
rhythmic ally

* * *

related
relating
relation
releasing
relentless
reliance
relieving
religion
religious
relinquish es
relinquished
reluctance
reluctant
remainder
remaining
remember ed
remembrance
reminded
reminder
remission
remittance
removal
removing
Renaissance
reneging
renewal
repeated
repeating
repellent
repelling
repentance
replacement
replacing
reported
reporter
reposing
repression
repressive
reprieving
republic
repulsive
requirement
requiring
researcher
resemblance
resemble d
resembling
resentful ly
resentment
reserving
resistance
resistor
resolving
resources
resourcing

* * * *

rhetorical ly
rhythmically

ridiculing
ridiculous
rigidity
rigorously
ritually

In these words you can hear the vowel sound i as in pig

85

R

**

ribbing
ribbon
richer
richest
richly
richness
riddance
ridded
ridden
ridding
riddle d
riddling
*rigger person who rigs
rigging
rigid
*rigor rigid state
*rigour severe
conditions
rimming
*ringer person who
rings / close likeness
ringing
ringtone
ripping
ripple d
rippling
risen
risky -ier, -iest
ritual ly
river
rivet ed / ted

wriggle d
wriggling
*wringer clothes dryer
with rollers
wrinkle d
wrinkling
written

***

respectful ly
respective
respiring
resplendent
respondent
responsive
restoring
restraining
restriction
restrictive
resultant
resulted
resulting
resuming
retarded
retention
retentive
retirement
retiring
retrieval
retrieving
returning
reversal
reversing
revising
revision
revival
reviving
revolver
revolving
revulsion
rewritten

rhythmical ly

rickety
ricochet ted / ed
ridicule d
rigorous
ringleader
risotto s
riskier
riskiest
ritual ly
riverside
riveted / rivetted
riveting / rivetting

In these words you can hear the vowel sound i as in pig

S

*

cinch es

cyst

schist
scrimp ed
scrip
script

shift
shin ned
ship ped
shit
shrill
shrimp
shrink
[shrank]
[shrunk / shrunken]

*****sic** written in this way
*****sick** unwell
sieve d
sift
silk
sill
silt
sin ned
since
sing
[sang]
[sung]
*****sink** slowly go down /
basin in kitchen
[sank] [sunk / sunken]
sip ped
sit
[sat]
six th

skid ded
skill ed
skim med
skimp ed
skin ned
skip ped
skit

slick
slid
slim med
sling
[slung]
slink
[slunk]
slip ped
slit
[slit]

**

cement

chiffon

cigar
cinder
cirrus [cirri]
cistern
citrus
city -ies
civic
civil ly

*****cygnet** young swan
*****cymbals** discs to clash
cynic
cystic

*****Scilly** Isles
scissors
scribble d
scribbling
scripture

seclude
secrete
secure d
select
settee
severe

shilling
shimmer ed
shingle
shipment
shipping
shipwreck ed
shipyard
shiver ed
shrinkage
shrivel led

sibling
sickening
sickness
sieving
signal led
*****signet** seal / ring
*****silly** -ier, -iest
lacking sense
silver ed
simmer ed
simple
simpler
simplest
simply

***

celestial
ceramic

chivalrous
chivalry

cigarette
*****cilia** more than one
cilium
ciliary
cilium [cilia]
cinema
cinnamon
citizen
civilian
civilise d
ze
civilly

cylinder
cynical ly
Cypriot
cystitis

sadistic ally

scriptural ly

secession
secluded
secluding
secreting
secretion
selected
selecting
selection
selective
selector
semantic ally
semantics
sequential ly
sequoia
severely

shipbuilding
shivering
shrivelling

Sicily
sickening
signalling
signature
signify -ies
signified

* * * **

celebrity -ies
celestial
certificate

ciliary
citizenship
civilian
civilisation
zation
civilising
zing

cylindrical
cynically
cynicism

sadistically
salinity
satirical ly

scenario
schizophrenia
schizophrenic ally

security -ies
selectively
semantically
sequentially
severity -ies

significance
significant ly
similarity -ies
similarly
simplicity
simplification
simplistically
simulating
simulation
simultaneous ly
sincerity
singularity -ies
sister-in-law
situated
situation

solicitor
solidify -ies
solidified
solidity
soliloquy -ies
sophisticated
sophistication

for Scots: i -r
is on page 252 ▷

In these words you can hear the vowel sound i as in pig

S

*

smith

sniff ed
snip ped

sphinx es
spill ed
[spilt]
spin
[span]
[spun]
spit
[spat]
[spit]
splint
split
[split]
sprig
spring
[sprang]
[sprung]
sprint

squib
squid
squint

stick
[stuck]
stiff
still ed
stilts
sting
[stung]
stink
[stank]
[stunk]
stint
stitch es
stitched
strict
string
[strung]
strip ped

swift
swill ed
swim
[swam]
[swum]
swing
[swung]

**

sincere
sinew
sinful ly
singer
singing
single d
singling
singly
sinning
sipping
siskin
sissy -ies
sister
sitcom
sitter
sitting
sixpence
sixteen th
sixty -ies
sizzle d
sizzling

skidded
skidding
skilful ly
skillet
skimming
skinhead
skinning
skinny -ier, -iest
skipper
skipping
skittle

slimming
slipper ed
slippery
slipping
slipstone
slither ed
slitting

smitten

sniffle d
sniffling
snigger ed
snippet
snivel led

sphincter
spilling
spinach
spindle
spinner
spinning
spinster

***

silhouette
silica
silicon
*sillier more silly
silliest
silverware
silvery
similar
simile
simplify -ies
simplified
simplistic ally
simulate
sincerely
sinfully
Singapore
singular
sinister
sixtieth

skilfully

slippery

smithereens

snivelling

specific ally
spiritual ly

statistic ally
statistics
stimulant
stimulate
stimulus [stimuli]
stinginess

submission
submissive
submitted
submitting
subscription
subsistence
succinctly
sufficient
suspicion
suspicious ly

Switzerland
swivelling

sycamore
syllabic ally
syllable
syllabus es [syllabi]

* * * * **

specifically
spirituality
spiritually

stability
statistical ly
stimulating
stimulation

subsidiary -ies
sufficiently
suspiciously

syllabically
syllabification
symbiosis [symbioses]
symbiotic ally
symbolically
symbolising
    zing
symbolism
symmetrical ly
sympathetic ally
symphonically
symposium s [symposia]
symptomatic ally
synchronising
    zing
syncopated
syncopation
synonymous
synthesiser
    zer
synthesising
    zing
synthetically
systematic ally
systemically

*for Scots: i -r
is on page 252* ▷

In these words you can hear the vowel sound i as in pig

S

*

swish es
swished
Swiss
switch es
switched

***sync** happening at the
same time

* *

spirit
spitting
splinter ed
splitting
springboard
springtime
sprinkle d
sprinkler
sprinkling
sprinter

squirrel

sticker
sticking
sticky -ier, -iest
stiffness
stigma
stillness
stingy -ier, -iest
stipple d
stippling
stirrup
stitches
stitching
stricken
strictly
stridden
stringent
stringy -ier, -iest
stripper
stripping
striptease
striven

submit ted
subsist
succinct

swiftly
swimmer
swimming
swimsuit
swindle d
swindling
swinging
switching
swivel led
swivelling

symbol
***symbols** signs
symptom
syndrome
syntax
syringe d
syrup
system

* * *

symbolic ally
symbolise d
            ze
symmetric al
symmetry -ies
sympathise d
            ze
sympathy -ies
symphonic ally
symphony -ies
synagogue
synchromesh
synchronise d
            ze
syndicate
synonym
synoptic
syntactic
synthesis [syntheses]
synthesise d
            ze
synthetic ally
syphilis
Syria
syringing
syrupy -ier, -iest
systemic ally

for Scots: i -r
is on page 252 ▷

In these words you can hear the vowel sound i as in pig

89

T

*

thick
thin ned
thing
think
[thought]
this
thrift
thrill ed

tick ed
till
tilt
tin ned
tint
tip ped
tit

trick ed
trim med
trip ped

twig ged
twin ned
twinge
twist
twit
twitch es
twitched

* *

terrain

thicket
thickness
thimble
thinker
thinking
thinner
thinning
thistle
thither
thrifty -ier, -iest
thriller
thriven

ticket
tickle d
tickling
ticklish
tiller
timber
timid
tinder
tingle d
tingling
tinkle d
tinkling
tinning
tinsel
tipping
tiptoe d
tissue
titter ed

tribune
tribute
trickle d
trickling
tricky -ier, -iest
trigger ed
trillion
trimming
trimmings
trinket
triple d
triplet
tripling
tripping

twiddle d
twiddling
twigging
twinkle d
twinkling
twinning
twisted
twisting
twitter ed

* * *

terrific ally

thematic ally
thesaurus es [thesauri]

tiara
tiddlywinks
timpani

tradition
tremendous
tributary -ies
trickery
trilogy -ies
Trinidad
Trinity
trivial

typical ly
tyrannise d
        ze
tyranny -ies

* * * * * *

telegraphy
telepathy
telephonist
terrestrial ly
terrifically

theatrical ly
thematically
theodolite
theological ly
theology -ies
theoretical ly

traditional ly
tremendously
tribulation
tributary -ies
trigonometric
trigonometry
triviality -ies

Tunisia

typically
tyrannical ly
tyrannising
         zing
tyrannosaurus es
[tyrannosauri]

for Scots: i -r
is on page 253 ▷

In these words you can hear the vowel sound i as in pig

U

*

* *

until
uplift

* * *

unwilling

* * * *

unthinkable
unwillingness
unwittingly

V

*

* *

vicar
vicious
victim
victor
victual
vigil
vigour
villa
village
*villain wicked person
*villein free villager in
medieval times
villus [villi]
vineyard
vintage
virile
visage
viscose
vision
visit ed
visual ly
vivid
vixen

* * *

vanilla

Venetian
vermilion

vibrato
vicarage
victimise d
ze
victory -ies
video s
Vietnam
vigilance
vigilant
vigorous
villager
vindicate
vinegar
viola
virulent
visible
visibly
visionary -ies
visited
visiting
visitor
visual ly
visualise d
ze
vitamin
vitreous
vivacious

volition

* * * * * *

validity

velocity -ies

vicinity
vicissitude
victimisation
zation
victimising
zing
Victorian
victorious
videotape d
videotaping
Vietnamese
vigilante
vigorously
visibility
visionary -ies
visualisation
zation
visualise d
ze
visualising
zing
visually

for Scots: i -r
is on page 254 ▷

In these words you can hear the vowel sound i as in pig

W

*	**	***	****

*ring ed circle
*ring sound
[rang]
[rung]

whelk
*which that /
which one
whiff ed
*Whig former political
party
whim
*whin gorse / type of
hard rock
whip ped
*whish ed make a
whishing sound
whisk ed
whist
*whit little bit
whiz zed

wick
width
*wig ged hairpiece
will ed
wilt
*win gain what you
aim for
[won]
wince d
winch es
winched
wind
wing ed
wink ed
*wish es want it to be
true
wished
wisp
*wit humour /
humorous person
*witch woman said
to use magic
with

*wring twist
[wrung]
wrist
writ

*ringer person who
rings / close likeness

whimper ed
whinny -ies
whinnied
whippet
whipping
whisker ed
*whiskey (Irish or
American)
*whisky -ies (Scotch)
whisper ed
whistle d
whistling
*whither to which
place
Whitsun
whittle d
whittling
whizzing

wicked
wicker
wicket
widow ed
wigging
wiggle d
wiggling
wigwam
wiki
wilful ly
willing
willow
wincing
windfall
windmill
window
windpipe
windscreen
windsurf ed
windward
windy -ier, -iest
winger
wingspan
winkle d
winkling
winner
winning
winter ed
wintry
wisdom
wishful
wishing
wistful ly

whichever
whispering

wilderness es
wilfully
willingly
willingness
windier
windiest
windowpane /
window-pane
windowsill /
window-sill
windsurfer
windsurfing
wintertime
wishfully
wistfully
withdrawal
wittier
wittiest

Wikipedia
witticism

for Scots: i -r
is on page 255

In these words you can hear the vowel sound i as in pig

W

**
witchcraft
withdraw
[withdrew]
[withdrawn]
withdrawal
withdrawn
***wither** ed become
dry and shrivelled
withhold
[withheld]
within
without
withstand
[withstood]
witness ed
witty -ier,-iest
wizard
wizened

women

wriggle d
wriggling
***wringer** clothes dryer
with rollers
wrinkle d
wrinkling
written

for Scots: *i -r*
is on page 255 ▷

Z

*	**	***	****
zinc	**zigzag** ged	**zigzagging**	
zip ped	**zipper**	**Zimbabwe**	
	zipping		
	zither		

In these words you can hear the vowel sound **i** as in **pig**

93

A

*	**	***	**** ****
*-all every one	-abroad	abolish es	abdominal
-alms	abscond	abolished	abominable
			abominate
*-aught anything at all	across	acknowledge d	abominating
*-awe fear and wonder	adopt	adoption	accommodate
*-awed made to feel			accommodating
awe	agog	-albeit	accommodation
*-awl boring tool		allotment	acknowledgement /
	allot ted	allotted	acknowledgment
*odd unusual	-almost	allotting	acknowledging
	aloft	-almighty	acropolis [acropoleis]
*-or marks choice	along	alongside	
	-alright	-already	-alteration
*-ought should	-also	-alternate	-alternating
	*-altar holy table		-alternative ly
	*-alter ed change	apostle	-alternator
	-although	-appalling	-altogether
	-always		
		astonish es	anonymous
	anon	astonished	
			apologetic ally
	-appal led	atomic	apologise d
	-applaud		ze
	-applause	-audible	apologising
		-audience	zing
	assault	-auditor	apology -ies
		-auditory	apostrophe
	-auburn	*-aurally by the ear	approximate ly
	-auction ed	-aurora	approximating
	-audit	-Austria	approximation
	*-auger tool	-authentic ally	
	*-augur suggest for	-authorise d	astonishment
	the future	ze	astrology
	*-August month	-autograph ed	astronomer
	*-august impressive		astronomy
	-aura s / -ae	-awfully	
	*-aural ly by the ear		atrocity -ies
	-austere	*-orally by the mouth	
	-author		-auditorium s [auditoria]
	-autumn		-auditory
			Australia
	-awesome / awsome		-authentically
	*-awful ly dreadful		-authorising
	-awkward		zing
			-authority -ies
	*-offal less valuable meat		-autobiographical ly
			-autobiography -ies
	*-oral ly by the mouth		-autocracy -ies
			-autocratic ally
			-automatic ally
			-automation
			-automobile
			-autonomic
			-autonomous
			-auxiliary -ies

for H . . .
see page 102 ▷

for Scots: o -r
is on page 256 ▷

In these words you can hear the vowel sound o as in dog

B

*

*-**bald** lacking hair
-**balk** / **baulk** ed
*-**ball** round object /
dance
*-**balled** made into a
ball
*-**balm** ointment
-**baulk** / **balk** ed
*-**bawl** yell
*-**bawled** did yell

blob
*__bloc__ group of allied
countries
*__block__ ed stop / solid
squared-off object
blog ged
*__blond__ man with
fair hair
*__blonde__ woman with
fair hair
blot ted

bob bed
bog ged
*__bomb__ explosive
device
bombed
bond
boss es
bossed
botch es
botched
-**bought**
box es
boxed

-**brawl** ed
-**brawn**
-**broad**
bronze d
broth
-**brought**

* *

-**ballpoint**
-**ballroom**
-**balmy** -ier, -iest
balsa
balti
Baltic
baroque
-**basalt**
-**bauxite**

because
-**befall**
[befell]
-[befallen]
belong ed
-**besought**
beyond

blancmange
blockade
blockboard
blocking
blogger
blogging
blossom ed
blotted
blotter
blotting

bobbing
bodice
body -ies
bodied
boggy -ier, -iest
bombard
bomber
bombshell
bondage
bonfire
bonnet
bonny -ier, -iest
borrow ed
bossy -ier, -iest
botching
bother ed
bottle d
bottling
bottom ed
boxer
boxing
boxplot

-**brawny** -ier, -iest
-**broadcast**
-[broadcast]
-**broadside**
bronchial
bronco

* * *

-**befallen**
belonging
belongings
besotted

bodily
bombardment
bombastic ally
borrowing
Bosnia
botanist
botany
Botswana
bottleneck
bottomless

-**broadcaster**
-**broadcasting**
broccoli
bronchial
bronchitis
brontosaur

* * * * *

barometer

binocular
binoculars
biographer
biography -ies
biologist
biology

bombastically

brontosaurus es

In these words the first letter 'o' is a neutral vowel. It sounds like the 'o' in 'occurring'.

Bolivia   botanical
bonanza   brocade

---

for Scots: o -r
is on page 257 ▷

In these words you can hear the vowel sound **o** as in **dog**

95

C

*

*-**call**ed shout / name
-**calm** ed
*-**caught** got / trapped
-**caulk** ed
*-**cause** bring about /
    reason
-**caused**
*-**caw** hard bird cry
*-**cawed** did caw
*-**caws** does caw

-**chalk** ed
chop ped

*-**clause** words in
    sentence / part of
    written agreement
-**claw** ed
*-**claws** curved nails
    or limbs
clock ed
clod
clot ted
cloth

*-**coarse** rough
cob
cock ed
***cod** fish
cog
cogged
*-**col** gap between
    mountains
cop ped
*-**cops** the police
*-**copse** small wood
*-**cord** string
*-**core** central part /
    take out the core from
*-**cored** did core
*-**corps** group
cost
[cost]
*-**cot** baby's bed
cough ed
*-**course** track /
    direction / part of
    meal / of course

-**crawl** ed
crock ed
croft
crop ped
cross es
crossed

*for Qu . . .
see page 109* ▷

* *

-**calling**
-**cauldron**
-**causal** ly
-**causing**
-**caustic** ally
-**caution** ed
-**cautious**

chocolate
*-**choler** anger
chopper
chopping
choppy -ier, -iest
chopsticks
*-**choral** for or by a
    choir
chronic ally

clockwise
clotted
clotting

cobbler
cobweb bed
cocker
cockerel
cockle
Cockney
cockpit
cockroach es
cocksure
cocktail
codfish
coffee
coffin
*-**collage** picture made
    by sticking on items
*-**collar** ed band or ring
    round a neck or shaft /
    seize by the neck
colleague
collect
*-**college** educational
    establishment
collie
collier
column ed
combat ed / ted
combine
comet
comic
comma
comment
commerce
common
Commons
commune ◄

* * *

cauliflower
-**causally**
-**causation**
-**caustically**
-**cautiously**

chloroform ed
chlorophyll
cholera
chorister
chronically
chronicle d
chronicling

cochlea
cockatoo
cockerel
cognition
cognitive
colliery -ies
colonise d
        ze
colonist
colony -ies
colossal ly
columnist
combated / combatted
combating / combatting
combining
comedy -ies
comical ly
commentary -ies
commonly
commonplace
commonwealth
communal ly
communist
comparable
compensate
competence
competent
*-**complement**
    something that
    completes
complicate
*-**compliment**
    expression of praise
    or politeness
composite
comprehend
compromise ◄

*for Scots: o -r
is on page 258* ▷

* * * * * * *

cauliflower
-**causality**
-**caustically**

choreographer
choreography
chronically
chronological ly
chronology -ies

-**claustrophobia**
-**claustrophobic**

colonisation
        zation
colonising
        zing
colossally
combination
comically
commentator
commodity -ies
communally
communism
commutative
commutator
comparable
compensating
compensation
competition
*-**complementary**
    making up a whole
complicated
complicating
complication
*-**complimentary**
    expressing praise
composition
compositor
comprehensible
comprehension
comprehensive
compromising
computation al
concentrating
concentration
concertina
condemnation
condensation
confidential ly
confidentiality
confidently
confirmation
confiscating
confrontation ◄

In these words you can hear the vowel sound O as in dog

C

* *

compact
complex es
compost
compound
comrade
concave
concept
concert
concoct
concord
concourse
concrete
condom
conduct
conflict
Congo
congress
conic
*conker horse chestnut
*conquer ed defeat
conquest
conscience
conscious
conscript
console
constant
contact
content
contents
contest
context
contour ed
contract
contrast
convent
converse
convert
convex
convict
convoy
copper
copping
copy -ies
copied
*coral substance
formed from bones
of sea creatures
*corral enclosure for
horses and cattle
cosmic ally
costly -ier, -iest
costume d
cottage
cottar / cotter
cotton ed

* * *

concentrate
concentric
concoction
concreting
conference
*confidant person
trusted to keep secrets
*confidants people
trusted to keep secrets
*confidence self-belief
*confident very sure
confiscate
confluence
congregate
congruence
congruent
conical
conifer
conjugate
connoisseur
conqueror
consciously
consciousness
consecrate
consequence
consequent
consonant
constantly
constitute
consulate
contemplate
continent
contraband
contradict
contrary
convalesce d
copulate
copying
copyright
coronary -ies
coroner
correspond
corridor
cosmetic ally
cosmetics
cosmically
cosmonaut
costuming
cottoning

crockery
crocodile
cross-section

Kosovo

* * * * *

conglomerate
conglomeration
congregating
congregation
conjugating
connotation
conquistador
conscientious
consecrating
consecration
consequently
conservation
consolation
consolidation
constellation
constipated
constipation
constitution al
constitutional ly
consultation
contemplating
contemplation
continental ly
continuity -ies
contraception
contraceptive
contradiction
contradictory
contribution
controversial ly
controversy -ies
convalescence
convalescent
conversation
copulating
copulation
coronary -ies
coronation
correlation
*correspondence
exchange of letters /
similarity
correspondent
*correspondents those
sending letters or
reports
corresponding ly
corrugated
cosmetically
cosmically

cross-sectional

kilometre

for Qu . . .
see page 109 ▷

-crawling

for Scots: o -r
is on page 258 ▷

In these words you can hear the vowel sound o as in dog

97

C

**
cropping
crossbar
crossfade
crosshatch ed
crossing
crossroads
crossword
crotchet

for Qu . . .
see page 109

for Scots: o -r
is on page 258

In these words the first letter 'o' is a neutral vowel. It sounds like the 'o' in 'occurring'.
CORRECT WORDS

cholesterol	comparing	concise ly	connecting	contest ant
chorale	comparison	conclude	connection	contingency -ies
cocoon ed	compartment	concluding	connector	continual ly
collapse d	compassion ate	conclusion	conscription	continuance
collapsible	compatible	conclusive	consecutive	continuation
collapsing	compel led	concurrent	consensus es	continue d
collect ing	compelling	concuss es	consent	continuing
collection	compete	concussed	conservatism	continuous ly
collective ly	competing	concussing	conservative	continuum
collector	competitive ness	concussion	conservatory -ies	contract ion
collide	competitor	condemn ed	conserve d	contractor
colliding	compile d	condense d	conserving	contractual ly
collision	compiling	condenser	consider ed	contralto s
colloquial ly	complacency	condensing	considerable	contraption
cologne	complacent	condition ed	considerate	contrary
colonial ly	complain ed	conditional ly	consideration	contrast
colonialism	complaint	conducive	consist ing	contribute d
combat ed / ted	complete ly	conduct	consistency -ies	contributing
combating / combatting	completing	conduction	consistent ly	contributor
combine d	completion	conductor	console d	control led
combining	complexion	confectioner	consoling	controller
combustible	complexity -ies	confectionery	conspicuous	controlling
combustion	comply -ies	confer red	conspiracy -ies	convection
comedian	complied	conferring	conspirator	convector
comedienne	component	confess es	conspire d	convenience
command er	compose d	confessed	conspiring	convenient ly
commandment	composer	confession al	constabulary -ies	convention al ly
commemorate	composing	confessor	constituency -ies	converge d
commemoration	composure	confetti	constituent	convergent
commence d	compress es	confide	constrain ed	converging
commencing	compressed	confiding	constraint	converse d
commercial ly	compression	confine d	construct ed	conversely
commission ed	compressor	confining	construction al	conversing
commissioner	comprise d	confirm ed	constructive	conversion
commit ted	comprising	conflict	consult ed	convert ible
commitment	compulsion	conform ed	consultancy -ies	convey ed
committee	compulsive	conformist	consultant	conveyor /
committing	compulsory	conformity	consume d	conveyer
commodity -ies	compute	confront	consumer	convict ion
commotion	computer ised	confuse d	consuming	convince d
communal ly	computing	confusing	consumption	convincing
commune d	conceal ed	confusion	contagious	convulse d
communicate	concede	congenital ly	contain ed	convulsing
communication	conceit ed	congested	container	convulsion
communing	conceive d	congestion	contaminate	convulsive
communion	conceiving	congratulate	contaminating	correct ed
community -ies	concentric	congratulating	contamination	correction
commutative	conception	congratulations	contemporary -ies	correctly
commute	conceptual ly	coniferous	contempt ible	corrode
commuter	concern ed	conjecture d	contemptuous	corroding
commuting	concerning	conjecturing	contend	corrosion
companion	concerto s	conjunction	content	corrosive
compare d	concession	connect ed	contention	corrupt ion

In these words you can hear the vowel sound O as in dog

D

*

-**daub** ed
-**daunt**
-**dawn** ed

dock ed
dodge d
dog ged
doll ed
don ned
dong ed
dot ted

*-**draw** pull / sketch
 [drew]
-[drawn]
*-**drawer** sliding
 container
-**drawl** ed
 drop ped

* *

-**daughter**
-**daunting**
-**dauntless**
-**dawdle** d
-**dawdling**

demob bed

dislodge d
dissolve d
-**distraught**

doctor ed
doctrine
dodgem
dodging
dodgy -ier, -iest
dogging
doghouse
dogma
doldrums
dollar
dollop
dolly -ies
dolphin
donkey
donning
dotcom
dotplot
dotted
dotting

-**drawback**
-**drawbridge**
-**drawing**
 droplet
 dropout
 dropping

* * *

demolish es
demolished
deposit ed
despondent

dishonest
dislodging
dissolving

doctrinal ly
document
doggedly
dogmatic ally
dominant
dominance
dominate
domino es

* * * * *

democracy -ies
demonstrative
denomination
denominator
deposited
depositing
derogatory
despondency

dichotomy -ies
dishonesty
dishonourable
disqualify -ies
disqualified

doctrinally
docu-drama
documentary -ies
documentation
dogmatically
dolphinarium
dominating
domination

dromedary -ies

> **In these words the first letter 'o' is a neutral vowel. It sounds like the 'o' in 'occurring'.**
>
> domain domestic ally domesticate

for Scots: o -r
is on page 259 ▷

E

*

* *

encore d
enthral led

evolve d

exalt
-**exhaust**

* * *

embody -ies
embodied

enthralling
envelope

erotic ally

evolving

* * * * * *

ecologist
ecology
economist
economy -ies

entrepreneur ial
entrepreneurship

equality

erotically

for I . . .
see page 102 ▷

for Scots: o -r
is on page 259 ▷

In these words you can hear the vowel sound o as in dog

E

SHORT VOWEL **O**

* * *

exalted
-exhausted
-exhaustion
exotic ally

* * * * *

esophagus es [esophagi]

exotically
exploratory

for Scots: o -r
is on page 259 ▷

F

*

-**fall**
  [fell]
-[fallen]
false
fault
*-**faun** goat-god
*-**fawn** young deer /
  colour / try to win
  favour
*-**fawned** did fawn

-**flaunt**
-**flaw** ed
flock ed
***flocks** more than one
  flock of animals
flog ged
flop ped
floss ed

fog
***fond** showing love
font
-**fought**
fox es
foxed

-**fraud**
-**fraught**
frock
frog
from
frond
frost
froth ed

***phlox** flowering plant

for th . . .
see page 113 ▷

* *

-**falcon**
-**fallen**
-**falling**
-**fallout**
-**falsehood**
falter ed
faulty -ier, -iest

-**flawless**
flogging
flopping
floppy -ier, -iest
floral
florist

fodder
foggy -ier, -iest
foghorn
follow ed
folly -ies
fondle d
fondling
forage d
forehead
foreign
forest
forgone / foregone
forgot
fossil
foster ed
foxglove
foxy -ier, -iest

frogman [frogmen]
frolic ked
frostbite
frosty -ier, -iest
frothy -ier, -iest

phosphate

* * *

-**falsify** -ies
  falsified
-**falsity**

*-**fiancé** man engaged
  to be married
*-**fiancée** woman
  engaged to be married

foggiest
follower
following
foraging
foreigner
forestry
forgotten
fossilise d
     ze

-**fraudulent**
frolicking
frostbitten

phosphorus

* * * * * *

ferocity

fossilising
     zing

frivolity

phenomenal ly
phenomenon
[phenomena]
philosopher
philosophical ly
philosophy -ies
photographer
photography

for Scots: o -r
is on page 260 ▷

In these words the first letter 'o' is a neutral
vowel. It sounds like the 'o' in 'occurring'.

forensic   forever   forget-me-not

In these words you can hear the vowel sound O as in dog

G

*

*-**gall** cheek /
bitterness / sore /
swelling
*-**Gaul** ancient region
of Europe
-**gaunt**
-**gauze**

genre

gloss es
glossed

*-**gnaw** keep biting
*-**gnawed** did gnaw

*-**god** superhuman being
or idol
*-**God** single all-powerful
being
golf ed
gone
gong
gosh
got
goth

*nod ded move the head
down and up
*-nor and not

* *

-**galling**
-**gaudy** -ier, -iest
-**gauntlet**

genre

globule
glossy -ies

gobble d
***gobbling** greedily
eating
goblet
***goblin** evil spirit
goddess es
goggles
golfer
golly
gosling
gospel
gossip ed
Gothic

grotto es / s
grotty -ier, -iest
grovel led
grovelling

* * *

galoshes

geography

-**Gibraltar**

globular
glockenspiel
glossary -ies

godparents
golliwog
gossiping

grovelling

* * * *

geography -ies
geology
geometry -ies

*for Scots: o -r
is on page 261* ▷

In this word the letter 'o' is a neutral vowel.
gorilla

In these words you can hear the vowel sound O as in dog

101

H

*

*-**hall** large room / passage
halt
*-**haul** drag / amount gained
-**hauled**
-**haunch** es
-**haunt**
-**haw**
*-**hawk** bird / carry and try to sell / clear the throat noisily
-**hawked**

hob
***hock** leg joint / wine / pawn
hog ged
honk ed
hop ped
hot

* *

-**halter**
-**haughty** -ier, -iest
-**haulage**
-**haunches**
-**hawthorn**

hobble d
hobbling
hobby -ies
hockey
hogging
Holland
hollow ed
holly
homage
honest
Hong Kong
honour ed
hopper
hopping
hopscotch
horrid
horror
hospice
hostage
***hostel** place to stay in
***hostile** unfriendly
hotch-potch
hotter
hottest
hovel
hover ed

* * *

-**haughtily**

historic ally

holiday
hollyhock
holocaust
hologram
holograph
homicide
homograph
homonym
homophone
honestly
honesty
honourable
horoscope
horrible
horribly
horrify -ies
horrified
hospital
hovercraft

hypnotic ally

* * * * *

historical ly

holography
homicidal
***homogeneous** of the same kind throughout
***homogenous** of the same genetic origin
honorary
honourable
horizontal ly
horrifying
hospitable
hospitalise d ze
hospitalising zing
hospitality
hostility -ies

hypnotically
hypocrisy
hypothesis [hypotheses]

> **In these words the 'o' is neutral.**
> horizon   horrendous   horrific ally

for Scots: o -r is on page 261

I

*

* *

-**instal** led / **install** ed
involve d

* * *

immoral ly
impromptu s
improper

-**installing**
-**instalment** / **installment**
involvement

* * * * * *

illogical ly

impossibility
impossible
impoverish ed

-**inaugural**
-**inauguration**
incongruous
inoculate
inoculation
insoluble
insomnia
intolerable
intolerance
intoxicate
intoxication
involuntary

for E . . . see page 99

for Scots: o -r is on page 262

In these words you can hear the vowel sound o as in dog

J

SHORT VOWEL O

*
-jaunt
-jaw ed

job bed
jog ged
jolt
jot ted

* *
-jaunty -ier, -iest
-jawing

jobbing
jobless
jockey ed
jockstrap
jodhpurs
jogger
jogging
jolly -ies
jollied
jostle d
jostling
jotted
jotter
jotting

* * *
geography -ies

-Gibraltar

jocular

* * * *
geography
geology
geometry -ies

◁ for dr . . .
see page 99

for Scots: o -r
is on page 262 ▷

K

*
knob
knock ed
*knot ted tied
fastening / hard part
of wood / sea mile
(per hour)

*-naught / nought zero

*not used in denial,
negation, refusal
*-nought / naught zero

* *
knocker
knockout
knotted
knotting
*knotty -ier, -iest full
of knots
knowledge

*-naughty -ier, -iest badly
behaved

* * *
Kosovo

* * * *
kilometre

knowledgeable

In these words the letter 'o' is a neutral vowel.	
Korea	Korean

◁ for C . . .
see page 96

for Qu . . .
see page 109 ▷

for Scots: o -r
is on page 262 ▷

In these words you can hear the vowel sound o as in dog

L

*

-**launch** es
-launched
*-**law** laws enforced
 in a country
-**lawn**

lob bed
*-**loch** Scottish word
 for 'lake'
*-**lock** fastening device
locked
lodge d
loft
log ged
long ed
lop ped
*-**lore** traditions and
 facts
loss es
lost
lot

* *

-**launcher**
-**launderette**
-**launder** ed
-**laundry** -ies
laurel
-**lawful** ly
-**lawyer**

lobbing
lobby -ies
lobbied
lobster
locker
locket
locus [loci]
lodger
lodging
lodgings
lofty -ier, -iest
logging
logic ally
longer
longest
longing
long-term
lopping
lorry -ies
lotto
lozenge

* * *

laconic ally
-**launderette**
-**lawfully**

logical ly
lollipop
longingly
longitude
lottery -ies

* * * * * *

laboratory -ies
laconically

logarithm
logically
longevity
longitudinal ly

*for Scots: o -r
is on page 263* ▷

In these words you can hear the vowel sound O as in dog

M

*

***mall** public walk /
walk lined with shops
malt
*-**maul**ed handle
roughly / heavy mallet
-**mauve**

mobbed
mocked
mod
***moll** gangster's girl
mopped
mosque
mosses
moth
motte

* *

Malta

mobbing
mocha
modelled
modelling
moderate
modern
modest
module
mollusc
monarch
mongooses
monsoon
monster
monstrous
mopping
***moral**ly concerning
right and wrong
***morale** confidence
morrow
mossy -ier, -iest
motley
mottled
motto es / s

* * *

melodic ally

mnemonic

moccasin
mockery -ies
modelling
moderate
modernise d
ze
modesty
modify -ies
modified
modular
molecule
monarchy -ies
monastery -ies
monitor ed
monochrome
monologue
monotone
monoxide
monument
moralise d
ze
morally
Morocco
mosquito es

*for Scots: o -r
is on page 263* ▷

* * * * * * *

mahogany
majority -ies

melodically
methodical ly
metropolis es

misogynist
misogyny

moderation
moderato
modernisation
zation
modernising
zing
modification
modifier
modulation
monochromatic ally
monogamous
monolithic
monopolise d
ze
monopoly -ies
monotheism
monotonous
monstrosity
monumental ly

mythology -ies

In these words the first letter 'o' is neutral.		
Mohammed	momentum	morality
molasses	Monsieur	morose
molecular	moraine	

N

*

*-**gnaw** keep biting
*-**gnaw**ed did gnaw

knob
knocked
***knot**ted tied fastening /
hard part of wood /
sea mile (per hour)

*-**naught** / **nought** zero

***nod**ded move head
down and up
*-**nor** and not
***not** used in denial,
negation, refusal
notches
notched
*-**nought** / **naught** zero

* *

knocker
knockout
knotted
knotting
***knotty** -ier, -iest full of
knots
knowledge

*-**naughty** -ier, -iest
badly behaved

nodding
nodule
nonsense
nonstop
nostril
novel
novice
noxious
nozzle

* * *

-**naughtier**
-**naughtiest**
-**naughtiness**
-**nausea**
-**nauseous**
-**nautical** ly

neurotic ally

nocturnal ly
nominal ly
nominate
nominee
nonchalant
nonfiction / **non-fiction**
nostalgia
nostalgic ally
novelist
novelty -ies

* * * * *

knowledgeable

-**nautically**

neurotically

nocturnally
nominally
nomination
nonconformist
nostalgically
notwithstanding

*for Scots: o -r
is on page 263* ▷

In these words you can hear the vowel sound **O** as in dog

O

*	* *	* * *	* * * * * * * *

*

*-all every one
-alms

*-aught anything at all

*-awe fear and wonder
*-awed made to feel awe
*-awl boring tool

*odd unusual

of
off

on

opt

*-**or** marks choice

*-**ought** should

ox [oxen]

* *

-almost
-alright
-also
*-altar holy table
*-alter ed change
-although
-always

-auburn
-auction ed
-audit
*-auger tool
*-augur suggest for the
  future
*-August month
*-august impressive
-aura s / -ae
*-aurally by the ear
-austere
-author
-autumn

-awesome / awsome
*-awful ly dreadful
-awkward

honest
honour ed

object
oblong

occult
o'clock
octane
octave

oddly
oddment

***offal** less valuable
  meat
offer ed
offering
office
off-line
offset
offshore
offside
offspring
offstage
often

olive

omelette ☞

* * *

-albeit
-almighty
-already
-alternate

-appalling

-audible
-audience
-auditor
-auditory
*-aurally by the ear
-aurora
  Austria
-authentic ally
-authorise d
  ze
-autism
-autistic ally
-autograph ed

-awfully

honestly
honesty
honourable

obnoxious
obsolete
obstacle
obstinate
obvious

occupant
occupy -ies
occupied
octagon
October
octopus es [octopi]
ocular
oculist

oddity -ies

offering
offertory -ies
officer

ominous
omnibus

oncoming
ongoing
onlooker ☞

* * * * * * * *

-alteration
-alternating
-alternative ly
-alternator
-altogether

-auditorium s [auditoria]
-auditory
  Australia
-authentically
-authorising
  zing
-authority -ies
-autistic ally
-autobiographical ly
-autobiography -ies
-autocracy -ies
-autocratic ally
-automatic ally
-automation
-automobile
-autonomic
-autonomous
-auxiliary -ies

entrepreneur ial
entrepreneurship

honorary
honourable

objectively
objectivity
obligation
observation
obsolescence
obsolescent
obstinacy
obstinately
obviously

occupation al
occupier
octagonal

oesophagus / esophagus
oesophagus es
[oesophagi]

offertory -ies

onomatopoeia ☞

for H . . .
see page 102

for Scots: o -r
is on page 264

In these words you can hear the vowel sound o as in dog

O

* *

online / on-line
onset
onslaught
onto
onward
onwards

opera
opted
optic ally
opting
option
opus es [opera]

*-oral ly by the mouth
orange

osprey
ostrich es

otter

oxen
oxide

* * *

opera
operate
ophthalmic
opossum
opposite
optical ly
optician
optimal ly
optimist
optimum
optional

oracle
*-orally by the mouth
orangeade
oration
orator
oratory
origin

oscillate
osmium
osmosis
ossicle

oxidise d
      ze
oxygen

* * * * * *

operated
operatic ally
operating
operation
operational ly
operator
opportunist ic
opportunity -ies
opposition
optically
optimally
optimism
optimistic ally

orientate
orientation
orienteering

oscillation
ostensible
ostensibly
ostinato

oxidation
oxidisation
      zation
oxidising
      zing
oxyacetylene

for H . . .
see page 102

for Scots: o -r
is on page 264

In these words the first letter 'o' is a neutral vowel.   It sounds like the 'o' in 'occurring'.

ORIGINAL WORDS

obedience
obedient
obey ed
obituary -ies
object ion
objectionable
objective
obligatory
oblige d
obliging
oblique
obliterate

obliterating
oblivion
oblivious
obscene
obscenity -ies
obscure d
obscuring
obscurity -ies
observable
observant
observatory -ies
observe d

observer
observing
obsess ed
obsession al ly
obsessive
obsidian
obstruct ion
obstructive
obtain ed
obtuse
occasion
occasional ly

occur red
occurrence
occurring
offence
offend
offender
offensive
official ly
omission
omit ted
omitting
opinion

opponent
oppose d
opposing
oppress es
oppressed
oppression
oppressive
oppressor
original ly
originality
originate
originating

In these words you can hear the vowel sound O as in dog

P

*

*flocks more than one
flock of animals

-palm ed
-paunch es
*pause brief gap /
hesitate
-paused
*paw foot of animal
*pawed examined by
paw
-pawn
*pawned left in return
for loan
*paws feet of animal

*phlox flowering plant

plot ted

*pod ded form pods /
casing
pomp
*pond pool
*poor badly off
pop ped
*pore tiny hole / study
closely
posh
pot ted
*pour flow out
*poured did pour

-prawn
prod ded
prompt
prong ed
prop ped

-psalm

* *

-palfrey
palsy -ied
-pausing
-pawpaw

phosphate

plotted
plotting

pocket
podcast
podded
podding
podgy -ier, -iest
polish es
polished
polka
pollen
pompom
pompous
poncho s
ponder ed
pontoon
popcorn
poplar
poplin
popping
poppy -ies
porridge
possum
posture d
pothole
potted
potter
potting

problem
prodded
prodding
produce
product
*profit ed gain
project
prolong ed
promise d
promptly
proper
*prophet inspired
religious leader
propping
prospect
prosper ed
prostate
prostrate
proverb
province
proxy -ies

* * *

peroxide

phosphorus

-plausible

podgier
podgiest
policy -ies
politics
pollinate
poltergeist
polygon
polythene
ponderous
*populace common
people
popular
populate
*populous full of
people
positive
possible
possibly
postulate
posturing
pottery -ies
poverty

-precaution
probable
probably
prodigal
prodigy -ies
profited
profiting
progeny
prognosis
promenade
prominence
prominent
promising
promontory -ies
propagate
properly
property -ies
*prophecy -ies statement
about a future event
*prophesy -ies make
a statement about
the future
prophesied
prosecute
prosperous
prostitute
Protestant
providence
provident

* * * * *

pathology

personification
personify -ies
personified

phenomenal ly
phenomenon
[phenomena]
philosopher
philosophical ly
philosophy -ies
photographer
photography

politician
pollination
polyester
Polynesia
polynomial
polyphonic ally
polystyrene
polytechnic
polytheism
polyurethane
pomegranate
popularity
populating
population
possibility -ies
postulating

predominant ly
prerogative
probability -ies
problematic ally
proclamation
productivity
profitability
profitable
promiscuity
promontory -ies
propaganda
propagating
proposition
prosecuting
prosecution
prosecutor
prosperity
prostitution
provocation
provocative
proximity

for Scots: o -r
is on page 265

In these words you can hear the vowel sound o as in dog

P

In these words the first letter 'o' is a neutral vowel. It sounds like the 'o' in 'occurring'.

PRO FOUND WORDS

phonetic ally
photographer
photography
polarity -ies
police
policeman
[policemen]
policewoman
[policewomen]
policing
polite ly
political ly
pollutant
pollute
polluting
pollution
polyphony
position ed
possess es
possessed
possession

possessive
potato es
potential ly
probation
procedure
proceed ing
proceedings
procession
proclaim ed
procure d
procuring
prodigious
produce d
producer
producing
production
productive
profane
profess es
professed
profession

professional ly
professionalism
professor
proficiency -ies
proficient
profound
profuse
profusion
progression
progressive ly
prohibit ed
prohibiting
prohibitive
project
projectile
projection
projector
proliferate
proliferating
prolific ally
promote

promoter
promoting
promotion
pronounce d
pronouncement
pronouncing
pronunciation
propel led
propeller
propelling
propensity -ies
proportion al ly
proportionate ly
propos
proposal
propose d
proposing
proprietor
propulsion
prospect
prospective

prospector
prospectus es
protect ed
protection
protective
protector
protest
protractor
protrude
protruding
provide
provided
providing
provincial
provision
provisional ly
provisions
provoke d
provoking

Q

*

quash es
quashed

* *

quadrant
quagmire
quandary -ies
quantum
quarrel led
quarry -ies
quarried

* * *

quadrangle
quadratic
quadriceps
quadruped
quadruple d
quadruplet
quadrupling
qualify -ies
qualified
quality -ies
quandary -ies
quantify -ies
quantified
quantity -ies
quarantine
quarrelling

* * * * *

quadrilateral
qualification
qualifier
qualitative
quantitative

In these words you can hear the vowel sound o as in dog

R

*	**	***	* * * **
-raw	-raucous	rendezvous	responsibility -ies
		resolving	responsible
rob bed	-recall ed	respondent	
rock ed	resolve d	responsive	rhetorical ly
rod ded	respond	revolver	rhinoceros es
romp ed	response	revolving	
*rot ted decay	revolt		robotically
	revolve d	risotto s	
wrath			
wrong ed	rhomboid	robbery -ies	
*-wrought made to fit	rhombus es [rhombi]	robotic ally	
		rockery -ies	
	robber	rollicking	
	robbing	rottweiler	
	robin		
	rocker	wrongdoing	
	rocket	wrongfully	
	rocky -ier, -iest		
	rodded		
	rodding		
	*rollick act with		
	enjoyment		
	*rollock / rowlock pivot		
	for oar		
	rosin ed		
	roster		
	rostrum s [rostra]		
	rotted		
	rotten		
	rotting		
	*rowlock / rollock pivot		
	for oar		
	wrongful ly		
	wrongly		

for Scots: o -r
is on page 266 ▷

> **In these words the first letter 'o' is a neutral vowel. It sounds like the 'o' in 'occurring'.**
>
> romance d   romancing   romantic ally

In these words you can hear the vowel sound o as in dog

S

*

-psalm

salt
-sauce
*-saw looked at /
  cutting tool
*-sawed did saw
-[sawn]

-scald
scoff ed
scone
Scot
scotch ed
Scotch
-scrawl ed

-shawl
shock ed
shod
shone
shop ped
shot

slog ged
slop ped
slosh es
sloshed
slot ted

-small
smock ed
smog

snob
snot

*-soar fly high
*-soared flew high
sob bed
sock ed
*sod turf
soft
solve d
song
*-sore painful
-sought

-spawn ed
spot ted
-sprawl ed

squad
squash es
squashed
squat ted
-squawk ed

* *

-salty -ier, -iest
-saucepan
-saucer
-saucy -ier, -iest
-sauna
-saunter ed
sausage
-sawdust

scholar
scoffing
Scotland
Scotsman [Scotsmen]
Scottish

shoddy -ier, -iest
shoplift
shopper
shopping
shotgun

-slaughter ed
slogging
slopping
sloppy -ier, -iest
slotted
slotting

-smaller
-smallest
-smallpox
-small-scale

snobbish
snotty -ier, -iest

sobbing
soccer
socket
sodden
soften ed
softer
softly
software
soggy -ier,-iest
solace
solder ed
solemn
solid
solvent
solving
sombre
sonic
sonnet
sorrow ed
sorry -ier, -iest
sovereign

* * *

-saucily

scholarly
scholarship
Scotswoman
[Scotswomen]

shopkeeper

snobbery
snottier
snottiest

soldering
solemnly
solenoid
solidly
solitary
solitude
soluble
sombrero s
sonorous
sovereignty -ies
soviet

sponsorship

stockbroker
stockmarket
-strawberry -ies
strontium

subconscious

swastika

symbolic ally
symphonic ally
synoptic

* * * * *

solidarity
solubility
sostenuto

spontaneity
spontaneous ly

subconsciously

symbolically
symphonically
synonymous

for Scots: o -r
is on page 267 ▷

In these words you can hear the vowel sound o as in dog

111

S

*

*-stalk stem / hunt / walk stiffly
-stalked
-stall ed
-staunch es
-staunched
*stock ed supply
stodge
stop ped
-straw
strong

swab bed
swamp ed
swan
swap / swop ped
*swat slap with a flat object
*-sword weapon
*swot study hard

* *

sponsor ed
spotlight
spotted
spotting
spotty -ier, -iest
sprocket

squabble d
squabbling
squadron
squalid
squalor
squander ed
squatted
squatter
squatting

-stalker
*-stalking hunting / walking stiffly
-stalling
-stalwart
stockade
*stocking ed leg covering
stocky -ier, -iest
stodgy -ier, -iest
stoppage
stopper
stopping
stopwatch es
-strawberry -ies
stronger
strongest
stronghold
strongly

swabbing
swallow ed
swapping / swopping
*swatted did swat
*swatting slapping with a flat object
*swotted did swot
*swotting studying hard

for Scots: o -r is on page 267

> **In these words the first letter 'o' is a neutral vowel. It sounds like the 'o' in 'occurring'.**
>
> society -ies
> solicitor
> solidify -ies
> solidified
> solidity
> soliloquy -ies
>
> solution
> Somalia
> sophisticated
> sophistication
> soprano s
> sporadic ally

In these words you can hear the vowel sound o as in dog

T

*

*-**talk** speak
-**talked**
-**tall**
*-**taught** instructed
-**taunt**
*-**taut** tight

-**thaw** ed
 thong
-**thought**
 throb bed
 throng ed

 tongs
 top ped
*-**torque** turning force /
 necklace
 toss es
 tossed
*-**tot** young child / small
 amount / add

 trod
 trot ted
 trough ed

* *

-**talking**
-**taller**
-**tallest**
-**tawny** -ier, -iest

-**thoughtful** ly
 throbbing
 throttle d

*-**tocsin** alarm bell
 toddle d
 toddler
 toddling
 toffee
 toggle
 toggling
 tomboy
 tomcat
 tonic
 tonsil
 topic
 topping
 topple d
 toppling
 topsoil
 torrent
 toxic
*-**toxin** poison

-**trauma** s [traumata]
 trodden
 trolley
 trombone
 tropic ally
 trotted
 trotting

* * *

-**talkative**

 tectonic

-**thoughtfully**

 toboggan
 tolerance
 tolerant
 tolerate
 tomahawk
 tommy-gun
 tomorrow
 topical

-**traumata**
-**traumatic**
 tropical ly

* * * *

 theodolite
 theology -ies
 thermometer

 tolerable
 tolerating
 toleration
 tonsillitis / tonsilitis
 topography
 topology
 topsy-turvy

 tropically

*for Scots: o -r
is on page 268* ▷

> In these words the first letter 'o' is a neutral
> vowel. It sounds like the 'o' in 'occurring'.
>
> | | |
> |---|---|
> | tobacco s | tomato es |
> | tobacconist | torrential ly |

U

*

* *

upon

* * *

* * * *

In these words you can hear the vowel sound ○ as in **dog**

V

*

***vault** gymnastic leap /
underground room /
arched roof

***volt** unit of electrical
force

* *

vodka
volley ed
voltage
volume
vomit ed

* * *

volatile
volcanic ally
volcano es / s
voluntary
volunteer ed

* * * * *

velocity -ies

volatility
volcanically
voluntarily

In this word the letter 'o' is a neutral vowel.

vocabulary -ies   vocation   vocational ly

W

*

***rot** ted decay

waft
***-walk** ed go in steps
-**wall** ed
waltz es
waltzed
wan
wand
want
was
wash es
washed
wasp
watch es
watched
***watt** unit of electric
power
***watts** units of electric
power

***what** that or those
which / which /
how much / I do not
understand
***what's** what is

***wok** cooking pan

wrath
wrong ed
***-wrought** made to fit

* *

wadding
waddle d
waddling
waffle d
waffling
-**walker**
-**walking**
wallet
-**wallflower**
wallow ed
-**walnut**
-**walrus** es
wander ed
wanted
wanting
wanton
warrant
warren
washer
***washers** means of
washing / sealing rings
***washes** cleans with
water
washing
wasn't
watchdog
watchful ly
watching
watchman [watchmen]
watchword
-**water** ed

-**withdraw**
[withdrew]
-**withdrawal**
-**withdrawn**

wobble d
wobbling
wobbly
wonky -ier, -iest

wrongful ly
wrongly

* * *

-**wallflower**
-**wallpaper** ed
wandering
warranty -ies
warrior
washable
washbasin
watchfully
-**waterfall**
-**waterfowl**
-**waterproof** ed
-**watershed**
-**watertight**
-**waterway**
-**watery**

whatever

-**withdrawal**

wrongdoing
wrongfully

* * * *

-**walkie-talkie**
-**watercolour**

whatsoever

---

for Scots: o -r
is on page 269

In these words you can hear the vowel sound o as in dog

Y

SHORT VOWEL O

*

yacht
-yawn ed

* *

yachting

yoghourt / yoghurt /
yogurt
yonder

* * *

* * * *

for Scots: o -r
is on page 269 ▷

Z

*

* *

zombi / zombie

* * *

* * * *

zoology

A

SHORT VOWEL **u**   SHORT VOWEL **oo**

*	**	***	* * * * *
	above	abruptly	accompaniment
	abrupt	abundance	accompany -ies
		abundant	accompanied
	-adjourn ed		accomplishment
	adjust	accomplice	
	adult	accomplish es	adultery
		accomplished	
	affront	accustom ed	
	-afoot		
		adjuster	
	among	adjustment	
	amongst		
		another	
	-assure d		
		assumption	
	august	-assurance	
		-assuring	

for *Scots: ur & ir* are on page 242 ▷

B

*	**	***	* * * * **
blood	because	becoming	brother-in-law
bluff ed	become	beloved	
blunt	[became]		budgerigar
blush es	[become]	bloodthirsty	budgetary
blushed	begun		Bulgaria
	beloved	-bookseller	-bureaucracy -ies
-book ed		-bourgeoisie	-bureaucratic ally
	bloodshed		
-brook ed	bloodstream	brotherhood	
brunt	bloody -ier,-iest		
brush es	blubber ed	buccaneer ed	
brushed	blunder ed	bucketful	
	bluntly	bucketing	
buck ed		-Buddhism	
bud ded	-bookcase	budgerigar	
budge d	-booking	budgetary	
buff ed	-booklet	budgeting	
bug ged	-bookmark ed	buffalo es	
bulb	-bookshelf [bookshelves]	-bulldozer ed	
bulge d	-bookshop	-bulletin	
bulk	*borough town or	bumblebee	
-bull	district with an MP	bungalow	
bum med	-bosom	Burundi	
bump ed	-bourgeois	buttercup	
bun		butterfly -ies	
bunch es	brother	buttermilk	
bunched	Brussels	butterscotch	
bung ed			
bunk ed			

for *Scots: ur & ir* are on page 243 ▷

-or oo as in woodpecker

116

In these words you can hear the sound u as in duck

B

*

bus es
-bush es
-bushed
*bussed carried by bus
*bust upper part of
  body / break / arrest
*but except / instead /
  yet
*butt large cask /
  person made fun of /
  thick end of tool or
  weapon / push with
  head
buzz es
buzzed

* *

bubble d
bubbling
bucket ed
buckle d
buckling
-Buddha
-Buddhist
budding
buddy -ies
budget ed
budgie
budging
buffer ed
*buffet ed push roughly
*buffet self-service meal
buffing
bugging
buggy -ies
bulbous
bulky -ier, -iest
-bulldog
-bullet
-bullfrog
-bullock
-bullseye
-bully -ies
-bullied
-bulrush es
bumming
bumper
bundle d
bundling
bungle d
bungling
bunion
bunker ed
bunny -ies
Bunsen
*burgh borough in
Scotland
burrow ed
-bushel
busker
bustle d
bustling
-butcher ed
butler
*butted pushed with
  head
*butter ed spread with
butter
buttocks
button ed
buttress es
buttressed
butty -ies
buzzard
buzzer

for *Scots: ur & ir*
are on page 243

-or oo as in woodpecker

In these words you can hear the sound u as in duck

117

C

*

chuck ed
chug ged
chum med
chump
chunk ed

club bed
cluck ed
clump ed
clung
clutch es
clutched

come
[came]
[come]
-cook ed
-could

-crook
crumb
crunch es
crunched
crush es
crushed
crust
crutch es
crux es [cruces]

cub
cuff ed
cult
cup ped
-cure d
cut
[cut]

* *

chuckle d
chuckling
chugging
chumming
chunky -ier, -iest
chutney

clubhouse
clumsy -ier, -iest
cluster ed
clutter ed

colour ed
comeback
comfort
coming
compass es
concuss es
concussed
conduct
confront
conjure d
construct
consult
convulse d
-cooker
-cookie
-cooking
corrupt
-couldn't
country -ies
couple d
coupling
courage
-courgette
cousin
cover ed

-crooked
crumble d
crumbling
crumpet
crumple d
crumpling
crunchy -ier, -iest
crusty -ier, -iest
crutches

* * *

chunkier
chunkiest

colander / cullender
colourful ly
colouring
colourless
combustion
comfortable
comfortably
comforting
company -ies
compulsion
compulsive
concurrent
concussing
concussion
conduction
conductor
conjunction
conjurer / conjuror
constable
constructed
construction
constructive
consultant
consulted
consumption
convulsion
convulsive
-cookery
corruption
countryman
[countrymen]
countryside
-courier
covenant
coverage
covering

crustacean

cul-de-sac
culinary
culminate
cultivate
cultural ly
cumbersome
-curator
-curio
-curious
currency -ies
currently
custody
customary
customer
cutlery

* * * * *

circumference

colourfully
combustible
comfortable
comfortably
compulsory
constructional
consultancy -ies

culinary
culminating
culmination
cultivation
culturally
-curiosity -ies
-curiously
custodial
customary

for *Scots: ur & ir*
are on page 244 ▷

-or oo as in woodpecker

In these words you can hear the sound u as in duck

C

* *
-cuckoo
cuddle d
cuddling
culprit
culture d
cunning
cupboard
cupful
cupping
-curate
-curing
*currant fruit
*current flowing
stream / present
curry -ies
curried
-cushion ed
custard
custom
customs
cutback
cutter
cutting

for *Scots: ur & ir* are on page 244 ▷

Here the first syllable vowel sounds are neutral.

courageous   curricular   curriculum [curricula]

-or oo as in woodpecker

In these words you can hear the sound u as in duck

119

D

*

does
*done finished
*dost old form of 'do',
used with 'thou'
doth
dove

drug ged
drum med
drunk

duck
*ducked did duck
*duct tube or pipe
dug
dull ed
dumb
dump ed
*dun grey-brown
dunce
dung
dusk
*dust particles of
earth or waste matter
Dutch

* *

deduct

discuss es
*discussed debated
*disgust strong
dislike
disrupt
distrust

doesn't
double d
doubling
doubly
dozen

drugging
drummer
drumming
drumstick
drunkard
drunken

duchess es
duckling
duffel / duffle
dugout
dummy -ies
dumpling
dungeon
-during
dustbin
duster
dusty -ier, -iest

* * *

deduction
deductive
destruction
destructive

discomfort
discourage d
discover ed
discussing
discussion
disgruntle d
disgruntling
disgusting
disruption
disruptive

drunkenness

dungarees

* * * * *

denunciation

discouraging
discovery -ies

for *Scots: ur & ir*
are on page 245

E

*

* *

-endure d
engulf ed
enough
*-ensure d make certain
entrust

erupt

-euro
-Europe

for I . . .
see page 123

*-insure d protect against
loss

* * *

emulsion ed

encourage d
-endurance
-enduring
*-ensuring making
certain

erupted
eruption

expulsion

*-insuring protecting
against loss

-or oo as in woodpecker

* * * *

encouragement
encouraging

-European

for *Scots: ur & ir*
are on page 245

    In these words you can hear the sound u as in duck

F

*	* *	* * *	* * * * *
flood	flooded	fluctuate	fluctuating
fluff ed	flooding	-fluorescence	fluctuation
flung	floodlight	-fluorescent	-fluorescence
flush es	floodlit		-fluorescent
flushed	flourish es	-footballer	-fluoridation /
flux es	flourished	forthcoming	fluoridisation
	fluffy -ier, -iest		zation
-foot	-fluoride	frontier	
	-fluorine	frustrating	functionality -ies
front	flurry -ies	frustration	functionally
	flurried		fundamental ly
fudge d	fluster ed	-fulfilling	-furiously
-full	flutter ed	-fulfilment	
fun		functional ly	
fund	-football	functioning	
fuss es	-footbridge	funnelling	
fussed	-footer	funnier	
	-foothill	funniest	
	-foothold	funnily	
	-footing	-furious	
	-footnote		
	-footpath		
	-footstep		
	-footwork		
	-forsook		
	frontage		
	frontier		
	frustrate		
	fudging		
	-fulcrum		
	-fulfil led		
	-full-back / fullback		
	-fuller		
	-fullest		
	-fullness		
	-full-scale		
	-full-time		
	-fully		
	fumble d		
	fumbling		
	function ed		
	funding		
	funfair		
	fungal		
	fungi		
	*fungous spongy or		
	in other ways like a		
	fungus		
	*fungus es [fungi] type		
	of plant		
	funnel led		
	funny -ier, -iest		
	furrow ed		
	-fury -ies		
	fuzzy -ier, -iest		

for th . . .
see page 133 ▷

for Scots: ur & ir
are on page 246 ▷

-or oo as in woodpecker

In these words you can hear the sound u as in duck

121

G

*	* *	* * *	* * * * *
glove d	gazump ed	gluttony	governmental ly
glum			
glut	glutton	-good-looking	gutturally
		-gooseberry -ies	
-good	-goodbye	government	
-goods	-goodness	governor	
-gourd	-goodnight		
	-goodwill	grudgingly	
grub bed	-gooseberry -ies		
grudge	-gourmet	gullible	
gruff	govern ed	gunpowder	
grunt		guttering	
	grubbing	guttural ly	
gulf	grubby -ier, -iest		
gull ed	grudging		
gulp ed	grumble d		
gum med	grumbling		
gun ned	grumpy -ier, -iest		
gush es			
gushed	gudgeon		
gust	gullet		
gut ted	gulley / gully -ies		
guts	gulling		
	gumboil		
	gumming		
	gunfire		
	gunman [gunmen]		
	gunner		
	gunning		
	gunpoint		
	gunshot		
	guppy -ies		
	-guru s		
	gusto		
	gusty -ier, -iest		
	gutsy -ier, -iest		
	gutter		
	gutting		
	guzzle d		
	guzzling		

for *Scots: ur & ir* are on page 246 ▷

-or **oo** as in woodpecker

In these words you can hear the sound **u** as in duck

H

*

-hood
-hook ed

hub
huff
hug ged
hulk
hull
hum med
hump ed
hunch es
hunched
hung
hunk
hunt
hush es
hushed
husk
hut
hutch es

* *

honey ed
-hoodie / hoody -ies
-hoummos / hommus /
hummous / hummus /
houmous / humus

hubbub
huddle d
huddling
hugging
hulky -ier, -iest
hullo
humble d
humbling
humming
hundred
hundredth
hunger ed
hungry -ier, -iest
hunted
hunter
hunting
-hurrah!
-hurray!
hurry -ies
hurried
husband
husky -ies
hustle d
hustling

* * *

honeybee
honeycomb
honeydew
honeymoon

hummingbird
Hungary
hungrier
hungrily
hurricane
hurriedly
hurrying

* * * *

honeysuckle

hullabaloo
Hungarian

for Scots: ur & ir
are on page 247

I

*

* *

*-ensured make certain

indulge d
instruct
insult
*-insure d protect
against loss
intrust / entrust

* * *

*-ensuring making certain

impulsive

induction
inductive
indulgence
indulgent
indulging
injunction
injustice
instruction
instructive
instructor
insulting
-insurance
*-insuring protecting
against loss

* * * * * * *

illustrious

-impurity -ies

-incurable
industrial ly
industrialisation
            zation
industrialise d
            ze
industrialist
industrious
-infuriate
-injurious

for Scots: ur & ir
are on page 247

for E . . .
see page 120

-or oo as in woodpecker

In these words you can hear the sound u as in duck

J

*

judge d
jug ged
jump ed
junk
just
jut ted

◁ for dr . . .
see page 120

* *

judgement / judgment
judging
juggle d
juggler
juggling
jumble d
jumbling
jumper
jumping
jumpy -ier, -iest
junction
juncture
jungle
-juror
-jury -ies
justice
justly
jutting

* * *

judgemental /
judgmental
juggernaut
jugular
justify -ies
justified
juxtapose d

* * * * *

-jurisdiction
-jurisprudence
justifiable
justifiably
justification
juxtaposing
juxtaposition

K

*

◁ for C . . .
see page 118

* *

knuckle d
knuckling

kung fu

* * *

* * * *

for Scots: ur & ir
are on page 248 ▷

-or oo as in **woodpecker**

In these words you can hear the sound **u** as in **duck**

L

*	**	***	****
-look ed	London	Londoner	luxuriant
love d	-lookout	-lookalike	luxurious
	lovely -ier, -iest	lovable	
luck	lover	loveliest	
lug ged	loving	lovingly	
lugs			
lull ed	lucky -ier, -iest	luckier	
lump ed	luggage	luckiest	
lunch es	lugging	luckily	
lunched	*lumbar lower back	lullaby -ies	
lung	*lumber junk / timber /	lumbago	
lunge d	move awkwardly	lumberjack	
-lure d	lumbered	Luxembourg /	
lush	lumpy -ier, iest	Luxemburg	
lust	luncheon ed	luxury -ies	
	lunchtime		
	lunging		
	luscious		
	lustre		
	lusty -ier, -iest		

*for Scots: ur & ir
are on page 248* ▷

-or **oo** as in woodpecker

In these words you can hear the sound **u** as in duck

M

SHORT VOWEL **u**   SHORT VOWEL **oo**

*

monk
month
-moor ed

much
muck ed
mud
muff ed
mug ged
mulch es
mum
mumps
munch es
munched
mung
mush
musk
must

* *

-manure d
-mature d

misjudge d
-mistook
mistrust

Monday
money ed
mongrel
monkey ed
monthly
-mooring
-moorland
-Moslem / Muslim
mother ed

muddle d
muddling
muddy -ier, -iest
mudguard
*muffin teacake
*muffing missing a
shot or catch
muffle d
muffling
mugger
mugging
muggy -ier, -iest
mulberry -ies
mumble d
mumbling
mummy -ies
mundane
*muscat wine / grape
*muscle body tissue
muscled
muscling
mushroom ed
*musket gun
-Muslim / Moslem
*muslin fine thin cotton
*mussel shellfish
mustang
*mustard plant with
hot-tasting seeds
muster
*mustered called
together
mustn't
musty -ier, -iest
mutter ed
mutton
muzzle d
*muzzling putting a
muzzle on

* * *

misjudging

monetary
motherhood

mulberry -ies
multiple
multiply -ies
multiplied
multitude
muscatel
muscular

* * * * * *

-maturity

monetary
mother-in-law
mother-of-pearl

multicultural ly
multilateral ly
multimedia
multi-million
multinational
multiplicand
multiplication
multiplicative
multiplicity
multiplier
musculature

> **Here the 'ou' is a neutral vowel.**
>
> moustache

for Scots: ur & ir
are on page 249 ▷

-or **oo** as in **woodpecker**

In these words you can hear the sound **u** as in **duck**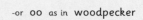

N

*
none not any
-**nook**

nudge d
null
numb ed
***nun** woman in
convent
nut

* *
knuckle d
knuckling

-**neural**
-**neuron** / **neurone**

nothing

nudging
nugget
number ed
nutmeg
nutty -ier, -iest
nuzzle d
nuzzling

* * *
nonetheless
nourishment

nullify -ies
nullified
nutcracker

* * * * **
-**neurological** ly
-**neurologist**
-**neurology**

for Scots: ur & ir
are on page 249 ▷

O

*
once
***one** 1
oops

***won** gained

* *
august

-**obscure** d
obstruct

one-off
oneself
one-way
onion

other

oven

* * *
-**obscuring**
obstruction
obstructive

occurrence

otherwise

* * * *
-**obscurity** -ies

◁ for H . . .
see page 123

for Scots: ur & ir
are on page 249 ▷

-or oo as in woodpecker

In these words you can hear the sound u as in duck

P

*

pluck ed
plug ged
*plum fruit
*plumb lead weight
on a cord / do work
of plumber
plumbed
plump ed
plunge d
plus es
plush

*-poor badly off
*-pore tiny hole / study
closely
*-pour ed flow out

pub
puff ed
pug
-pull ed
pulp ed
pulse d
pump ed
pun ned
punch es
punched
punk
punt
pup
*-pure unmixed
*pus liquid from
poisoned place
-push es
-pushed
*-puss es cat
*-put place
-[put]
*putt gentle golf shot
on a green

* *

plover
plugging
plumber
plumbing
plunder ed
plunging
-plural ly

-poorer
-poorest
-poorly

-procure d

public ly
publish es
published
-pudding
puddle d
puddling
puffin
-pulley
-pulpit
pulsar
pulsing
pumice
pumpkin
punctual ly
puncture d
pungent
punish es
punished
punning
puppet
puppy -ies
-purely
*-purest cleanest
*-purist perfectionist
-pushchair
-pussy -ies
putted
putter
*-putting placing
*putting doing putts
putty -ies
puttied
puzzle d
puzzling

* * *

percussion
percussive

-pluralist
-plurally

presumptuous
-procuring
production
productive
propulsion

publican
publicise d
publicly
publisher
publishing
-pullover
punctually
punctuate
puncturing
punishment
-purify -ies
-purified
-Puritan / puritan
-purity

* * * * *

-pluralism

presumptuous
pronunciation

publication
publicity
publicising
pulmonary
punctually
punctuating
punctuation
-purification
-puritanical
-puritanism

*for Scots: ur & ir
are on page 250* ▷

Q

*

* *

Qur'an / Koran

* * *

* * * *

-or oo as in woodpecker

In these words you can hear the sound u as in duck

R

*

-rook
-room
*rough uneven /
 harsh / crude
roughed

rub bed
ruck
*ruff collar
rug
rum
rump
run
[ran]
[run]
*rung step of ladder /
 sounded
runt
rush es
rushed
rusk
rust
rut ted

*wrung twisted

* *

refund
result

roughage
roughen ed
roughly
roughness

rubber
rubbing
rubbish
rubble
rucksack
rudder
ruddy -ier, -iest
ruffle d
ruffling
Rugby
rugged
rugger
rumba
rumble d
rumbling
rummy
rumpus es
runner
running
runny -ier, -iest
runway
rupture d
rushing
Russia
Russian
rustic
rustle d
rustling
rusty -ier, iest
rutted
rutting

* * *

recover ed
recurrence
recurrent
reduction
redundant
reluctance
reluctant
republic
repulsive
resultant
resulted
resulting
revulsion

-rookery -ies

ruffian
runaway
runner-up
rupturing

* * * * *

recovery -ies
redundancy -ies
reluctantly
republican
resuscitate
resuscitating
resuscitation

-Romania / Roumania /
 Rumania

for Scots: ur & ir
are on page 251

-or oo as in woodpecker

In these words you can hear the sound u as in duck

S

*	* *	* * *	* * * * *
scrub bed	scrubbing	scullery -ies	circumference
scruff	scruffy -ier, -iest		
scrum	scuffle d	seduction	-security -ies
*scull ed row / oar	scuffling	seductive	
sculpt	sculptor		structurally
scum	sculptress es	shrubbery -ies	
	sculpture	shuttlecock	subcommittee
-shook	scumbling		subconsciously
-should	scurry -ies	slovenly	subdividing
shove d	scurried		subjectivity
shrub	scuttle d	somebody	subsequently
shrug ged	scuttling	somersault	subsidising
shrunk		son-in-law	zing
shunt	-secure d		substituting
shush es		-spurious	substitution
shushed	-shouldn't		subterranean
shut	shovel led	structural ly	subtropical
[shut]	shrugging	structuring	suffocating
	shudder ed	studying	summarising
*skull bone of the head	shuffle d		zing
skunk	shuffling	subconscious	supplementary -ies
	shutdown	subdivide	
sludge	shutter ed	submarine	
slug	shutting	subsection	
slum med	shuttle d	subsequent	
slump ed	shuttling	subsidence	
slunk		subsidise d	
slush	sluggish	ze	
	slumber ed	subsidy -ies	
smudge d	slumming	substantive	
smug	slurry	substitute	
smut		subtitle d	
	smother ed	subtitling	
snub bed	smudging	subtlety -ies	
snuff ed	smuggle d	subtrahend	
snug	smuggler	suddenly	
	smuggling	sufferer	
*some a certain		suffering	
number or amount	snubbing	suffocate	
*son male child	snuffing	suffragette	
-soot	snuffle d	sulphuric	
	snuffling	sultana	
sponge d	snuggle d	summarise d	
sprung	snuggling	ze	
spun		*summary -ies brief	
	somehow	account	
	someone	summertime	
	something	*summery like summer	
	sometime	sumptuous	
	sometimes	sunflower	
	somewhat	sunglasses	
	somewhere	supplement	
	*sonny laddie	suppleness	
	southern		

-or oo as in woodpecker

130

In these words you can hear the sound u as in duck

for Scots: ur & ir are on page 252

S

*	**
-stood	**splutter** ed
struck	**sponging**
strum med	**spongy** -ier, -iest
strung	-**sputnik**
strut ted	
stub bed	**stomach** ed
stuck	**structure** d
stud ded	**struggle** d
stuff ed	**struggling**
stump ed	**strumming**
stun ned	**strutting**
stung	**stubbing**
stunk	**stubble**
stunt	**stubborn**
	stubby -ier, -iest
such	**studding**
suck ed	**study** -ies
suds	studied
sulk ed	**stuffing**
***sum** med total /	**stuffy** -ier, -iest
exercise with numbers	**stumble** d
***sun** source of sunlight	**stumbling**
sung	**stunning**
sunk	**stutter** ed
sunned	
-**sure**	**subject**
	subset
swung	**subsoil**
	substance
	subtle
	subtly
	suburb
	subway
	***succour** help
	***sucker** person or
	thing that sucks /
	shoot from stem or
	root / person who
	is easily tricked
	suckle d
	suckling
	suction
	sudden
	suffer ed
	suffix es
	suffrage
	-**sugar** ed
	sulky -ier, -iest
	sullen
	sully -ies
	sullied
	sulphate
	sulphur
	sultan

for Scots: ur & ir
are on page 252 ▷

-or **oo** as in **woodpecker**

In these words you can hear the sound **u** as in **duck**

131

S

* *

summer
summing
summit
summon ed
summons
sumptuous
sunbathe d
sunburn ed
[sunburnt]
***sundae** sweet dish
***Sunday** day
sundry -ies
sunflower
sunken
sunlight
sunlit
sunning
***sunny** -ier, -iest   light
and pleasant
sunrise
sunset
sunshade
sunshine
sunstroke
suntan ned
supper
supple
-**surely**
suspect

for Scots: ur & ir are on page 252 ▷

In these words the first letter 'u' is a neutral vowel.   It sounds like the 'u' in 'suspicious'.

S*U*CCESSFUL WORDS

subdue d	subscribing	succeed	supplied	surround ed
subduing	subscription	success es	supplier	surrounding s
subject ed	subside	successful ly	supply -ies	susceptibility -ies
subjection	subsidiary -ies	succession	support ed	susceptible
subjective	subsiding	successive	supporter	suspect ed
submerge d	subsist	successor	supporting	suspend
submerging	subsistence	succinct ly	suppose d	suspense
submission	substantial ly	sufficient ly	supposedly	suspension
submissive	subtend	suggest ed	supposing	suspicion
submit ted	subtract	suggestible	suppress es	suspicious ly
submitting	subtracting	suggesting	suppressed	sustain ed
subordinate	subtraction	suggestion	suppression	sustainable
subscribe d	suburban	suggestive	surrender ed	sustainably

-or oo as in **woodpecker**

In these words you can hear the sound u as in **duck**

T

*

thrush es
thrust
[thrust]
thud ded
thug
thumb ed
thump ed
thus

*ton measure of
weight
tongue d
*tonne 1000 kilos
-took
touch es
touched
tough
-tour ed

truck
trudge d
trunk
truss es
*trussed tied up
firmly
*trust faith

tub
tuck ed
tuft
tug ged
*tun large barrel
tusk

* *

thorough
thudded
thudding
thumbnail
thunder ed

tongue-tied
touchdown
touching
touchline
touchy -ier, -iest
toughen ed
tougher
toughest
-tourist

trouble d
troubling
trudging
trumpet ed
truncheon
trundle d
trundling
trussing
*trustee agent legally
controlling money or
property
*trusty -ier, -iest reliable

tubby -ier, -iest
tugging
tumble d
tumbler
tumbling
tummy -ies
tundra
tungsten
tunnel led
turret
tussle d
tussling

* * *

thoroughbred
thoroughfare
thoroughly
thunderbolt
thunderclap
thundercloud
thunderous
thunderstorm
thunderstruck

-tournament

troublesome
trumpeted
trumpeting
trustworthy

tunnelling

* * * *

thoroughgoing

*for Scots: ur & ir
are on page 253* ▷

-or oo as in **woodpecker**

In these words you can hear the sound u as in duck

133

U

*	**	***	* * * * **
up ped	onion	otherwise	**ultimately**
	other	**ugliest**	**ultimatum**
us		**ugliness**	**ultrasonic** ally
	oven		**ultraviolet / ultra-violet**
		ultimate	
	udder		**unabated**
		umbrella	**unacceptable**
	ugly -ier, -iest	**umpiring**	**unaccountably**
			unaffected
	ulcer	**unable**	**unambiguous** ly
	Ulster	**unabridged**	**unattractive**
		unafraid	**unavailable**
	umpire d	**unaided**	**unavoidable**
		unaware	**unbearable**
		unbeaten	**unbelievable**
	unarmed	**unbroken**	**unbreakable**
	unbend	**unbutton** ed	**uncannier**
	[unbent]	**uncanny** -ier, -iest	**uncanniest**
	unbind	**uncertain**	**uncertainty** -ies
	[unbound]	**unchallenged**	**uncomfortable**
	unblock ed	**uncommon**	**uncomfortably**
	unbolt	**unconcerned**	**uncompromising**
	unborn	**unconscious**	**unconditional** ly
	unchanged	**uncontrolled**	**unconsciously**
	uncle	**uncover** ed	**uncontrollable**
	unclean	**undamaged**	**unconventional** ly
	unclear	**undaunted**	**uncooperative**
	under	**undefined**	**undecided**
	***undo** reverse an act	**underclothes**	**undeniable**
	[undid]	**underfoot**	**undercover**
	[undone]	**undergo**	**undercurrent**
	undress es	[underwent]	**underdeveloped**
	undressed	[undergone]	**underestimate** d
	***undue** beyond normal	**underground**	**underestimating**
	limits	**undergrowth**	**undergraduate**
	unearth ed	**underlie**	**underlining**
	unfair	[underlay]	**underlying**
	unfit ted	[underlain]	**undermining**
	unfold	**underline** d	**understandable**
	unharmed	**undermine** d	**understandably**
	unheard	**underneath**	**understanding**
	unhurt	**underscore** d	**understudy** -ies
	unjust	**undersell**	understudied
	unkind	[undersold]	**undertaken**
	unknown	**understand**	**undertaker**
	unlatch es	[understood]	**undertaking**
	unlatched	**undertake**	**underwater**
	unless	[undertook]	**underwriting**
	unlike	[undertaken]	**underwritten**
	unload	**underwear**	**undesirable**
	unlock ed	**underworld**	**undoubtedly**
	unpack ed	**underwrite**	
	unpaid	[underwrote]	
	***unreal** not actual	[underwritten]	
	***unreel** unwind	**undisturbed** -or oo as in woodpecker	
	unrest	**undoing**	
	unroll ed		

for H . . .
see page 123

for Scots: ur & ir
are on page 254

In these words you can hear the sound u as in duck

U

* *

unsafe
unscathed
unscrew ed
unseen
unskilled
unsolved
unsure
untie d
until
unto
untold
untouched
untrained
untrue
unused
unveil ed
unwell
unwind
[unwound]
unwise
unwrap ped

update
upgrade
uphill
uphold
[upheld]
upkeep
upland
uplift
upload
upper
upright
uproar
uproot
upset
[upset]
upside
upstairs
upstream
upsurge
uptake
upturn ed
upward
upwards

usher ed

utmost
utter ed

* * *

unduly
uneasy -ier, -iest
unemployed
unending
unequal led
uneven
unexplored
unfasten ed
unfinished
unfriendly -ier, -iest
unfurnished
ungrateful ly
unguarded
unhappy -ier, -iest
unhealthy -ier, -iest
unhelpful
uninjured
uninstal led /
uninstall ed
unlawful ly
unlikely
unlucky -ier, -iest
unmarried
unnatural
unnoticed
unpleasant
unravel led
unravelling
unreal
unscramble d
unscrambling
unselfish
unsettled
unstable
unsteady
untangle d
untangling
untidy -ier, -iest
untying
unusual ly
unwanted
unwelcome
unwilling
unworthy
unwrapping

upbringing
upheaval
upholster ed
uprising
upsetting
upside down
up-to-date

-Uranus

utterance
utterly

* * * * * * *

uneasily
unemotional ly
unemployment
unequivocal ly
unexpected ly
unfamiliar
unfavourable
unforgettable
unfortunate ly
ungratefully
unhappily
unhappiness
unidentified
unimportant
uninhabitable
uninhabited
uninstalling
unjustified
unlawfully
unlimited
unmistakable
unnecessarily
unnecessary
unoccupied
unofficial ly
unorthodox
unpopular
unprecedented
unpredictable
unprotected
unqualified
unquestionably
unravelling
unrealistic ally
unreasonable
unrelated
unreliable
unsanitary
unsatisfactory
unscrupulous ly
unsociable
unspecified
unsuccessful ly
unsuitable
unthinkable
unusually
unwillingness
unwittingly

upholstery

for Scots: ur & ir
are on page 254

-or oo as in **woodpecker**

| Here the 'u' has a neutral sound. |
| upon |

for H . . .
see page 123

In these words you can hear the sound u as in duck

135

V

*

* *
vulgar
vulture

* * *
vulnerable

* * * * * *
vulgarity -ies
vulnerability
vulnerable

for Scots: ur & ir
are on page 254 ▷

W

*
once
*one 1

*rung step of ladder /
sounded

-wolf wolves
-wolfed
*won gained
*-wood timber / area
with many trees
*-woof! bark of dog
*-woof weft
-wool
*-would was willing to /
used to / was going to

*wrung twisted

* *
oneself

-woman [women]
wonder ed
wondrous
-wooden
-woodland
-woodwind
-woodwork
-woollen
-woolly
worry -ies
worried
-worsted
-would-be
-wouldn't

* * *
-womanhood
wonderful ly
wondering
-woodcutter
-woodpecker
worrying

* * * *
wonderfully

for Scots: ur & ir
are on page 255 ▷

Y

*
young
*-your belonging to
you
*-you're you are
-yours

* *
younger
youngest
youngster
-yourself
-yourselves

yummy -ier, -iest

* * *

* * * *

-or oo as in **woodpecker**

In these words you can hear the sound u as in duck

A

*

ace d
ache d

age d

*aid help
*aide helper
*aids sources of help /
  does help
*Aids / AIDS acquired
  immune deficiency
  syndrome
*ail ed grow weak
aim ed
ain't

*ale beer

ape d

*ate did eat

eh

*eight 8
eighth

* *

abate
ablaze
able
ably
abstain ed

acclaim ed
aching
acorn
acquaint
acre

afraid

again
against
aged
ageing / aging
agent

ailment

amaze d
amen

ancient
angel
anus es

apex es [apices]
appraise d
April
apron

arrange d
array ed

ashamed
Asia
Asian
assail ed
astray

attain ed

avail ed

await
awake d
[awoke]
[awoken]
away

éclair

eighteen th
eighty -ies

élite

* * *

abating
abeyance
abrasive

acquaintance
acreage

adjacent

agency -ies

alien

amazement
amazing
amiable

aorta s / -ae

appraisal
appraising
apricot

aqueous

arrangement
arranging

asexual
assailant

atheist
attainment

availing

awaken ed
awaking

eightieth
eisteddfod

élitist

* * * * * *

Albania
alienation

amiable

Arabia

asymmetric al
asymmetry -ies

atheism
atypical ly

Australia

availability
available
aviation
aviator

awakening

élitism

for H . . .
see page 144

for Scots: ae -r
is on page 236

In these words you can hear the vowel sound ae as in snail   **137**

B

LONG VOWEL ae

*

babe
*bail bar on
cricket stumps /
payment for release /
bail out
bailed
bait
*baize cloth
bake d
*bale bundle /
bale out
baled
*base foot / central
establishment /
worthless
*based established
*bass low sound
*baste cover with
melted fat /
tack together
bathe d
bay ed
*bays more than
one bay

beige

blade
blame d
blaze d

brace d
*brae hillside
*braes more than one
brae
*braid plait /
edging cloth
braille
brain ed
*braise d gently
cook in liquid
*braise / braize fish
*brake means of
slowing or stopping
brave d
*bray hee-haw
*brayed did bray
*braze d join with
hard solder
*break smash in
pieces / interrupt /
suddenly change
[broke]
[broken]

* *

babied
baby -ies
babied
bacon
bailey
bailiff
baker
baking
baling
basal
baseball
baseline
basement
basic ally
basin
basing
basis [bases]
basting
bathing

became
behave d
betray ed

blameless
blaming
blatant
blazer
blazing

bracelet
braces
bracing
brainy -ier, -iest
braising / braizing
braking
bravely
braving
brazen
brazier
brazing
breakage
breakdown
breakers
breaking
breakthrough
break-up
brigade
brocade

* * *

babysit / baby-sit
bakery -ies
basically
bayonet ed / ted

behaving
behaviour
belated
betrayal

blatantly

bravery
brazier
breakable
breakaway
breakwater

* * * *

babysitter
babysitting
basically
bayoneted / bayonetted

behavioural
belatedly

*for Scots: ae -r
is on page 236* ▷

In these words you can hear the vowel sound ae as in snail

C

*

caged
caked
came
caned
cape
cased
caved

chafed
chained
changed
chase
*chased did chase
*chaste pure

claimed
clay

craned
crate
craved
craze
crèche / creche
crêpe / crepe

* *

cabled
cabling
caging
caking
canine
caning
casin
catered
caving

ceilidh

chafing
chamber
changing
chaos
chasing

claimant

cocaine
complained
complaint
constrained
constraint
contained
conveyed

cradled
cradling
craning
cratered
craving
crayoned
crazy -ier, -iest
create
cremate

* * *

capable
catering
causation

changeable
chaotic ally

complacent
contagious
container
conveyor / conveyer
courageous

crayoning
craziest
crazily
created
creating
creation
creative
creator
cremating
cremation
Croatia
crustacean

* * * * *

Canadian
capability -ies

chaotically

complacency

for Qu . . .
see page 148

for Scots: ae -r
is on page 236

In these words you can hear the vowel sound ae as in snail

D

*

dale
dame
*Dane citizen of Denmark
date
day
*days more than one day
*daze state of not thinking clearly
dazed

*deign pretend to lower oneself socially

drain ed
drake
drape d

* *

dahlia
daily
dainty -ier, -iest
daisy -ies
danger
Danish
data
dated
dating
daybreak
daydream ed
daylight
daytime

debate
debris
début / debut
*decade ten years
decay ed
*decayed did decay
décor
defame d
deflate
deist
delay ed
derail ed
detain ed
détente

dictate
disdain ed
disgrace d
dismay ed
displace d
display ed
distaste

domain
donate

drainage
draper
draping

* * *

dahlia
daintily
dangerous
database

debating
defaming
deflated
deflating
deflation
deism
deity -ies
derailment

dictating
dictation
dictator
disable d
disabling
disgraceful ly
disgracing
displacement
displacing
distasteful

donated
donating
donation

drapery -ies

* * * *

dangerously

disablement
disdainfully
disgracefully
distastefully

for Scots: ae -r is on page 237 ▷

In these words you can hear the vowel sound ae as in snail

E

*
*ate did eat

eh

***eight** 8
 eighth

**
éclair

eighteen th
eighty -ies

élite

embrace d

encase d
engage d
engrave d
enrage d
enslave d
entail ed

equate

erase d

escape d
estate
estranged

evade

exchange d
exclaim ed
exhale d
explain ed

for H . . .
see page 144

for I . . .
see page 144

***
eightieth
eisteddfod

elated
elation
élitist

embracing

enable d
enabling
encasing
endanger ed
engagement
engaging
engraving
enraging
enslaving

equating
equation
equator

eraser
erasing

escaping

evading
evasion
evasive

exchanging
exhaling
explaining

****
élitism

extraneous

for Scots: ae -r
is on page 237

F

*

face d
fade
fail ed
*faint weak
faith
fake d
fame d
*fate destiny
*fay fairy
*fays more than one
fairy
*faze d unnerve d

feign ed
*feint mock attack
*fete festival
*fey strange and
otherworldly

flake d
flame d

frail
frame d
fray ed
*frays noisy fights /
wears away at edges
freight

*phase d stage d
*phrase meaningful
sequence of words, notes
or movements in dance
phrased

* *

fable d
facecloth
facial
facing
faded
fading
failing
failure
fainter
faintest
faintly
faithful ly
*faker fraud
faking
*fakir begging holy
man (Muslim or Hindu)
famous
fatal ly
favour ed
favourite

flagrant
flaking
flaming
flavour ed

forgave
forsake
[forsook]
[forsaken]

fragrance
fragrant
framework
framing
freighter
Fresnel
frustrate

phasing
phrasing

* * *

faithfully
fallacious
fatally
favourable
favourite

filtration
fixation

flavouring
flotation

formation
forsaken
forsaking

frustrating
frustration

* * * * * *

fatalism
fatalistic ally
favourable
favourably
favouritism

phraseology

for th . . .
see page 151

for Scots: ae -r
is on page 238

In these words you can hear the vowel sound ae as in snail

G

*   *** ***   *** * ***   *** * * ***

*Gael Celt
gain ed
*gait way of
walking
*gale strong wind
game
gaol / jail
gaoled / jailed
gape d
*gate entrance
gauge d
gave
gay
*gays homosexuals
*gaze d stare d

glaze d

grace d
*grade standard
grain ed
grape
*grate grid / rub
hard
grave
gray / grey
*graze d eat growing
grass / scrape the skin
*great big /
important
grey / gray
*greyed turned grey
*greys / grays neutral
colours between white
and black

gable
Gaelic
gaily
gaining
gala
gaming
gaoler / jailer
gaping
gaseous
gatecrash es
gatecrashed
gatehouse
gatepost
gateway
gauging
gazing

glacial
glazing

graceful ly
gracing
gracious
graded
gradient
grading
grapefruit
grapevine
grateful ly
*grater gadget for
grating
grating
gratis
graveyard
gravy -ies
grazing
*greater more great
greatest
greatly
greatness
grenade
greyhound
grimace d

gaiety

glacial
*glacier mass of
slow-moving ice
*glazier worker
who fits glass
in windows

gracefully
gradation
gradient
gratefully
grimacing

geranium

gymnasium s [gymnasia]

for Scots: ae -r
is on page 238

In these words you can hear the vowel sound **ae** as in **snail**

H

*

***hail** hard frozen
rain / call name
or greetings /
come from
hailed
***hale** very healthy
haste
hate
***hay** dried grass
haze

***hey!** ho!

* *

Haiti
halo ed
hasten ed
hasty -ier, -iest
hated
hateful ly
hating
hatred
haven
haystack
hazel
hazy -ier,-iest

heinous
heyday

humane
hurray!

* * *

halfpenny -ies
hastily

herbaceous

hiatus es

for Scots: ae -r
is on page 238

* * * *

I

*

for E . . .
see page 141

* *

inflame d
inflate
inhale d
innate
insane
invade

* * *

impatience
impatient

inflaming
inflating
inflation
inhaler
inhaling
invaded
invader
invading
invasion

Israeli

* * * * *

impatiently

incapable
inflationary
insatiable

Iranian

for Scots: ae -r
is on page 239

In these words you can hear the vowel sound ae as in snail

J

LONG VOWEL **ae**

*	**	***	****
jade	jaded	**Jamaica**	geranium
jail / gaol	jailer / gaoler	**Jamaican**	
jailed / gaoled	jailhouse		gymnasium s [gymnasia]
jay			

◁ for dr . . .
see page 140

K

*	**	***	****
*****knave** rascal			
*nave part of church			

◁ for C . . .
see page 139

for Qu . . .
see page 148 ▷

L

*	**	***	****
lace d	**label** led	**labelling**	
laid	**labour** ed	**labourer**	
*****lain** rested	**lacing**	**ladybird**	
lake	**laden**	**laserjet**	
lame d	**ladies**	*****lazier** more lazy	
*****lane** narrow road	**ladle** d	**laziest**	
late	**ladling**	**lazily**	
lathe	**lady** -ies	**laziness**	
lay	**Laos**		
[laid]	*****laser** apparatus	**liaising**	
*****lays** does lay / poems	making light beams	**liaison**	
*****laze** take it easy	that can cut		
	lately	**location**	
	lateness		
	latent	**lumbago**	
	later		
	latest		
	latex		
	lay-by		
	layer		
	laying		
	layman [laymen]		
	layout		
	lazing		
	lazy -ier, -iest		

for Scots: ae -r
is on page 239 ▷

liaise d

In these words you can hear the vowel sound **ae** as in snail

M

*

mace
***made** formed
***maid** girl
***mail** post /
armour
mailed
maimed
***main** chief / strength
***maize** corn
make
[made]
***male** masculine
***mane** hair, as on
neck of horse or lion
mate
may
***maze** puzzle with
many paths

* *

maelstrom
maiden
mailboxes
mailer
mainframe
mainland
mainly
mainsail
mainstream
maintained
major
maker
makeshift
make-up
making
manger
mangy-ier, -iest
mania
maple
mason
mating
matrixes [matrices]
matron
maybe
maypole

mislay
[mislaid]
mistake
[mistook]
[mistaken]

moraine

mundane

* * *

maintenance
majorette
Malaya
Malaysia
mammalian
mania
maniac
masonry
matriarch
mayonnaise

mistaken
mistaking

* * * *

Malaysia
matriarchal
matriarchy -ies

for Scots: ae -r
is on page 239 ▷

N

*

*knave rascal

nailed
named
*nave part of
church
*nay no

*née born with
the name...
*neigh noise made
by horses
neighed

* *

naked
namely
naming
narrate
nasally
nation
native
nature
*naval concerning
warships
*navel tummy-button
navy-ies

negate
neighbour

* * *

narrating
narration
narrator
nasally
nationwide

negating
negation
neighbourhood
neighbouring
neighbourly

* * * *

146

In these words you can hear the vowel sound ae as in snail

O

*	**	***	*****
	obey ed	occasion	Australia
	obtain ed		
		oration	obtainable
		outrageous	occasional ly

P

*   ******   *******   ****** ****

*faze d unnerve d
*fays more than one
fairy

*frays noisy fights /
wears away at edges

pace
*paced did pace
page d
paid
*pail bucket
*pain suffering
paint
*pale whitish
*pane sheet of glass
*paste mixture of
powder and liquid
pave d
pay
[paid]

*phase d stage d
*phrase meaningful
sequence of words,
notes or movements in
dance
phrased

*place d position
plague d
*plaice fish
*plain area of
level land / simple
*plane aeroplane /
flat surface /
smoothing tool / tree
plate
play ed

*praise d glorify /
high approval
*pray ask for help
*prays asks for help
*prey victim
*preys hunts to feed

pagan
painful ly
painted
painter
painting
papal
paper ed
parade
pastry -ies
patent
*patience ability to
wait for results
patient
*patients people under
medical treatment
patron
pavement
paving
paying
payment
payroll

persuade
pervade

phrasing

placement
placing
plainly
*plaintiff person who
takes legal action
*plaintive sad-sounding
player
playful ly
playground
playgroup
playing
playmate
playtime
playwright

portray ed

prevail ed
proclaim ed
profane

pacemaker
painfully
painkiller
painstaking
palatial ly
papacy -ies
paperback
paperboy
paperclip
papergirl
paperwork
parading
patiently
patriarch
patriot
payable

persuading
persuasion
persuasive
pervading
pervasive

plagiarist
playfully

potato es

prevailing
probation

palaeontologist /
paleontologist
palatially
papier-mâché
patriarchal
patriarchy -ies
patriotic ally
patriotism

phraseology

plagiarism

for Scots: ae -r
is on page 239

In these words you can hear the vowel sound **ae** as in snail

Q

*

quail ed
quaint
quake d

* *

quailing
Quaker
quaking
quasar
quaver ed

* * *

quotation

* * * *

R

*

race d
rage d
raid
rail ed
*rain water falling
from clouds
rained
*raise d lift up
rake d
range d
rape d
rate
rave d
ray
*rays beams
*raze d tear down

*reign rule
*rein strap to control
an animal

* *

rabies
racecourse
racehorse
racial ly
racing
racist
*radar radio detection
raging
*raider person who
raids
railing
railway
rainbow
raincoat
raindrop
rainfall
raining
rainy -ier, -iest
raises
raisin
raising
raking
rampage d
rapist
rating
raven
raving
rayon
razor

reclaim ed
refrain ed
regain ed
regime / régime
reindeer
relate
remain ed
renege d
repay
[repaid]
replace d
restrain ed
restraint
retain ed

* * *

racially
racism
radial ly
radiant
radiate
radio s
radioed
radium
radius [radii]
rainforest
rainier
rainiest
rampaging
rapier
rateable
ratio s

reagent
related
relating
relation
remainder
remaining
Renaissance
reneging
replacement
replacing
restraining

rotation

* * * * * * *

radially
radiation
radiator
radioactive
radioactivity
radiographer
radiography
radiologist
radiology

relationship

Romania / Roumania /
Rumania

*for Scots: ae -r
is on page 240* ▷

In these words you can hear the vowel sound **ae** as in **snail**

S

*

safe
sage
*sail travel by boat /
sheet fixed to mast
sailed
saint
sake
*sale selling
same
*sane of sound mind
saved
say
[said]

scaled
scraped

*seine weighted fishnet
*Seine French river

shade
*shake move quickly
in different directions
[shook]
[shaken]
shale
shamed
shaped
shaved
*sheikh / sheik Arab
ruler

skate
skein

slain
slate
slaved
*slay kill
[slew]
[slain]
*sleigh sledge

snail
snaked

spaced
*spade tool
Spain
spate
*spayed operated
on to remove ovaries
sprained
sprayed

* *

sable
sabre
sacred
sadist
safeguard
safely
safer
safest
safety
sago
sailing
sailor
salesgirl
salesman [salesmen]
saline
Satan
*saver person or
thing that saves
saving
savings
*saviour rescuer
*savour enjoy a
taste or smell
saying

*scalar measurable on
a scale
scalene
*scaler pulse counter
scaling
scaly
scapegoat
scathing
scraper
scraping

séance

shaded
shading
shady -ier, -iest
shaker
shaking
shaky -ier, -iest
shameful ly
shaming
shaver
shaving

skateboard
skater
skating

slater
slaving

snaking

* * *

sadism
salesperson
saleswoman
[saleswomen]
salient
savoury -ies

shakily
shamefully

slavery

spacewoman
[spacewomen]
spatially / spacially

stabilised
ze
stadiums [stadia]
*stationary still
*stationery writing
materials
straightaway
straightforward

surveillance
surveying
surveyor

* * * *

stabiliser
zer
stabilising
zing
*stationary still
*stationery writing
materials

sustainable
sustainably

for Scots: ae -r
is on page 240

In these words you can hear the vowel sound ae as in snail   **149**

S

*

stage d
***staid** serious and
dull
stain ed
***stake** stick /
bet / prize
staked
stale
state
stave d
[stove]
stay
***stayed** did stay
***steak** meat
***straight** without
curves
strain ed
***strait** channel
straits
strange
stray ed

***suede** soft undressed
leather

sway
***swayed** did sway

* *

spacecraft
spaceman [spacemen]
spaceship
spacesuit
spacing
spacious
spatial / spacial

stable d
stabling
stagecoach
staging
stainless
staking
stalemate
stamen
staple d
stapling
stated
stately
statement
statesman [statesmen]
station ed
status es
staving
staying
straighten ed
strangely
stranger
stratus [strati]

survey ed
sustain ed

*for Scots: ae -r
is on page 240*

In these words you can hear the vowel sound **ae** as in **snail**

T

*

*tail part at the back
tailed
taint
take
[took]
[taken]
*tale story
tamed
taped
taste

they
they'd
they'll
they've

traced
trade
trailed
trained
*trait characteristic
*tray board with
raised edges, for
carrying things

**

tabled
tabling
tailored
taken
takeoff
taking
takings
taming
*tapered become
thinner towards
one end / waxed
spill or wick
taping
*tapir animal
tasted
tastefully
tasting
tasty -ier, -iest

terrain

today

tracing
traded
trademark
trader
trading
trailer
trainee
trainer
trainers
training
traitor

***

tablecloth
tablespoon
takeaway
takeover
tastefully

tenacious

****

titanium

for Scots: ae -r
is on page 241

U

*

**

***

Uranus

****

V

*

vague
*vain conceited
*vale valley
*vane blade
vaned

*veiled cover
*vein blood vessel /
mood / streak

**

vacant
vacate
vaguely
vagueness
valence
vapour

***

vacancy -ies
vacating
*vacation holiday /
process of leaving
valency -ies

vivacious

*vocation calling /
occupation
volcano es / s

*****

vocationally

for Scots: ae -r
is on page 241

In these words you can hear the vowel sound **ae** as in snail

151

W

| * | ** | *** | **** |

*wade walk in water
wage d
waif
*wail ed cry
*wain old farm wagon
*waist narrow part
of body
*wait stay
*waive no longer
enforce
wake d
[woke]
[woken]
*Wales country
*wane d grow smaller
*waste rubbish
*wave hand signal /
surge
waved
*way path

*weigh find the
weight of
*weighed found the
weight of
*weight heaviness /
value

*whale sea-mammal
*whales more than
one whale
*whey watery part
of sour milk

wading
wader
wafer
wager ed
waging
*wailer loud-crying
mourner
waistcoat
*waited did wait
waiter
waiting
waitress es
*waiver releasing
statement
*waiving no longer
enforcing
waken ed
waking
waning
wastage
wasted
wasteful ly
wasteland
wasting
wavelength
*waver ed hesitate d
*waving using the hand
to signal
wavy -ier, -iest
waylay
[waylaid]
wayside

weighbridge
weighing
*weighted having
added weight
weightless
weighty -ier, -iest

*whaler ship for whale-
hunting
whaling

wastefully
wastepaper

weightlessness

for Scots: ae -r
is on page 241 ▷

Y

| * | ** | *** | **** |

yea

In these words you can hear the vowel sound ae as in snail

A

*	**	***	**** *
	achieve d	achievement achieving	abbreviation
	adhere d		aesthetically
	afield	adhering adhesive	agreeable
	agree d	Aegean aesthetic ally	amenable amenity -ies
	anneal ed antique	agreement	anaemia / anemia anaesthetist / anesthetist
	appeal ed appear ed appease d	allegiance amino amoeba	appreciable appreciate appreciating
	asleep	anaemic / anemic	appreciation appreciative
	austere	appearance appeasement appeasing	
		arena	

B

*

*be to be / exist
*beaches shore
beached
bead
beaked
beamed
*bean vegetable
beard
beast
*beat batter / defeat
[beat]
[beaten]
*bee insect
*beech tree
beefed
*been from 'to be'
*beer drink
*beet plant with
sweet root

*bier frame to bear
coffin

bleaches
bleached
bleak
bleat
bleed
[bled]
bleeped

*breaches gap / break
breached
bream
breathed
*breeches bottom
part of gun
breed
[bred]
breezed
briefed

* *

batik

beacon
beagle
beagling
beaker
beanbag
beanstalk
beastly
beaten
*beater person or
thing that beats
beating
beavered
beehive
beeswax
*beetle insect
beetroot
being
belief
believed
beneath
bereaved
[bereft]
beseeches
beseeched
[besought]
besieged
*beta Greek letter b
*betel leaves and nut
between

bleeding

*breaches gaps /
does breach
breathing
*breeches trousers
for riding / bottom
parts of guns
breeder
breeding
breezing
briefcase
briefly

* * *

beefburger
beefeater
believer
believing
bereavement
besieging

bikini

* * * *

bacterial
bacterium [bacteria]

believable

Here the first letter 'e' has a short 'i' sound.

B*E*HAVING WORDS

beatitude	belatedly
became	belonged
because	belongings
become	beloved
[became]	below
[become]	bemused
becoming	bemusing
befall	benevolent
[befell]	benign
[befallen]	bereft
before	beset
beforehand	[beset]
befriend	besetting
begin	beside
[began]	besides
[begun]	besotted
beginner	besought
beginning	bestowed
behalf	betrayed
behaved	betrayal
behaving	betwixt
behaviour	beware
behavioural	bewildered
behead	bewilderment
beheld	bewitches
behind	bewitched
behold	beyond
[beheld]	

---

154   In these words you can hear the vowel sound ee as in eagle

*

cease d
*cede give up

*cheap at low cost
cheat
cheek ed
*cheep chirp
cheeped
cheer ed
cheese d
chic
chief

clean ed
clear ed
cleat
cleave d
[cleft]
[clove]
[cloven]
clique

*creak make a high-
pitched noise
creaked
cream ed
crease d
creed
*creek inlet / stream
creep
[crept]

keel ed
keen
keep
[kept]
*key lever for lock or
other mechanism /
important / musical scale
keyed

*quay wharf

*seed part of a plant
from which a new one
can grow / selected
player in a tournament
draw

for Qu . . .
see page 167

* *

career ed

ceasefire
ceasing
*cedar tree
*ceiling inner roof
of room

cheaper
cheapest
cheaply
*cheater deceiver
cheating
cheeky -ier, -iest
cheerful ly
*cheetah animal
chiefly
chieftain

cleaner
cleaning
clearance
clearer
clearest
clearing
clearly
cleavage
cleaving
cliché

compete
complete
conceal ed
concede
conceit
conceive d

creasing
creature
creeper
critique

cuisine

keeper
keeping
Kenya
keyboard
keyhole
keynote

kilo
kiosk
kiwi

*sealing fastening
*seeder device for sowing
or removing seeds

* * *

casino s
cathedral

*cereal food from
grain / plant
producing grain

cheerfully
cheeseburger

clientele

coeliac
competing
completely
completing
completion
conceited
conceiving
concerto s

creosote
critiquing

Korea
Korean

*serial parts in order

* * * * *

chameleon
chemotherapy

comedian
comedienne
congenial ly
convenience
convenient ly

creativity
creosoting
criterion [criteria]

Here the first letter 'e' has a short 'i' sound.

CREATIVE WORDS
celestial
cement
create d
creating
creation
creative
creator

credential
cremate
cremating
cremation
crescendo s
crevasse

In these words you can hear the vowel sound ee as in eagle

155

*	**	***	***** **
deal	dealer	deceitful ly	deceitfully
[dealt]	decease d	deceiving	decelerate
*dean presiding	deceit	decency -ies	decelerating
officer	deceive d	decoding	deceleration
*dear beloved /	decent	decompose d	decentralisation
expensive	decode	decreasing	zation
deed	decrease d	defeated	decomposer
deem ed	decree d	deflated	decomposing
deep	deepen ed	deflating	decomposition
*deer [deer] animal	deeper	deflation	decompression
*dene small valley	deepest	defragment	deformation
	deeply	deism	denitrify -ies
dream ed	defeat	deity -ies	denitrified
[dreamt]	defect	deleting	deodorant
	deflate	deletion	departmental
	defrost	demeanour	deposition
	degree	detainee	depreciate
	deist	devalue d	depreciating
	delete	deviance	depreciation
	demean ed	deviant	deregulation
	demon	deviate	deteriorate
	deplete	devious	deteriorating
	detail ed		deterioration
	detour		devaluation
			devaluing
	diesel		deviating
	*discreet tactful		deviation
	*discrete separate		devolution
	disease d		
	displease d		
	dreary -ier, -iest		

In these words the first letter 'e' is pronounced like the short 'i' in 'pig'.

D**E**LIGHTFUL WORDS

debate	defend ant	demand ed	depending	deserter	detective
debating	defender	demanding	deploy ed	deserve d	detector
decamp ed	defensive	demise	deployment	deserving	detention
decay ed	defer red	demob bed	deport	design ed	deter red
December	deferring	democracy -ies	deposit ed	designer	detergent
deception	defiance	demolish es	depositing	desirable	determination
deceptive	defiant	demolished	depress es	desire d	determine d
decide	deficiency -ies	demonstrative	depressed	desiring	determining
deciding	deficient	denial	depression	despair ed	deterrence
deciduous	define d	denomination	depressive	despatch es	deterrent
decipher ed	defining	denominator	deprive d	despatched	deterring
decision	deflect ion	denote	deriving	despise d	detest
decisive	deform ed	denoting	derail ed	despising	detract
declare d	defy -ies	denounce d	derailment	despite	develop ed
declaring	defied	denouncing	derivative	despondency	developer
decline d	delay ed	denunciation	derive d	despondent	developing
declining	deliberate ly	deny -ies	deriving	dessert	development al
decry -ies	deliberating	denied	derogatory	destroy ed	device
decried	delicious	depart ure	descend ed	destroyer	devise d
deduce d	delight ed	department	descendant	destruction	devising
deducing	delightful ly	depend ed	descendent	destructive	devoid
deduct ion	delirious	dependable	descent	detach es	devote d
deductive	deliver ed	dependant s	describe d	detached	devoting
defect or	deliverance	dependence	describing	detain ed	devotion
defective	delivery -ies	dependency -ies	description	detect able	devour ed
defence	delusion	dependent	descriptive	detection	devout
			desert ed		

In these words you can hear the vowel sound **ee** as in **eagle**

E

*

each
ear
ease d
east
eat
[ate]
[eaten]
eaves

eel

eke d

eve

* *

eager
eagle
earache
eardrum
earmark ed
earring
easel
Easter
eastern
eastward / eastwards
easy -ier, -iest
eaten
eating

*eerie / eery weird

ego
Egypt

*either one or the other

élite

email / e-mail
emu

endear ed

equal led

era

esteem ed

*ether solvent
ethos

even
evening
evil ly

exceed
excrete
extreme

*eyrie / eyry -ies   nest of bird of prey

* * *

aesthetic ally

eagerly
eagerness
easier
easiest
easily

egoist / egotist

élitist

endearment

equalise d
ze
equalling
equally

ethernet

evening
evenly

exceeding
excreting
excretion
extremely
extremist

Oedipal
Oedipus
oestrogen

* * * * * * *

aesthetically

easygoing

ecclesiastical ly
ecological ly
economic
economical ly
economics
economy -ies
ecosystem

egoism / egotism
egoistic / egotistic

élitism
elongation

equalising
zing
equatorial ly
equiangular
equidistant
equilateral
equilibrium s [equilibria]

esophagus / oesophagus
esophagus es [esophagi]

Ethiopia

evangelical
evangelist
evolution
evolutionary

exceedingly
expediency
expedient
experience d
experiencing
experiential ly
exterior

First sound = 'i'.
EFFECTIVE WORDS

eclipse d
eclipsing
ecologist
ecology
economist
edition
effect ive ly
effectiveness
efficient ly
Egyptian
eject or
elaborate
elaboration
elastic ally
elasticity
elated
elation
elect ion
elector
electoral ly
electorate
electric al ly
electrician
electricity
electrocute
electrode
electrolysis
electrolyte
electrolytic ally
electromagnetic ally
electron
electronic ally
electronics
eleven th
elicit ed
eliciting
eliminate
eliminating
elimination
Elizabethan
ellipse
elliptical ly
elope d
eloping
elucidate
elude
eluding
elusive
emancipate d
emancipating

See also E on page 65
for H . . . see page 160
See also I on page 72
for I . . . see page 161

emancipation
emerge d
emergence
emergency -ies
emerging
emission
emit ted
emitting
emotion al ly
emotive
emulsion ed
enable d
enabling
enact
enamel led

enamelling
enamour ed
enormous ly
enough
enumerate
epitome
equality
equate
equation
equator
equip ped
equipment
equipping
equivalence
equivalent

erase d
eraser
erasing
erect ion
erode
eroding
erosion
erotic ally
erratic ally
erroneous ly
erupt ed
eruption
escape d
escaping
escarpment

especially
essential ly
establish es
established
establishment
estate
estrange d
etcetera
eternal ly
eternity
evacuate
evacuation
evacuee
evade
evading

evaluate
evaluating
evaluation
evaporate
evaporating
evaporation
evasion
evasive
event
eventual ly
evict
evoke d
evoking
evolve d
evolving

In these words you can hear the vowel sound ee as in eagle

F

*	**	***	**** *
fear ed	faeces	facetious	feasibility
feast	fatigue d		
*feat act		fearfully	
fee	fearful ly	feasible	
feed	fearless	featuring	
[fed]	fearsome	feverish	
feel	feature d		
[felt]	feeble	fiasco s	
*feet more than one	feedback	fiesta	
foot	feeding		
	feeler	freelancing	
field	feeling	frequency -ies	
fiend	female	frequently	
fierce	fever ed		
fiord / fjord			
	fielder		
*flea insect	fiercely		
*flee run away	Fiji		
[fled]	fiord / fjord		
fleece d			
fleet	fleecing		
	fleecy -ier, -iest		
freak ed			
free d	foetal / fetal		
*frees releases	foetus es / fetus es		
*freeze chill /change	foresee		
from liquid to solid /	[foresaw]		
hold steady	[foreseen]		
[froze]			
[frozen]	freebie		
*frieze decorated	freedom		
band / type of cloth	freehand		
	freehold		
	freelance d		
	freely		
	freeman [freemen]		
	freer		
	freestyle		
	freeware		
	freewheel ed		
	freezer		
	freezing		
	frequent		

> Here the first letter 'e' has a short 'i' sound.
>
> ferocious   ferocity   frenetic ally

for th . . .
see page 172 ▷

phenyl

In these words you can hear the vowel sound ee as in eagle

G

*

gear ed
gee
geek
geese
gene
*genes more than
one gene

ghee

gleam ed
glean ed
glee

*grease oily substance
greased
*greave armour to
protect the lower leg
*Greece country
greed
Greek
green
greet
grief
*grieve d feel sadness

*jeans trousers
jeep
jeer ed

* *

gearbox es
gee-gee
geekish
geeky
genie
genome
geyser

greasing
greasy -ier, -iest
greedy -ier, -iest
greenbelt
greengage
greenhouse
Greenland
greeted
greeting
grievance
grieving
grievous

Jesus

* * *

galena

genial ly
genius es [genii]
genotype

graffiti
greedily
greenery
Greenlander

* * * * *

genealogy -ies
genially
geographic al ly
geological ly
geometric al ly

Here the first letter 'e' has a short 'i' sound.

genetic ally
geography
geology

geometry -ies
geranium
gregarious

H

*

he
*heal ed cure /
get better
heap ed
*hear receive by ear
[heard]
*hears does hear
heat
heath
heave d
[hove]
heaved
*he'd he had / he
would
*heed notice / take
seriously
*heel part of foot /
shoe
heeled
*he'll he will
*here in this place
*here's here is
he's

* *

healer
hearing
hearsay
heated
heater
heathen
heating
heatwave
heaving
Hebrew
heedless
heinous
helix es [helices]
hereby
herein
hero es

* * *

haematite / hematite

helium
hereabouts
hereafter
heretofore

* * * *

hysteria

Here the first letter 'e' has a short 'i' sound.

heroic ally

In these words you can hear the vowel sound ee as in eagle

I

*	**	***	* * * * **
	idea	idea	idealise d
	ideal ly	ideal ly	ze
		idealise d	idealising
	impede	ze	zing
			idealism
	increase d	illegal ly	ideally
	indeed		
	intrigue d	immediate	illegally
		impeachment	
		impeding	immediate
			immediately
		increasing	imperial ly
		indecent	imperialism
		infrequent	imperious
		ingenious	
		intriguing	increasingly
			inferior
			inferiority
			ingenious
			ingredient
			interior

for E . . .
see page 157

See also E
on page 65

See also I
on page 72

In these words you can hear the vowel sound *ee* as in *eagle*

J

LONG VOWEL ee

*

gee
gene
*genes more than one
gene

*jeans trousers
jeep
jeer ed

for dr . . .
see page 156

* *

gee-gee
genie
genome

Jesus

* * *

genial ly
genius es [genii]
genotype

* * * * *

genealogy -ies
genially

K

*

keel ed
keen
keep
[kept]
*key lever for lock
or other mechanism /
important / musical
scale
keyed

*knead press with
hands
knee
*kneed hit with the
knee
kneel ed
[knelt]

*need require

*quay wharf

for C . . .
see page 155

for Qu . . .
see page 167

* *

keenly
keeper
keeping
Kenya
keyboard
keyhole
keynote
keypad
keyword

kilo
kiosk
kiwi

kneeler

* * *

Korea
Korean

* * * *

In these words you can hear the vowel sound ee as in eagle

L

*

*lea meadow
*leach es cause a liquid
to pass through
*lead show the way
by going first / leash
[led]
leaf [leaves]
league
*leak unwanted
escape
leaked
lean ed
[leant]
leap ed
[leapt]
lease
*leased rented
leash es
leashed
*least smallest amount
leave
[left]
leaves
*lee shelter /
sheltered side
*leech es bloodsucker
*leek vegetable
leer ed

*lied German song

* *

leaching
*leader leading
person or thing
leading
leaflet
leafy -ier, -iest
leaning
leapfrog ged
leasehold
leasing
*leaver person
who leaves
leaving
leeward
leeway
legal ly
legion
lesion
lethal ly
*lever tool
levered

*lieder German songs
litre

* * *

leadership
leafier
leafiest
legalise d
ze
legally
lenient
leotard
leverage

liaison
Lima-bean

* * * * *

legalisation
zation
legalising
zing
legalistic ally
leniency

Liberia

Here the first letter 'e' has a short 'i' sound.

legality -ies   legitimate
legato   lethargic
legitimacy

M

*

*me myself
mead
meal
*mean intend /
miserly / poor
[meant]
means
*meat flesh of
animal
meek
*meet be in contact /
encounter
[met]
mere
*mete deal

*mi third note in a
musical scale
*mien bearing /
look of person

* *

machine d
marine

meagre
mealtime
meaning
meanness
meantime
meanwhile
measles
meaty -ier, -iest
meeting
merely
*meter measuring
machine
metered
methane
*metre unit of
length / verse
rhythm

migraine
misdeal
[misdealt]
mislead
[misled]

mystique

* * *

machining
machinist
Madeira
marina

meaningful ly
meaningless
*meatier more
substantial
media
median
mediate
medium s [media]
*meteor shooting star
meteorite

misleading

* * * * * * * *

machinery
material ly
materialism
materialist
materialistic

meaningfully
mediation
mediator
mediocre
meteorite
meteorological ly
meteorology

mysterious ly

Here the first letter 'e' has a short 'i' sound.

meander ed
mechanic ally
medicinal ly
melodic ally
melodious
memento es / s
memorial

meniscus es [menisci]
meridian
methodical ly
meticulous
metropolis es
mnemonic

In these words you can hear the vowel sound **ee** as in **eagle**

N

LONG VOWEL **ee**

*

*knead press with hands
knee
*kneed hit with the knee
kneel ed
[knelt]

near ed
neat
*need require

niche
niece

* *

kneeler

nearby
nearer
nearest
nearing
nearly
neatly
needed
needle d
needless
needling
needy -ier, -iest
negro es
neither
neon

* * *

needlessly

* * * * *

neolithic
Neapolitan

Here the first letter 'e' has a short 'i' sound.

necessity -ies
negate
negating
negation

neglect
neglectfully
negotiable
negotiate

negotiating
negotiation
negotiator

O

*

* *

oblique
obscene

* * *

Oedipal
Oedipus
oestrogen

* * * *

obedience
obedient

oesophagus / esophagus
oesophagus es
[oesophagi]

In these words you can hear the vowel sound ee as in eagle

P

*

*pea vegetable
*peace period
without war
peach es
*peak highest point
*peaked reached a
maximum / pinched
*peal ringing
*pealed rang
peat
*pee urinate
*peek peep
*peel rind / skin
*peeled removed
the rind or skin
peen ed
peep ed
*peer ed look hard /
person of equal
rank / lord

*piece part
*pieced correctly fitted
*pier upright support /
structure extending
into the sea
pierce d
*pique hurt pride
*piqued annoyed
*piste ski run

plea
plead
*pleas requests
*please used when
asking / give pleasure
pleased
pleat

police d

*pre- prefix meaning
'before'
preach es
preached
preen ed
priest
*prix French for 'prize'

* *

peaceful ly
peacetime
peacock
peahen
peanut
peevish
penal
penis es
people d
perceive d

phenyl
phoenix

pianist
piano s
piecing
pierrot

pleasing

police d
policeman [policemen]
policing

preacher
precede
precinct
prefect
prefix es
prefixed
pre-school / preschool
pretext
preview
pre-war / prewar
priestess es
priesthood
proceed

* * *

paedophile
paprika

peaceable
peacefully
penalise d
ze
period

pianist
piano s
pierrot

placebo s

policeman [policemen]
policewoman
[policewomen]
policing

preceded
preceding
premature
premium
premolar
presuppose d
previous
procedure
proceeding
proceedings

* * * * *

paediatric
paediatrician
paedophilia

penalising
zing
periodic
periodical
periodically

pianoforte

policewoman
[policewomen]

predecessor
prefabricate
prehistoric ally
presupposing
previously
proscenium s [proscenia]

In these words the first letter 'e' is pronounced like the 'i' in 'pig'.
PHƐNOMENAL WORDS

peculiar	precaution	prepare d	presumably
peculiarity -ies	precipitate	preparing	presume d
pedestrian	precipitating	prerogative	presuming
peninsula	precipitation	prescribe d	presumptuous
peninsular	precise ly	prescribing	pretence
perimeter	precision	prescription	pretend ed
peripheral ly	preclude	present ed	pretentious
periphery -ies	precocious	presentable	prevail ed
peroxide	predict able	presenting	prevailing
petition ed	prediction	preservative	prevent ion
petroleum	predominant ly	preserve d	preventive
phenomenal ly	prefer red	preserving	
phenomenon	preferring	preside	
[phenomena]	preliminary -ies	presiding	

In these words you can hear the vowel sound ee as in eagle

Q

*

*key lever for lock or
other mechanism /
important / musical scale

*quay wharf
queen ed
queer ed
quiche

* *

quayside
queasy -ier, -iest
query -ies
quinine

* * *

* * * *

R

*

reach es
reached
*read look at and
understand
[read]
*real genuine
ream ed
reap ed
rear ed
*reed plant /
vibrating strip
reef ed
*reek ed stink
*reel ed spool /
wind / stagger

*wreak ed bring about
wreath ed

* *

ravine

reaches
reaching
react
reader
reading
realise d
      ze
really
reamer
rearm ed
reason ed
rebate
rebound
rebuild
[rebuilt]
recede s
receipt
receive d
recent
recess es
recessed
reclaim ed
recoil ed
recount
redeem ed
redo
[redid]
[redone]
refill ed
reflex es
refuel led
refund
regain ed
regal
regent
regime / **régime**
region
regroup ed
reject

* * *

reaction
reactor
readable
readjust
reagent
realising
      zing
realism
realistic ally
reappear ed
rearrange d
reasoning
reassure d
recapture d
receding
receiver
receiving
recently
reconstruct
recycle d
recycling
refuel led
refuelling
regional ly
reinforce d
releasing
relieving
renaming
repayment
repeated
repeating
replacement
replacing
reproduce d
researcher
retailer
retrial / **re-trial**
retrieval
retrieving
reunion
rewiring
rewritten
rewriting

rheostat

* * * * * *

reactionary -ies
realistically
reality -ies
rearranging
reasonable
reasonably
reassemble
reassurance
reassuring
recapturing
rechargeable
reconstitute
reconstruction
redevelopment
refuelling
regionally
rehabilitation
reincarnation
reinforcement
reinforcing
reiteration
relaxation
remedial
reorganisation
      zation
reorganise d
      ze
reorganising
      zing
repatriate
repatriating
repatriation
repercussion
reproducing
reproduction
reproductive
restructuring
reunification
reunion

In these words you can hear the vowel sound ee as in eagle

167

R

* *
*relaid laid again
relapse
relay
[relaid]
*relayed sent on as
received
release d
relief
relieve d
relive / re-live
remake
[remade]
remit
renal
rename d
repay
[repaid]
repeal ed
repeat
replace d
replay
reprieve d
research es
researched
reset
[reset]
retail ed
retell
[retold]
retread
retreat
retrial / re-trial
retrieve d
reveal ed
rewire d
rewrite
[rewrote]
[rewritten]

routine

Here the first letter 'e' has a short 'i' sound.

REFRESHING WORDS

rebel led	rehearsal	resembling
rebelling	rehearse d	resent ful ly
rebellion	rehearsing	resentment
rebellious	reject ion	reserve d
rebound	rejoice d	reserving
rebuke d	rejoicing	reside
rebuking	rejoin ed	residing
recall ed	relate d	resign ed
receptacle	relating	resilience
reception ist	relation ship	resilient
receptive	relax es	resist ance
receptor	relaxed	resistor
recession	relent less	resolve d
recessive	reliability	resolving
recipient	reliable	resort
reciprocal ly	reliance	resource d
reciprocate	religion	resources
reciprocating	religious	resourcing
recital	relinquish es	respect able
recite	relinquished	respectful ly
reciting	reluctance	respective ly
reclaim ed	reluctant ly	respire d
recline d	rely -ies	respiring
reclining	relied	respond
recoil ed	remain ed	response
record ed	remainder	responsibility -ies
recorder	remaining	responsible
recording	remark ed	responsive
recount	remarkable	restore d
recourse	remember ed	restoring
recover ed	remembering	restrain ed
recovery -ies	remembrance	restraint
recruit	remind ed	restrict ion
recuperate	reminder	restrictive
recur red	remote	result ed
recurrence	removable /	resultant
recurrent	removeable	resulting
recurring	removal	resume d
redemption	remove d	resuming
reduce d	removing	resuscitate
reducing	remuneration	resuscitating
reduction	Renaissance	resuscitation
redundancy -ies	renege d	retain ed
redundant	reneging	retard ed
refer red	renew ed	retire d
referral	renewal	retirement
referring	renown ed	retiring
refine d	repair ed	retort
refinery -ies	repel led	return ed
refining	repellent	returnable
reflect ed	repelling	returning
reflection	repent ance	revenge d
reflector	repetitive	revenging
reflexive	reply -ies	reverberate
reform ed	replied	reverberating
refract ion	report er	reversal
refractive	repose d	reverse d
refrain ed	reposing	reversible
refresh es	repress ed	reversing
refreshed	repression	review ed
refreshment	repressive	revise d
refrigerator	reprisal	revising
refund	reproach es	revision
refusal	reproached	revival
refuse d	republic an	revive d
refusing	repudiate	reviving
refute	repudiating	revolt
refuting	repulsive	revolve d
regain ed	repute	revolver
regard ed	request	revolving
regardless	require d	revue
regatta	requirement	revulsion
regret ted	requiring	reward
regretful ly	resemblance	
regretting	resemble d	

In these words you can hear the vowel sound **ee** as in **eagle**

S

*

cease d
*cede give up

*scene part of play /
display / place / view
schemed
screamed
screeches
screeched
screened

*sea very large area of
water / part of an
ocean
sealed
*seamed join
*sear burn the surface
with sudden heat
*seas very large areas
of water / parts of
oceans
seat
*see register by eye /
understand
[saw]
[seen]
*seed part of a plant
from which a new
one can grow /
selected player in a
tournament draw
*seek look for
[sought]
*seemed appear
*seen registered by
eye / understood
seeped
*seer prophet
*sees does see
seethed
*seize grab
seized
*sere withered

* *

*cedar tree
*ceiling inner roof of
room

scenic ally
schemas [schemata]
scheming
screening
screenshot

seabed
seafood
seafront
seagull
*sealing fastening
sealskin
*seaman sailor
*seamen sailors
seaport
seashore
seasick
seaside
seasoned
seatbelt
seated
seaweed
*secret kept hidden
*secrete produce
liquid in body / hide
*seeder device for
sowing or removing
seeds
seedling
seeing
seeking
seesaw
seething
seizing
seizure
*semen sperm-carrying
liquid
sepal
sequel
sequence
sequinned
serene
series
serum
settee
severe

shearer
sheepdog
sheepish
sheepskin

* * *

*cereal food from grain /
plant producing grain

coeliac

scenery
scenically
sclerosis
screensaver

seafarer
seasickness
seasonal
seasoning
secrecy
secreting
secretion
secretive
secretly
seemingly
*senior older / more
important
sequencing
*serially parts in
order
serious
severely

signoras
Sikhism
sincerely

sleepier
sleepiest
sleepily

speedily

strategic ally

* * * * * *

scenically

seniority
serially
seriously
seriousness

signorina

Slovenia

speedometer

stereotype
strategically

superior
superiority

S

*

she
sheaf [sheaves]
*sheared cut off
wool or hair
[shorn]
shears
sheathed
she'd
sheen
sheep [sheep]
*sheer pure / very
steep / very thin / go
off at an angle
sheered
sheet
she'll
she's
shield
shrieked

siege
*Sikh member of
an Indian religious
group

skied

sleek
sleep
[slept]
sleet
sleeved

smeared

sneaked
sneered
sneezed

speak
[spoke]
[spoken]
speared
speeches
speed
[sped]
sphere
spree

squeaked
squealed
squeezed

* *

*signori Italian for 'Mr.'
sincere

skier
skiing

sleeper
sleeping
sleepless
sleepy -ier, -iest
sleeving

sneaky -ier, -iest
sneezing

speaker
speaking
species
speechless
speeding
speedos
speedy -ier, -iest

squeegee
squeezing

stealing
steamer
steeple
steering
steroid
streaky -ier, -iest
streamer
streaming
streamlined

succeed

Sweden
Swedish
sweeper
sweeping
sweetheart
sweetly
sweetness

In these words you can hear the vowel sound ee as in eagle

S

*

***steal** thieve /
move quietly
[stole]
[stolen]
steam ed
steed
***steel** metal
steeled
steep
steer ed
streak ed
stream ed
street

***suite** pieces that
go together

***Swede** Swedish person
***swede** type of turnip
sweep
[swept]
***sweet** of sugary
taste / nice

Here the first letter 'e' has a short 'i' sound.

S*E*LECTED WORDS

scenario s	selection
secession	selective ly
seclude d	selector
secure d	semantic ally
security -ies	semantics
seduce d	sequential ly
seducing	sequoia
seduction	serenity
seductive	severity -ies
select ed	specific ally
selecting	

T

*

*tea drink / meal
teach es
[taught]
teak
*team working
group / playing
side
*teamed made a team
*tear sign of distress
*teas drinks / meals
*teased mock in fun /
comb
teat
*tee support for
golf ball
*teem swarm
*teemed swarmed
teens
*tees more than one
tee
teeth

thee
theme d
these
thief [thieves]
three

*tier one of a
number of levels
tiered

treat
tree

tweed
tweet

* *

T-shirt / tee-shirt

teabag
teacher
teaching
team-mate
teamwork
teapot
tearful ly
teasing
teaspoon
teatime
teeming
teenage
teepee / tepee
teeshirt / T-shirt
teething

theatre
theorem
theorist
theory -ies
thesis [theses]

trapeze
treacle
treason
*treaties written
agreements between
countries
treating
*treatise formal piece
of writing
treatment
treaty -ies
treetops
trio

tweezers

* * *

tearfully
teaspoonful
tedious
tedium
teenager

three-quarters

trachea

* * * * * *

theatrical ly
theodolite
theologian
theological ly
theology -ies
theoretical ly

trapezium s [trapezia]

Here the first letter 'e' has a short 'i' sound.

T**E**RRIFIC WORDS

telegraphy
telephonist
terrestrial ly
terrific ally

thematic ally
thesaurus es [thesauri]
tremendous ly

In these words you can hear the vowel sound *ee* as in *eagle*

V

*

veal
*veer ed swing around

*via by way of

* *

vehement
vehicle
veneer ed
*venous con concerned
with veins
*Venus planet /
goddess of love
veto es
vetoed

*via by way of
visa

* * *

vehement ly
vehicle
Venetian
vetoing

viola

* * * *

vehemently

In these words the first 'e' is a neutral vowel.

velocity -ies   veranda / verandah

In these words you can hear the vowel sound *ee* as in *eagle*

173

W

*   * *   * * *   * * * *

*reek ed stink

weaken ed   **wearily**
weaker   **weariness**
weakest
we people speaking   **weakling**
weak feeble   ***weakly*** feebly   **wheelbarrow**
weal mark left on   **weakness** es
skin by whip   **weary** -ier, -iest
weald open or   **weasel**
wooded country   **weaver**
weave interlace   **weaving**
threads   **weekday**
[wove]   **weekend**
[woven]   ***weekly*** every week /
we'd we had / we   a weekly magazine
would   **weeping**
wee small / pass   **weevil**
water   **werewolf** [werewolves]
weed passed water
weed unwanted   **wheelchair**
wild plant   **wheeler**
week seven days   **wheelie** s
weep   **wheezing**
[wept]
weir dam across
river
weird
we'll we will
we're we are
we've we have

wheat
wheel round rotating
frame or disc
wheeled did wheel
wheeze d

wield have and use

wreak ed bring about
wreath ed

In these words you can hear the vowel sound ee as in **eagle**

Y

*	**	***	****
ye	year-old		
year	yearly		
yeast			
	yielding		
yield			

Z

*	**	***	****
zeal	Zaire		
	zebra		
	zero es / s		

In these words you can hear the vowel sound ee as in eagle

175

A

*

*aisle part of
church / gangway

*aye yes

*eye visual organ

*I the person speaking
*I'll I will

for H . . .
see page 182

* *

abide

acquire d

admire d
advice
advise d

alight
align ed
alike
alive
ally -ies
allied

apply -ies
applied

arise
[arose]
[arisen]
arrive d

ascribe d
aside
aspire d
assign ed

awhile
awry

* * *

abided
abiding

acquiring

admirer
admiring
adviser
advising

alignment
alliance
almighty

appliance
applying

arising
arrival
arriving

ascribing
aspiring
assignment
asylum

* * * * *

advisable
advisory

annihilate
annihilating
annihilation

In these words you can hear the vowel sound **ie** as in **lion**

B

*

bide d
[bode]
*bight broad bay /
loop
bike d
bile
bind
[bound]
*bite tear with teeth
[bit]
[bitten]

blight
blind

bribe d
bride
bright
brine

*buy purchase
[bought]
*buyer purchaser

*by beside / not
after / past /
through / on
*bye goodbye / pay-off
for not playing
*byre cow-house
*byte unit of
information

* *

behind
benign
beside
besides

bias ed / sed
*Bible holy book for
Christians
*bible copy of Bible /
best reference book
biceps
biking
binder
binding
biped
biro
bisect
bison
biting

blimey!
blindfold
blindly
blindness

bribing
*bridal of the bride
bridegroom
bridesmaid
*bridle headgear for
controlling a horse
bridled
bridling
brighten ed
brighter
brightest
brightly
brightness

*buyer purchaser
buying

bye-bye
bygone
bypass ed
byway

* * *

biasing / biassing
bicycle d
bicycling
bifocal
bilingual
binary
biofuel
biopsy -ies
bisector

bribery

by-product
bystander

* * * * * *

biennial ly
bifurcated
bilateral ly
binomial
biochemical
biochemist
biochemistry
biodiesel
biographer
biographical ly
biography -ies
biological ly
biologist
biology
biotechnology

by-election

In these words you can hear the vowel sound **ie** as in **lion**

177

C

*

child
chime d
*choir singing
group / part of
church
Christ

*cite give as an
example / quote

*climb ed go up /
upward slope
*clime climate

cried
cries
crime
cry -ies
cried

kind
kite

*quire 24 sheets of
writing paper

*sight vision
*site place

for Qu . . .
see page 189 ▷

* *

childbirth
childhood
childish
chiming
*china porcelain
*China country
Chinese

cider
*citing quoting

client
climate
climax es
climaxed
climber
climbing

collide
combine d
compile d
comply -ies
complied
comprise d
concise
confide
confine d
conspire d

crisis [crises]
crying

cycle d
cycling
cyclist
cyclone
*cypress es tree
*Cyprus island

kayak

kindly
kindness

psychic ally

*sighting act of spotting
*siting placing

* * *

climatic
clitoris

colliding
combining
compiling
comprising
concisely
confiding
confinement
confining
conspiring

cybershop
cyberspace

kinetic ally

psychical ly
psychosis [psychoses]
psychotic ally

* * * * * *

climatology

criterion [criteria]

cybercafé
cyclorama
cytoplasm

kaleidoscope

kinetically

psychiatric ally
psychiatrist
psychiatry
psychically
psychoanalyse d
psychoanalysis
psychoanalyst
psychological ly
psychologist
psychology
psychotherapist
psychotherapy
psychotically

D

*

dial led
dice d ⌐

* *

decide
decline d
decry -ies
decried ⌐

* * *

decided
deciding
decipher ed
decisive
declining ⌐

* * * *

delightfully
desirable

In these words you can hear the vowel sound **ie** as in **lion**

D

*

die cease living /
small cube / tool
for stamping or
shaping
died
dike / dyke
dine have dinner
dined
dire desperate
dive d

dried
drive
[drove]
[driven]
dry -ies
dried

dye d stain
dyer person using
dyes
dyke / dike
dyne unit of force

**

define d
defy -ies
defied
delight
demise
deny -ies
denied
deprive d
derive d
describe d
design ed
desire d
despise d
despite
device gadget /
plan
devise d invent /
work out

dial led
dialling
diamond
diary -ies
dicey
dicing
diecast
diet
digest
digraph
dilute
dining
direct
disguise d
dislike d
dissect
diver
diverge d
diverse
divert
divide
divine d
divine

drier more dry /
machine that dries
driest
drily / dryly
driver
driveway
driving
dryer / drier person,
substance or
machine that dries
drying
dryly / drily

dyeing using dye
dying ceasing to live

***

defiance
defiant
defining
defying
delighted
delightful ly
denial
depriving
deriving
describing
designer
desiring
despising
devising

diagnose d
diagram
dialect
dialling
dialogue
diamond
diaphragm
diarrhoea
diatom
dicier
diciest
didactic
dietary
digestion
dilemma
diluted
diluting
dilution
dimension
dining-room
dinosaur
dioxide
directed
direction
directive
directly
director
disciple
disguising
disliking
divergent
diverging
diversion
diverted
divided
dividers
dividing
divining
divisor

dynamic ally
dynamite
dynamo s

**** ***

diabetes
diabetic
diabolical ly
diagnosing
diagnosis -es
diagnostic ally
diagonal ly
diagrammatic ally
dialectic al ly
diameter
diarrhoea
dichotomy -ies
dietary
digestible
dimensional
directory -ies
diversification
diversify -ies
diversified
diversity

dynamically
dynamometer

In these words you can hear the vowel sound **ie** as in **lion**

179

E

*

*aye yes

*eye visual organ
*eyed looked at
 with interest

*I the person speaking
*I'd I would / I had

for H . . .
see page 182 ▷

for I . . .
see page 183 ▷

* *

eider
either

enquire / inquire d
entire

esquire

excite
expire d

eyeball
eyebrow
eyeing / eying
eyelash es
*eyelet small hole
eyelid
eyesight

*islet small island

* * *

eisteddfod

enlighten ed
enquiring / inquiring
enquiry / inquiry -ies
entirely
entitle d
entitling

excited
excitement
exciting
expiring

eyewitness es

* * * * * * *

encyclopedia
entitlement
environment
environmental ly
environmentalism
environmentalist

excitable
excitedly

In these words you can hear the vowel sound ie as in lion

F

*

fight
[fought]
*file tool / information
system / line of people
filed
*find discover
[found]
fine
*fined made to pay
a fine
fire d
five

flier / flyer
flies
flight
fly -ies
[flew]
[flown]

*friar religious man
who lived by begging
fried
*frier / fryer person or
equipment that fries
fright
fry -ies
fried
*fryer / frier person or
equipment that fries

*phial small vessel or
bottle

* *

fibre
fibrous
fiery
fighter
fighting
filename
filing
final
finance d
finding
finely
finer
finest
fining
finite
firearm
firefly -ies
firelight
fireman [firemen]
fireplace
firepower
fireproof
fireside
firewall
firewood
firework
firing
fiver

flier / flyer
flying
flywheel

*friar religious man
who lived by begging
Friday
*frier / fryer person or
equipment that fries
frighten ed
frightening
frightful ly
*fryer / frier person or
equipment that fries

*phial small vessel or
bottle
phylum [phyla]

* * *

fibreglass
fibrosis
finalise d
ze
finalist
finally
financial ly
financing
fire-engine
firefighter
firepower
firewoman [firewomen]

frightening
frightfully

* * * *

finalising
zing
finality
financially
financier

forsythia s

for th . . .
see page 192 ▷

In these words you can hear the vowel sound **ie** as in **lion**

181

G

*

*gibe / jibe taunt

glide

*gneiss rock

grime
grind
[ground]

*guide show the
way
*guise appearance
guy
*guyed ridiculed
*guys more than one
guy / does guy

*gybe / gibe / jibe
alter course by
swinging sail

jive d

*nice pleasant

* *

Geiger

giant
*gibing / jibing taunting

glider
gliding

goodbye
goodnight

grimy -ier, -iest
grinder

guidance
guideline
guiding

*gybing / gibing / jibing
altering course by
swinging sail
gyrate

jiving

* * *

gigantic
ginormous

Guyana

gyrating
gyroscope

* * * * * * *

gynaecological ly
gynaecologist
gynaecology
gyroscopic

H

*

height

*hi greeting
hide
[hid]
[hidden]
*high tall / great
*higher taller / greater
hike d
hind
*hire d grant or obtain
use if a payment is
made / employ
hive d

hype d

* *

haiku

heighten ed

hiding
hi-fi
*higher taller / greater
highest
highlands
highlight
highly
Highness
highrise
highroad
highway
hijack ed
hiker
hiking
hindsight
hiring
hiving
*hiya greeting

hybrid
hygiene
hyphen

* * *

Hawaii
Hawaiian

hiatus es
hibernate
highwayman

horizon

hyacinth
hydraulic ally
hydrofoil
hydrogen
hydroxide
hygienic ally
hyperlink
hypertext
hyphenate

* * * * * * *

hibernating
hibernation
hierarchical
hierarchy -ies
hieroglyphics

hydraulically
hydrocarbon
hydrochloric
hydroelectric ally
hydrometer
hygienically
*hyperbola form of
curve
*hyperbole
exaggeration
hyphenated
hyperactive
hypochondria
hypochondriac
hypotenuse
hypothesis [hypotheses]
hypothetical ly

In these words you can hear the vowel sound ie as in lion

I

*	**	***	**** ***
*aisle part of church / gangway	eider either	eisteddfod	idealism idealistic ally idealise d
*aye yes	*eyelet small hole	icicle	ze
		idea	idealising
*eye visual organ	iceberg	ideal ly	zing
*eyed looked at with interest	ice-cream	idealise d	ideally
	ice-floe	ze	identical ly
	Iceland	idolise d	identifiable
*I the person speaking	icing	ze	identification
	icon / ikon		identified
ice d	icy -ier, -iest	ignited	identifier
		igniting	identify -ies
*I'd I would / I had	idea		identified
	ideal ly	incisive	identity -ies
	*idle lazy	incisor	ideological ly
*I'll I will	idly	incited	ideology -ies
	*idol image for worship	inciting	idolising
I'm		inclining	zing
	ignite	indictment	
*ion charged particle		inquiring / enquiring	ironical ly
	ikon / icon	inquiry / enquiry -ies	ironmonger
		inscribing	
*iron metal	imply -ies	insider	isolated
ironed	implied	inspiring	isolation
		invited	isometric ally
*isle island	*incite urge	inviting	isomorphic
	incline d		isosceles
I've	indict	iodine	isotopic
	inquire / enquire d	iota	
	inscribe d		itinerant
	inside	Irishman [Irishmen]	itinerary -ies
	*insight understanding	ironic ally	
	inspire d	ironing	
	invite	ironmonger	
		ironwork	
	*ion charged particle	irony -ies	
	irate	islander	
	Ireland	isolate	
	iris es	isotope	
	Irish		
	*iron metal	itemise d	
	ironed	ze	
	ironing		
	ironwork	ivory -ies	
	island		
	*islet small island		
	item		
	ivy		

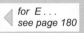for E . . .
see page 180

In these words you can hear the vowel sound ie as in lion

183

J

LONG VOWEL **ie**

*

*gybe / gibe / jibe alter
course by swinging sail

*jibe / gibe taunt
jive d

for dr . . .
see page 179

* *

giant

*gybing / gibing / jibing
altering course by
swinging sail
gyrate

*jibing / gibing taunting
jiving

* * *

gigantic
ginormous

gyrating
gyroscope

* * * *

gyroscopic

K

*

kind
kite

knife [knives]
knifed
*knight Sir --- /
chess piece

*night hours of darkness

for C . . .
see page 178

for Qu . . .
see page 189

* *

kayak

kindly
kindness

knifing
knighthood

* * *

kinetic ally

* * * * *

kaleidoscope

kinetically

In these words you can hear the vowel sound ie as in lion

L

*

*liar person who
tells lies
lice
*lie d tell untruth
*lie place oneself in a
horizontal position
[lay]
[lain]
life [lives]
light
[lit]
like d
lime d
line d
lion
lithe

*lye caustic solution
*lyre musical
instrument

* *

*liar person who
tells lies
*libel harmful
statement
*licence official
permission
*license d give
official permission
*lichen plant
lido s
lifeboat
lifeless
lifelike
lifelong
lifespan
lifestyle
lifetime
lighted
lighter
lightest
lighthouse
lighting
lightly
*lightning electric
flash in the sky
lightweight
likely
*liken ed point out
similarities
likeness es
likewise
liking
lilac
limeade
limelight
limestone
liner
linesman [linesmen]
line-up / lineup
lining
lino s
lion
lively -ier, -iest
livestock

lying
*lyre musical
instrument

* * *

*liable likely /
under obligation
library -ies
licensing
*lightening making
lighter
likelihood
livelihood
liveliness

* * * * *

liability -ies
Liberia
librarian
librarianship

In these words you can hear the vowel sound ie as in lion   **185**

*

mice
***might** would
perhaps / power
mild
mile
mime d
***mind** system of
thought and feeling /
look after /
watch / object
mine
***mined** did mine
mire d
***mite** tiny thing

my

* *

maestro s

mica
micro s
microbe
mighty
migraine
migrant
migrate
mildly
mileage
milestone
miming
mindful ly
mindless
***miner** worker in
mine
mining
***minor** less
important
minus es
minute
miser
mitre d
mitring

myself

* * *

Messiah

microchip
microphone
microscope
microwave
mightily
migrating
migration
migratory
mindfully

* * * *

microcomputer
micrometer
microprocessor
microscopic
minority -ies
mitochondria

In these words you can hear the vowel sound **ie** as in **lion**

N

*

*gneiss rock

knife [knives]
knifed
*knight Sir — / chess
piece

*nice pleasant
nigh
*night hours of
darkness
nine
ninth

* *

knifing
knighthood

naive

neither

nicely
nicer
nicest
nightclub
nightdress
nightfall
nightie
nightmare
night-time
nineteen th
ninety -ies
nitrate
nitric

nylon

* * *

nightingale
ninetieth
nitrify -ies
nitrified
nitrogen

* * * * *

Nigeria
nitrification
nitrifying

O

*

* *

alright

oblige d

* * *

almighty

obliging

* * * *

P

*

*file tool / information
system / line of people

*phial small vessel
or bottle

*pi 3·142 / Greek
letter
*pie meat or fruit
baked in pastry
pied
pike
pile d
pine d
pint
pipe d

pliers
plight
ply -ies
plied

price d
*pride high opinion
of oneself
*pried did pry
*pries does pry or
prise
prime d
prior
*prise / prize lever
with a metal bar
*prised did prise
*prize reward /
hold dear / prise
*prized did prize
pry -ies
pried

pyre

* *

perspire d

*phial small vessel
or bottle
phylum [phyla]

piling
pilot
pining
pious
pipeline
piper
piping
pirate

pliers
plywood

polite

precise
prescribe d
preside
priceless
pricing
priding
primal
primate
priming
prior
priory -ies
*prising levering
with a metal bar
private
*prizing holding dear /
prising
provide

psyche
psychic ally

pylon
python

* * *

papyrus es [papyri]

perspiring

piety
pineapple
pioneer
pirated
pirating

politely

precisely
prescribing
presiding
primacy
primary -ies
primeval
priory -ies
privacy
privately
privatise d
            ze
provided
provider
providing

psychical ly
psychosis [psychoses]
psychotic ally

pyrites

* * * * * * * *

primarily
priority -ies
privatisation
            zation
proprietor

psychiatric ally
psychiatrist
psychiatry
psychically
psychoanalyse d
psychoanalysis
psychoanalyst
psychoanalytic ally
psychological ly
psychologist
psychology
psychotherapist
psychotherapy
psychotically

pyrotechnic

In these words you can hear the vowel sound ie as in lion

Q

*

*choir singing group /
part of church

quiet
***quire** 24 sheets of
writing paper
quite

* *

quietly
quietened
quietness

* * *

quietly
quietened
quietness

* * * *

R

*

Reich

***rhyme / rime** to
end with the
same sound
rhymed

rice
ride
[rode]
[ridden]
***right** correct /
direction
riled
***rime** hoar-frost
rind
ripe
rise
[rose]
[risen]
***rite** ceremony

***rye** grain

***write** set down on
paper
[wrote]
[written]
writhe d
***wry** twisted

* *

recite
reclined
refined
rely -ies
relied
remind
reply -ies
replied
required
reside
resigned
respired
retired
revised
revived
rewrite
[rewrote]
[rewritten]

rhyming

ribald
rider
riding
rifled
rifling
righteous
rightfully
right-hand
rightly
right-wing
riling
rioted
ripened
rising
rivalled

writer
writing
wryly

* * *

recital
reciting
reclining
refining
reliance
relying
reminded
reminder
replying
reprisal
requirement
requiring
residing
respiring
retirement
retiring
revising
revival
reviving
rewriting

rightfully
rioted
rioting
riotous
rivalling
rivalry -ies

* * * * * *

refinery -ies
reliability
reliable

rhinoceros es

riboflavin

In these words you can hear the vowel sound ie as in lion

189

S

*

*cite give as an example / quote

scribe
scythe d

shine
[shone]
*****shire** county
shrine
shy -ies
shied
*****shyer** more shy

*****side** edge / surface / aspect / team
sigh
*****sighed** did sigh
*****sighs** more than one sigh
*****sight** vision
*****sign** ed mark with a meaning
*****sine** function of an angle
sire d
*****site** place
*****size** spatial extent / a weak glue
sized

sky -ies

*****sleight** quickness
slice d
slide
[slid]
*****slight** small / thin and delicate / treat without respect
slime
sly

smile d
smite
[smote]
[smitten]

snide
snipe d

* *

cider
cipher ed
*****citing** quoting

cycle d
cycling
cyclist
*****cypress** es tree
*****Cyprus** island

psychic ally

science
scientist
scriber
scribing
scything

seismic

shining
shiny -ier, -iest
*****shyer** more shy
shyly / shily
shyness

Siam
sideboard
sidelight
sideline d
sidelong
sidetrack ed
sideways
siding
*****sighting** act of spotting
signing
signpost
silage
silence d
silent
silo s
sinus es
siphon
siren
siring
sisal
*****siting** placing
sizing

skylark
skyline

* * *

psychically
psychosis [psychoses]
psychotic ally

saliva

scientist

seismograph

Siamese
sidelining
silencer
silencing
silently
sizable / sizeable

skydiving
skyscraper

society -ies

spiralling
spirally
spitefully

stylistic ally

subscribing
subsidence
subsiding
sufficing
supplier
supplying
surprising
survival
surviving
survivor

* * * * * *

cybercafé
cytoplasm

psychiatric ally
psychiatrist
psychiatry
psychically
psychoanalyse d
psychoanalysis
psychoanalyst
psychoanalytic ally
psychological ly
psychologist
psychology
psychotherapist
psychotherapy
psychotically

salivary

scientific ally

seismology

Siberia

society -ies

stylistically

surprisingly

In these words you can hear the vowel sound ie as in lion

S

*

spice d
spike d
spine
spire
spite
splice d
spline d
spy -ies
spied

squire

***stile** barrier
with steps
stride
[strode]
[stridden]
strife
strike
[struck]
[stricken]
stripe d
strive
[strove]
[striven]
***sty** -ies pen for pigs /
eye infection
***stye** s eye infection
***style** manner
styled

swine
swipe d

* *

slicing
sliding
slightest
slightly
slimy -ier, -iest
slyly / **slily**

smiley
smiling
smiting

sniper
sniping

spicing
spicy -ier, -iest
spider
spiking
spiky -ier, -iest
spinal
spiral led
spiral ly
spiteful ly
splicing
sprightly -ier, -iest
spying
spyware

stifle d
stifling
stipend
strident
striding
striker
striking
striving
styling
stylish
stylist
stylus es [styli]

sublime
subscribe d
subside
suffice d
supply -ies
supplied
surprise d
survive d

swiping

In these words you can hear the vowel sound **ie** as in **lion**

T

*

*Thai citizen of
  Thailand
*thigh upper part
  of leg
thine
thrice
thrive d
[throve]
[thriven]
*thy your
*thyme herb

*tide ebb and flow
*tie fasten with knot
*tied fastened
  with knot
tight
tights
tile d
*time period
timed
*tire make weary /
  ring fitted to wheel
tired

trial led
tribe
tripe
try -ies
tried

twice
twine d

type d
*tyre ring fitted
  to wheel

* *

Taiwan

Thailand
thriving
thyroid

tidal
tiding
tidings
tidy -ies
tidied
tiger
tighten ed
tightly
tiling
timeless
timely -ier, -iest
timer
timescale
timing
tiny -ier, -iest
tiredness
tiresome
tiring
title d

tonight

triad
trial led
trialling
tribal ly
tribesman
triceps
trifle d
tripod
triumph ed
trying

twilight

tycoon
tying
typhoon
typing
typist
tyrant

* * *

thiamine

tidier
tidiest
tidily
tidying
timetable d
timetabling
tinier
tiniest

trialling
triangle
tribunal
tricycle
tripartite
triumphal ly
triumphant

typewriter

* * * * *

titanium

triangular
triangulation
triceratops
triumphally
triumphantly

In these words you can hear the vowel sound **ie** as in **lion**

V

*
via
***vial** small bottle
vibe s
vice
vie d
***vile** disgusting
vine
***viol** stringed
instrument

* *
via
***vial** small bottle
vibrant
vibrate
Viking
vinyl
***viol** stringed
instrument
violence
violent
violet
viper
viral
virus es
viscount
visor
vital ly

vying

* * *
vagina
vaginal

viable
viaduct
vibrating
vibration
violate
violence
violent ly
violet
violin
vitally
vitamin

* * * * *
variety -ies

viability
vicarious ly
vice-president
vice-versa
vicissitude
violating
violation
violently
vitality
vivarium

W

*
***right** correct / direction
***rite** ceremony

***rye** grain

***while** time / during
the time that
***whiled** did while
whilst
***whine** d complain
white
why
***whys** causes / reasons

wide
wife -ves
***wild** untamed
***wile** trick
***wind** move by
turning
[wound]
***wine** drink
***wined** supplied
with wine
wipe d
wire d
***wise** very sensible

***write** set down on
paper
[wrote]
[written]
writhe d
***wry** twisted

* *
whiling
whining
Whitehall
whitewash es
whitewashed
whiting
whitish

widely
widen ed
wider
widespread
wi-fi
wildlife
wildly
wily -ier, -iest
winding
wining
wiper
wiping
wireless es
wiring
wiry -ier, -iest
wisely
wiser
wisest

writer
writhing
writing
wryly

* * *

* * * *

In these words you can hear the vowel sound **ie** as in **lion**

193

X

*
**
***
xylophone
****

Z

*
**
Zaire
***
xylophone
****

In these words you can hear the vowel sound **ie** as in **lion**

A

LONG VOWEL **oe**

*	* *	* * *	* * * * *
	abode	aerobic	ammonia
			ammonium
	afloat	approaching	
			appropriate ly
	ago	aroma	
			associate d
	alone	atonement	associating
	although	atoning	association
		atrocious	associative
	approach es		
	approached	awoken	
	arose		
	atone d		
	awoke		

for Scots: oe -r
is on page 256 ▷

B

*	* *	* * *	* * * *
*beau dandy	behold		
	[beheld]		
bloke	below		
blow	bestow ed		
[blew]			
[blown]	blokey		
	blower		
boast	blowing		
boat	blowlamp		
*bode did bide	*blowup / blow-up		
*bold brave	enlargement / big row		
*bole tree-trunk	*blow-up inflatable		
*boll seed capsule	*blow up enlarge /		
bolt	inflate / destroy by		
bone d	explosion		
both			
*bow wood and	boatman [boatmen]		
string / knot /	*bogey / bogie / bogy		
bend	evil spirit		
*bowed curved like	*bogey one stroke		
a bow	over par / dried snot		
*bowl container /	*bogie trolley		
send a ball	bogus		
*bowled rolled /	bolster ed		
bowled out	boning		
bowls	bonus es		
	bony -ier, iest		
*broach es open up	boulder		
broached	bouquet		
broke	bowler		
*brooch es ornament	bowling		
	brocade		
	brochure		
	broken		
	broker		

In these words the first letter 'o' is a neutral
vowel. It sounds like the 'o' in 'policeman'.

Bolivia	bonanza	botanical

for Scots: oe -r
is on page 257 ▷

In these words you can hear the vowel sound oe as in goat

C

LONG VOWEL oe

*

choke d
chose
chrome d

cloak ed
clone d
close
closed
*clothe d provide
with clothes
*clothes garments
*clove spice / did
cleave
*cloves spice

coach es
coached
coal
coast
coat
*coax es gently
persuade
coaxed
code
coke d
*Cokes more than one
Coca Cola
cold
colt
comb ed
cone
cope d
cove

croak ed
crow ed
[crew]
[crown]

for Qu . . .
see page 206

* *

chauffeur ed
choking
-choral
-chorus es
-chorused
chosen
chroming

cloakroom
closely
closing
closure
clothesline
clothing
clover

coastal
coastguard
coastline
coating
cobalt
cobra
cocaine
cocoa
coding
coerce d
colder
coldness
coleslaw
cologne
colon
coma
compose d
console d
control led
coping
corrode
cosine
cosy -ier, -iest

crochet ed
crocus es [croci]
croquet
crowbar

kosher

* * *

chauvinist
chromatic
chromium
chromosome

cirrhosis

coconut
coercing
coherent
coincide
commotion
component
*composer writer of
music
composing
*composure calmness
conifer
consoling
controller
controlling
corroding
corrosion
corrosive
cotangent

Croatia

kimono s

koala

* * * * * *

chauvinism
chauvinistic

coagulate
coagulating
coalition
coefficient
coincidence
collinear
colloquial ly
colonial ly
colonialism
coniferous
cooperate
cooperating
cooperation
cooperative
coordinate
coordinating
coordination
coordinator

custodial

for Scots: oe -r
is on page 258

In these words the first letter 'o' is a neutral vowel. It sounds like the 'o' in 'policeman'.

C**O**MMUNICATING WORDS

cholesterol	comedian	committing
chorale	comedienne	communal ly
cocoon ed	command er	commune d
collapse d	commandment	communicate
collapsible	commemorate	communicating
collapsing	commemoration	communication
collect ing	commence d	communing
collection	commencing	communion
collective ly	commercial ly	community -ies
collector	commission ed	commutative
collide	commissioner	commute
colliding	commit ted	commuter
collision	commitment	commuting
colossal ly	committee	corrupt ion

In these words you can hear the vowel sound oe as in goat

D

LONG VOWEL oe

*

doe female deer
does more than one
female deer
doh keynote
doh! how stupid!
dole d
dome d
don't
dope d
dose d
dough flour and
water
doze d snooze d

droll
drone d
drove

* *

decode
denote
devote

disclose d
disown ed
dispose d

docile
doling
domain
donate
donor
dosage
dosing
doughnut
dozing

droning

* * *

decoding
denoting
devoted
devoting
devotion

diploma
disclosing
disclosure
disposal
disposing

domestic ally
donated
donation

* * * * *

deodorant

diplomacy
disposable

domestically
domesticate

for Scots: oe -r
is on page 259 ▷

E

*

for H . . .
see page 200 ▷

for I . . .
see page 200 ▷

* *

elope d

enclose d
encroach es
encroached
enfold
engross es
engrossed
enrol led

erode

evoke d

explode
expose d

* * *

eloping

emotion
emotive

enclosing
enclosure
enrolling
enrolment

eroding
erosion

evoking

exploding
explosion
explosive
exponent
exposing
exposure

* * * * *

eau-de-cologne

emotional ly

erroneous ly

euphonium

for Scots: oe -r
is on page 259 ▷

In these words you can hear the vowel sound oe as in goat

F

*

float
*__floe__ floating ice-sheet
*__flow__ ed run

foal
*__foaled__ given birth
to a foal
foam ed
foe
*__fold__ bend double /
crease / sheep
enclosure
folk

fro
froze

phone d

**

floated
floating
flowchart
flowing

foamy -ier, -iest
focal
focus es [foci]
focused / focussed
folded
folder
folding
folklore
foretold
forgo / forego
[forwent / forewent]
[forgone / foregone]

frozen

phobic
phoneme
phoning
photo s

***

ferocious

fibrosis

flotation

focuses / focusses
focusing / focussing
foliage
folio s
fovea
foveal

phobia
photograph ed

* * * * **

photocopier
photocopy -ies
photocopied
photoelectric
photofinish
photographic ally
photosynthesis

for th . . .
see page 208 ▷

for Scots: oe -r
is on page 260 ▷

In these words you can hear the vowel sound oe as in goat

G

*	**	***	****
ghost	ghostly -ier, -iest	globally	

gloat	global ly	goalkeeper
globe	glowing	
glow ed	glow-worm	grocery -ies

gnome

go	goalie
[went]	goalpost
[gone]	goatskin
goad	gobo
goal	going
goat	golden
goes	goldfish
gold	goldsmith
	gopher

*grocer shopkeeper
selling food and other
goods

*groan deep moan	
groaned	
grope d	groping
gross ed	*grosser fatter / more
grove	disgusting
grow	grossly
[grew]	grotesque
*[grown] developed	grower
growth	growing
	grown-up

for Scots: oe -r
is on page 261 ▷

In these words you can hear the vowel sound **oe** as in **goat**

H

LONG VOWEL **oe**

*

hoax es
hoaxed
hoe d
*hoes more than
one hoe
*hold grip /
support / continue
[held]
*hole opening
*holed hit ball
into hole
holt
home d
hope d
*hose flexible
water-pipe / stockings
hosed
host
hove

*whole total / complete

* *

hallo / hello / hullo

holder
holding
hold-up
*holey full of holes
holing
holster
*holy -ier, -iest
sacred
homeland
homeless
homely -ier, -iest
homepage
homemade
homesick
homestead
homeward
homework
homing
hopeful ly
hopeless
hoping
hosepipe
hosing
hostess es
hotel

wholegrain
wholemeal
wholesale
wholesome
*wholly totally /
completely

* * *

heroic ally

holiness
holistic ally
hologram
holograph
homelessness
hopefully
hopelessly
hopelessness
hosiery

hypnosis

* * * * * * *

heroically

holistically
homeopathic ally
homeopathy
homogeneous
homophobia
homophobic
homosexual ly
homosexuality
hotelier

for Scots: oe -r
is on page 261

Here the first letter 'o' has a neutral sound.

holography   horizon   horrendous   horrific ally

I

*

for E . . .
see page 197

* *

impose d

invoke d

* * *

immobile
imposing

invoking

* * * *

for Scots: oe -r
is on page 262

In these words you can hear the vowel sound **oe** as in **goat**

J

LONG VOWEL **oe**

*
joke d

**
joker
joking

***
jovial ly

****
jovially

for dr . . .
see page 197

K

*
knoll
***know** understand
[knew]
[known]
***knows** does know

*no not any
*nose part of face

**
know-how
knowing

kosher

***
kimono s

knowingly

koala

****

> **In these words the first letter 'o' is a neutral vowel. It sounds like the 'o' in 'policeman'.**
>
> Korea   Korean

for C . . .
see page 196

for Qu . . .
see page 206

L

*
***lo** behold
***load** amount carried
loaf [loaves]
loafed
loam
***loan** ed lend /
amount lent
***loath / loth** unwilling
***loathe** d hate
lobe
***lode** vein of metal
ore / ditch
***lone** single
lope d
***low** not high / moo
***lowed** mooed

*
loaded
loathing
loathsome
local ly
locate
locus [loci]
locust
lodestone
logo s
lonely
loner
lonesome
loping
lotion
lotus
low-cost
lower ed
lowest
lowland
lowlands
lowly

***
locally
located
localise d
ze
location
loneliness

*****
localisation
zation
localising
zing
locality -ies
locomotion
locomotive
loganberry -ies

for Scots: oe -r
is on page 263

In these words you can hear the vowel sound oe as in goat

M

*

mauve

****mo** moment
****moan**ed complain
****moat** surrounding
defensive ditch
****mode** way / fashion
mole
moped
most
****mote** speck
mould
moult
****mow** cut with blades
[mowed] cut
[mown] cut

* *

mobile
mocha
modem
molar
molten
moment
moping
morose
Moses
mostly
motel
****motif / motive** theme /
figure
****motion**ed
****motive** cause of
action
motored
mouldy-ier, -iest
mower

* * *

mobilised
ze
Mohammed
molasses
momentary
momentous
momentum
****mosaic** a design made
up of small pieces
****Mosaic** Moses-related
motionless
motivate
motorbike
motorist
motorway

* * * * *

melodious

mobilisation
zation
mobility
momentarily
momentary
motivation
motorcycle

*for Scots: oe -r
is on page 263* ▷

> **In these words the first letter 'o' is a neutral
> vowel. It sounds like the 'o' in 'policeman'.**
>
> molecular   moraine
> morale   morality

N

*

gnome

knoll
****know** understand
[knew]
[known]
****knows** does know

****no** not any
node
****nose** part of face
nosed
note

* *

know-how
knowing

noble
Noel
nomad
no-one
nosebleed
nosey / nosy -ier, -iest
nosing
notebook
noted
noticed
notion
nova
nowhere

* * *

knowingly

neurosis -es

nobleman [noblemen]
nobody
nomadic
notable
notably
notation
noteworthy
notify -ies
notified
November

* * * * *

negotiable
negotiate
negotiating
negotiation
negotiator

nobility
noticeable
noticeably
notification
notoriety
notorious

In these words you can hear the vowel sound oe as in goat

O

*	**	***	***** *
oak	oatmeal	oasis [oases]	eau-de-cologne
oath			
oats	obese	odious	obedience
	obey ed		obedient
*ode long poem	oblique	old-fashioned	obesity
	oboe	Olympic	obituary -ies
*oh! exclamation			
	ocean	omission	oceanic
old	ochre	omitted	oceanography
		omitting	
*owe must pay	odour		overcoming
*owed did owe		opening	overlapping
own ed	ogre	openly	overlooking
	ogress es	openness	overwhelming ly
		opium	
	okay ed	opponent	
		opposing	
	older		
	oldest	-orally	
	omen	ovary -ies	
	omit ted	ovation	
		overall	
	only	overalls	
	onus es	overarm	
		overboard	
	opal	overcast	
	opaque	[overcast]	
	open ed	overcoat	
	opening	overcome	
	oppose d	[overcame]	
	opus es [opera]	[overcome]	
		overdo	
	-oral ly	[overdid]	
		[overdone]	
	*ova eggs	overdose	
	oval	overdraft	
	*over above	overdrive	
	overt	overdue	
	ovum [ova]	overeat	
		[overate]	
	owing	[overeaten]	
	owner	overfeed	
		[overfed]	
	ozone	overflow ed	
		overgrow	
		[overgrew]	
		[overgrown]	
		overhang	
		[overhung]	
		overhaul ed	
		overhead	
		overhear	
		[overheard]	
		overjoyed	
		overlap ped	
		overload	
		overlook ed	

for H . . .
see page 200

for Scots: oe -r
is on page 264

In these words you can hear the vowel sound oe as in goat

203

O

In these words the first letter 'o' sounds like the neutral 'o' sound in 'policeman'.

OBLIGING WORDS

obligatory	offend
oblige d	offender
obliging	offensive
obliterate	official ly
obliterating	opinion
oblivion	opossum
oblivious	oppression
occasion	oppressive
occasional ly	oppressor
occur red	original ly
occurrence	originality
occurring	originate
o'clock	originating
offence	

* * *

overnight
overpower ed
override
[overrode]
[overridden]
overrun
[overran]
[overrun]
overseas
oversee
[oversaw]
[overseen]
overshoot
[overshot]
oversize
oversleep
[overslept]
overspill
overtake
[overtook]
[overtaken]
overthrow
[overthrew]
[overthrown]
overtime
overtone
overture
overturn ed
overview
overweight
overwhelm ed
overwork ed

ownership

◀ for H . . .
see page 200

for Scots: oe -r
is on page 264 ▶

P

*

phone d

poach es
poached
poke d
***pole** long rod
***poll** number of
voters / head /
cut off top
polled
pope
pose d
post
☛

* *

patrol led

phobic
phoneme
phoning
photo s
☛

* * *

pagoda
patrolling

phobia
photograph ed

poetic ally
poetry
polarise d
    ze
polio
postmaster
postponing
potency
☛

* * * * **

petroleum

photocopier
photocopy -ies
photocopied
photoelectric
photofinish
photographic ally
photosynthesis

for Scots: oe -r
is on page 265 ▶

In these words you can hear the vowel sound oe as in goat

P

*

pro s
probe d
prone
***pros** points in favour /
professionals
***prose** text that is not
poetry

* *

poacher
poem
poet
poetry
poker
poking
Poland
polar
pole-vault
Polish
polo
pony -ies
posing
postage
postal
postcard
postcode
poster
posting
postman [postmen]
postpone d
postscript
post-war / postwar
posy -ies
potent
potion
poultry

probing
proceeds
process es
processed
profile d
***program** instructions
for computer
***programme** plan of
performance /
broadcast
programmed
progress es
progressed
project
prologue
promote
pronoun
propos
propose d
protein
protest
proton
proven
provoke d

* * *

precocious
processor
profiling
programmer
programming
prognosis
promoter
promoting
promotion
proposal
proposing
prosaic ally
protocol
prototype
provoking

* * * * *

plutonium

pneumonia

poetically
polarising
           zing
polarity -ies
postgraduate

prohibition
proletariat
proscenium s [proscenia]
protoplasm
protozoa

In these words the first letter 'o' is a neutral vowel. It sounds like the 'o' in 'policeman'.

PROGRESSIVE WORDS

phonetic ally
photographer
photography
police
policeman
[policemen]
policewoman
[policewomen]
policing
polite
politely
political ly
pollutant
pollute
polluting
pollution
polyphony
position ed
possess es
possessed
possession
possessive
potato es
potential ly
probation
procedure
proceed ing
proceedings
procession
proclaim ed
procure d

procuring
prodigious
produce d
producer
producing
production
productive
profane
profess es
professed
profession al ly
professionalism
professor
proficiency
proficient
profound
profuse
profusion
progression
progressive ly
prohibit ed
prohibiting
prohibitive
projectile
projection
projector
proliferate
proliferation
proliferating
prolific ally
prolong ed

pronounce d
pronouncement
pronouncing
pronunciation
propel led
propeller
propelling
propensity -ies
proportional ly
proportionate ly
proprietor
propulsion
prospect ive
prospector
prospectus es
protect ed
protection
protective
protector
protractor
protrude
protruding
provide d
provider
providing
provincial
provision s
provisional ly
provocative

---

for Scots: oe -r
is on page 265 ▷

Q

*
quote
quoth

* *
quota
quotient

* * *
quotation

* * * *

R

*
roach [roach]
*road track
*roam ed wander
roan
roast
robe d
*rode travelled on / by
*roe fish eggs or
sperm / small
deer
*roes more than one
roe
rogue
*role actor's part
*roll ed turn over
and over
*Rome city
rope d
*rose flower / did
rise
*rote repetition
rove
*row line / move
with oars
*rowed moved with
oars
*rows lines / moves
with oars

*wrote set down on
paper

* *
remote
repose d
reproach es
reproached
revolt
rewrote

roadblock
roadside
roadworks
robing
robot
robust
rodent
role-play
roller
rolling
Roman
romance d
roping
rosebud
rosette
rosewood
rosy -ier, -iest
*rota system of taking
turns to perform tasks
rotate
*rotor rotating shaft
and attachment
roving

* * *
reposing

robotic ally
rococo
rodeo
rolling-pin
romancing
romantic ally
rotary
rotating
rotation

* * * * *
rhododendron

robotically
romantically

for Scots: oe -r
is on page 266 ▷

In these words you can hear the vowel sound oe as in goat

S

*

scold
scone
scope
scroll ed

*sew ed stitch
[sewn]

shoal
show ed
[shown]

*sloe blackthorn
fruit or bush
slope d
sloth
*slow at a low speed
slowed

smoke d
smote

snow ed

*so therefore / to
such a degree /
in that way
soak ed
soap ed
*sold given for
money
*sole only / part of
foot and shoe / fish
*soled fitted with
new sole
*soul spirit
*sow ed plant
[sown]

spoke

stoat
stoke d
stole
stone d
stove
stow ed
strobe
strode
stroke d
stroll ed
strove

**

chauffeur

sauté

scrolling

sewing

shoulder ed

slogan
sloping
Slovak
slower
slowly

smoking
smoky -ier, -iest
smoulder ed

snowball ed
snowdrop
snowfall
snowflake
snowman [snowmen]
snowstorm
snowy -ier, -iest

sober ed
so-called
social ly
soda
sofa
solar
*solder ed join metal
*soldier ed serve in an
army / army person
solely
solo s
sonar

spoken
spokesman [spokesmen]

stoking
stolen
stoma s [stomata]
stoneware
stony -ier, -iest
*-storey floor
*-story -ies tale
stowing
stroking
strolling

suppose d

swollen

***

chauvinist

samosa

sclerosis [scleroses]

showjumper
showjumping

sociable
socialise d
ze
socialist
socially
sodium
*soldering joining
metal
*soldiering acting as
an army person
soloist
soviet

spokesperson
spokeswoman
[spokeswomen]

stomata
stowaway

supposing

**** *****

chauvinism
chauvinistic

Slovakia

socialisation
zation
socialism
socioeconomic ally
sociological ly
sociologist
sociology
Somalia

supposedly

symposium s [symposia]

In these words the first letter 'o' is a neutral
vowel. It sounds like the 'o' in 'policeman'.

society -ies
solicitor
solidify -ies
solidified
solidity
soliloquy -ies

solution
sonorous
sophisticated
sophistication
soprano s
sporadic ally

---

for Scots: oe -r
is on page 267 ▷

In these words you can hear the vowel sound **oe** as in **goat**

207

T

LONG VOWEL oe

*

those
though
throat
*throe sharp pain
*throne state chair
throned
throve
*throw hurl
[threw]
*[thrown] hurled

*toad animal
toast
*toe part of foot
*toed placed toes
against / fitted
with a toe
*told did tell
toll
*tolled did toll
tone d
tote
*tow pull behind
*towed pulled behind

troll

* *

throwing

toadstool
toasted
toaster
toastie
tofu
token
tonal ly
toning
topaz
-Tory -ies
total led
totem

*trojan harmful
computer program
*Trojan native of
ancient Troy
trophy -ies

* * *

tonally
totalling
totally

> In these words the first letter 'o' is a neutral
> vowel. It sounds like the 'o' in 'policeman'.
>
> tobacco s   topography
> tobacconist   topology
> tomato es   torrential ly

* * * *

totality

for Scots: oe -r
is on page 268

U

*

* *

unbolt
unfold
unknown
unload
unroll ed
untold

uphold
[upheld]
upload

* * *

unbroken
unnoticed
unopened
unspoken

upholster ed

* * * *

euphonium

unsociable

upholstery

V

*

*-vault gymnastic leap /
underground room /
arched roof

vogue
vole
*volt unit of
electrical force
vote

* *

vocal ly
vocals
voltage
voted
voter
voting

* * *

viola

vocalist
vocally
voltmeter

* * * *

> Here the first letter 'o' has a neutral sound.
> vocabulary -ies   vocation   vocational ly

In these words you can hear the vowel sound oe as in goat

W

LONG VOWEL oe

*

*hole opening

*rote repetition

*whoa! stop!
*whole total /
complete

*woe distress
woke
won't
wove

*wrote set down on
paper

* *

*holey full of holes
*holy sacred

wholegrain
wholemeal
wholesale
wholesome
*wholly totally /
completely

woeful ly
woken
woven

* * *

wholehearted ly

woefully

* * * *

wholeheartedly

for Scots: oe -r
is on page 269 ▷

Y

*

*yoke neck-piece
yoked
*yolk yellow part
of egg

* *

yeoman [yeomen]

yodel led / ed
yoga
yoghourt /
yoghurt / yogurt
yogi
yokel

* * *

yodelling / yodeling

* * * *

euphonium

for Scots: oe -r
is on page 269 ▷

Z

*

zone d

* *

* * *

zodiac

* * * * * *

zoological ly
zoology

In these words you can hear the vowel sound oe as in goat

A

*	* *	* * *	* * * * *
	-about	abusing	accumulate
	abuse d		accumulating
		accruing	accumulation
	accrue d	accusing	accumulator
	accuse d	acoustic	accusative
	acute		acoustical ly
		*allusion reference	
	*adieu goodbye		adjudicate
	*ado confused activity	amusement	adjudicating
		amusing	adjudication
	-afoot		adjudicator
		approval	
	*allude refer	approving	alluvial
	aloof		alluvium [alluvia]
		assuming	
	amuse d	-assurance	
		-assuring	
	anew		
		*illusion false belief or	
	approve d	appearance	

for H . . .
see page 215 ▷

assume d
-assure d

*elude avoid

In these words you can hear oo as in smooth   or ue as in newt

B

*

balloon ed

***blew** puffed
bloom ed
***blue** colour

boo ed
-**book** ed
boom ed
-**boor**
***boos** disapproving
cries
boost
boot
booth
***booze** d consume
alcohol / strong drink

brew
***brewed** fermented
***brews** does brew
***brood** offspring
-**brook** ed
broom
***bruise** injury
bruised
***bruit** spread rumours
***brute** beast

-**bull**
-**bush** es
-**bushed**

* *

baboon
balloon ed
bassoon

***beauty** -ies pleasing
example / loveliness
bemuse d

bluebell
blueprint
bluetit

booby -ies
booing
-**bookcase**
-**booklet**
-**bookshelf** [bookshelves]
booster
***bootee** baby's
woollen boot
***booty** stolen goods
boozer
boozing
-**bosom**
bouquet
-**bourgeois**
boutique

brewer
bruiser
bruising
brunette
brutal ly

-**Buddha**
-**Buddhist**
bugle
-**bulldog**
-**bullet**
-**bullfrog**
-**bullock**
-**bully** -ies
-**bullied**
-**bulrush** es
-**bureau** s / x
-**bushel**
-**butcher** ed

* * *

bazooka

beautiful ly
bemusing
Bermuda

blueberry -ies

boulevard
-**bourgeoisie**

brewery -ies
brutalise d
ze
brutally

-**Buddhism**
-**bulldozer** ed
-**bulletin**

* * * * *

beautifully

brutality

-**bureaucracy** -ies
-**bureaucratic** ally

C

*

chew ed
*chews does chew
*choose select
[chose]
[chosen]
*chute slope for
things to slide down

clue d

*coo ed speak softly /
sound made by pigeon
-cook ed
cool ed
coop
-could
*coup stroke /
successful action
-course d
-court

crew
*crewed acted as a
crew member
*crewel tapestry yarn
*crews more than
one crew
-crook
croon ed
*crude untreated /
done without skill
*cruel ly vicious
*cruise voyage
cruised

cube d
*cue rod / signal
*cued did cue
-cure d
cute

*queue waiting line
*queued did queue

*shoot fire / hit with
bullet / move very fast /
new growth from plant

for Qu . . .
see page 219 ▷

* *

canoe d
cashew

chewing
choosing

clueing

cocoon ed
commune d
commute
compute
conclude
confuse d
consume d
-cooker
-cooking
coolant
cooler
coolly
coolness
-couldn't
coupé
coupon
-courgette
-coursing

*crewel tapestry yarn
-crooked
crucial ly
*cruel ly vicious
cruelty -ies
cruet
cruiser
cruising
crusade

Cuba
cubic
cuboid
-cuckoo
*cueing / cuing
prompting
culottes
-curate
-curing
-cushion ed

Kuwait

*queueing / queuing
waiting in a line

* * *

canoeing

communal ly
communing
communion
commuter
commuting
computer
computing
concluding
conclusion
conclusive
conducive
confusing
confusion
consumer
consuming
-courier

crucially
crucible
crucifix es
cruciform
crucify -ies
crucified
cruelly
cruelty -ies
crusading

*cubical cube-shaped
*cubicle small room
cubism
cucumber
cumulus [cumuli]
-curating
-curator
-curio s
-curious

* * * * *

circuitous

communally
communicate
communicating
communication
communicative
communion
community -ies
commutative
computerise d
ze

crucifixion

cumulative
-curiosity -ies
-curiously

In these words you can hear oo as in smooth   or ue as in newt

D

*

deuce
*dew moisture

do
[did]
[done]
*doer active person
doom ed
*dour unsmiling

drew
droop ed

*dual double
*due owing
*duel led fight
duke
dune

* *

deduce d
dewdrop

diffuse d
disprove d
dispute
disused

doer
doing
doodle d
doodling

*dual double
ducal
*duel led fight
duelling
duet
duly
duo s
-during
duty -ies
duvet

* * *

deducing
delusion

diffusing
diffusion
disproven
disproving
disputing

dubious
duelling
duplicate
-durable
-duration
dutiful ly

* * * * *

disunity

duodenal
duplicating
duplication
-durability
dutifully

E

*

*ewe female sheep
*ewes more than
one ewe

*use employ

*yew tree
*yews yew trees

*you person / people

* *

*allude refer

*elude avoid

-endure d
*-ensure d make certain

-euro s
-Europe

exclude
excuse d
extrude

*insure d protect against
loss

* * *

eluding
*elusive hard to find

-endurance
-enduring
*-ensuring making
certain

eucharist
-eureka!

excluding
exclusion
exclusive
excusing
extruding
extrusion
extrusive

*illusive deceptive

*insuring protecting
against loss

* * * * * * *

elucidate

enthusiasm
enthusiast
enthusiastic ally
enumerate
enumerating

eucalyptus es
euphemism
euphonium
euphoria
-European
euthanasia

exclusively
excruciating
exuberance
exuberant

for H . . .
see page 215

for I . . .
see page 215

In these words you can hear **oo** as in **smooth**   or **ue** as in **newt**

F

*	* *	* * *	* * * * * *
feud	feudal ly	feudally	feudalism
*few not many	fewer		
		fluency	-fluorescence
*flew passed in	fluent	flugelhorn	-fluorescent
flight	fluid	-fluorescence	-fluoridation /
*flu influenza	-fluoride	-fluorescent	fluoridisation
*flue pipe	-fluorine		zation
fluke		foolhardy	
flute	foodstuff		foolhardiness
	foolish	fruiterer	fortuitous ly
food	foolproof	fruitfully	
fool ed	-football	fruition	frugality
-foot	-foothill		
-fourth	-foothold	fuelling	fumigating
	-footpath	fugitive	fumigation
fruit	-footstep	-fulfilling	-furiously
	-forsook	fumigate	futility
fuel led		funeral	futuristic ally
fugue	frugal	-furious	
-full	fruitful ly	fuselage	
fume d	fruitless		
fumes			
fuse d	fuchsia		
	fuel led		
*phew / whew relief!	fuelling		
	-fulcrum		
	-fulfil led		
	-fully		
	fuming		
	-fury -ies		
	fusing		
	fusion		
	futile		
	future		

for th . . .
see page 222 ▷

G

*	* *	* * *	* * * *
gloom	gloomy -ier, -iest	gloomily	gratuitous
glue d	glucose		
	gluten	-gooseberry -ies	
*gnu horned animal			
	-goodbye	gruelling	
-good	-goodness		
-goods	-goodnight		
goose [geese]	google d		
gourd	googling		
	googly -ies		
grew	-gooseberry -ies		
groom ed	gourmet		
groove d			
group ed	grouping		
	gruelling		
*knew understood	gruesome		
*new unused	-guru s		

214

H

*

**hew ed cut down
[hewn]

-hood
hoof [hooves]
hoofed
-hook ed
*hoop large ring or
band
hoop ed
hoot
hooves
-house

*hue colour
huge

*who which person or
people
who'd
who'll
whom
*whoop ed shout joyfully
*who's who is
*whose belonging to
whom or what

* *

hoover ed
*-hoummos / hommus /
hummous / hummus /
houmous / humus
chickpea spread

hugely
hula
*human person
*humane showing
concern for others
humid
humour ed
*humous containing
humus
*humus organic matter
in soil
-hurrah!
-hurray!

* * *

hooligan

humanist
humankind
*humerus [humeri] bone
in upper arm
humorist
*humorous funny

whoever
whooping-cough

* * * * *

hallucination

humanism
humanistic
humanitarian
humanities
humanity
humidity
humiliate
humiliating
humiliation
humility

I

*

* *

*-ensure d make certain

immune
improve d
-impure

include
induce d
*-insure d protect
against loss
intrude

* * *

*allusion reference

*elusive hard to find
*-ensuring making certain

*illusion false belief
or appearance
*illusive deceptive

improvement
improving

included
including
inclusion
inclusive
inducement
inducing
inhuman
-insurance
*-insuring protecting
against loss
intruder
intrusion
intrusive

* * * * *

illuminate
illuminating
illumination
illusory

immovable
immunity
impunity
-impurity -ies

-incurable
-infuriate
-infuriating
-injurious
innumerable
inscrutable
insuperable
intuitive

◁ for E . . .
see page 213

In these words you can hear **oo** as in smooth   or **ue** as in newt

215

J

*

*deuce tennis score / devil
*dew moisture

drew

*dual double
*due owing
*duelled fight
duke
*dune hill of sand

*Jew Jewish person
*jewel gem

*joule unit of energy

*juice liquid from fruit,
meat and vegetables
*June month

for dr . . .
see page 213

* *

*dual double
ducal
*duelled fight
duelling
duet
duly
during
duty -ies
duvet

*jewelled gem
jeweller
jewellery / jewelry
Jewess es
Jewish
*Jewry all Jews

judo
juicy -ier, -iest
jukebox es
July
-juror
*-jury -ies judging panel

* * *

duelling
duplicate
durable
duration
dutifully

Jacuzzi s

jeweller
jewellery / jewelry

jubilant
jubilee
judicially
judicious
juicier
juiciest
jujitsu
junior
Jupiter
juvenile

* * * * *

durability
dutifully

jubilation
Judaism
judicially
judiciary -ies
judiciously
-jurisdiction
-jurisprudence

K

*

*gnu horned animal

*knew understood

*new unused

* *

Kuwait

for C . . .
see page 212

* * *

for Qu . . .
see page 219

* * * *

L

*

*lieu place

*loo toilet
-looked
loom
looped
*loos toilets
loosed
*loot stolen goods
*lose have no longer /
fail to win
[lost]

-lured
*lute musical
instrument

* *

lagoon
lasso s / es

-lookout
loophole
loosely
loosened
loser
losing
louvre

lucid
ludo
lukewarm
lunar
lupin
-luring

* * *

lubricant
lubricate
lucrative
ludicrous
luminous

* * * *

leukaemia / leukemia

lubricating
lubrication

In these words you can hear **oo** as in smooth   or **ue** as in newt

M

*

mew ed
*mewl ed mew
*mews houses
converted from
stables

moo
*mood state of
feeling
*mooed went 'moo'
moon ed
-moor ed
*moose large northern
deer
-mourn ed
*-mouse small animal /
computer device
*mousse sweet dish
move d

*mule animal
*muse think deeply
mute

* *

-manure d
maroon ed
-mature d

-mistook
misuse d

moody -ier, -iest
moonlight
moonlit
-mooring
-moorland
-Moslem / Muslim
-mournful ly
-mourning
movement
mover
movie
moving

*mucous of / covered
with mucus
*mucus slimy liquid
muesli
-mural
music ally
musing
-Muslim / Moslem
mutant
mutual ly

* * *

manoeuvre d

-mournfully
movable / moveable

museum
musical ly
musician
mutation
mutilate
mutineer
mutiny -ies
mutinied
mutually

* * * * *

-maturity

mercurial

municipal ly
musically
mutilating
mutilation

N

*

*gnu horned animal

*knew understood

*new unused
*news reported
information
newt

-nook
noon
*noose loop that can
be tightened
-now

nude

* *

-neural
-neuron / neurone
neutral ly
neutron
newborn
newer
newest
newly
newscast
newsgroup
newton

noodle
nougat

nuance
nudist
nuisance

* * *

-neurosis -es
-neurotic ally
neutralise d
ze
neutrally
newcomer
newsagent
newsletter
newspaper
New Zealand

nuclear
nucleus [nuclei]
nudism
nudity
numeral
numeric al
numerous
nutrient
nutrition
nutritious
nutritive

pneumatic

* * * * * *

-neurological ly
-neurologist
-neurology
-neurotically
neutralising
zing
neutrality

numeration
numerator
numerical ly
nutritional
nutritionist

pneumonia

O

*

ooh
oops
ooze d

for H . . .
see page 215

* *

-obscure d
obtuse

oozes
oozing

* * *

-obscuring

* * * *

-obscurity -ies

In these words you can hear oo as in smooth   or ue as in newt

P

*	**	***	******
*few not many	**perfume** d	peculiar	**peculiar** ly
	Peru	perfuming	**peculiarity** -ies
pew	**pewter**		
		-pluralist	-pluralism
*phew / whew relief!	**platoon**	-plurally	plutonium
	plumage		
plume d	-plural ly	pneumatic	pneumonia
	Pluto		
		pollutant	presumably
pool ed		polluting	
*poor badly off	**pollute**	pollution	pugilistic ally
*-pour ed flow out	**poodle**		-purification
	-poorer		-puritanical
proof	-poorest	presuming	-puritanism
prove d	-poorly	-procuring	
[proven]	-pouring	producer	
prune d		producing	
	preclude	profusion	
-pull ed	**presume** d	protruding	
*-pure unmixed	-procure d		
-push es	**produce** d	pseudonym	
-pushed	**profuse**		
-puss es	**proofread**	puberty	
-put	**protrude**	pubescent	
-[put]	**proven**	-pullover	
	prudence	punitive	
	prudent	-purify -ies	
	pruning	-purified	
		-puritan / Puritan	
	-pudding	-purity	
	-pulley	pursuant	
	-pulpit	pursuer	
	puma	pursuing	
	puny -ier, -iest	putrefy -ies	
	pupa [pupae]	putrefied	
	pupil		
	-purée		
	-purely		
	*-purest cleanest		
	*-purist perfectionist		
	pursue d		
	pursuit		
	-pushchair		
	-pussy -ies		
	putrid		
	-putting		

Q

*	**	***	****
*cue rod / signal	*cueing / cuing prompting	**quintuplet**	
cued			
	*queueing / queuing		
*queue waiting line	waiting in a line		
queued			

In these words you can hear **oo** as in smooth   or **ue** as in newt   **219**

R

*

*rood crucifix / quarter
of an acre
roof ed
-rook
room ed
roost
*root part of
plant / origin
rouge
*route way

ruche d
*rude impolite
rue d
*rued regretted
*rues does regret
rule d
rune
*ruse trick

* *

raccoon / racoon

rebuke d
recoup ed
recruit
reduce d
refuse d
refute
remove d
renew ed
repute
-resource d
resume d
*review survey
reviewed
*revue theatrical
entertainment

rhubarb

rooftops
roommate
rooster
rouble / ruble
roulette
routine

ruby -ies
rudeness
ruin ed
ruler
ruling
rumour ed
rupee
-rural ly
ruthless

* * *

rebuking
recruitment
reducing
refusal
refusing
refuting
removal
removing
renewal
renewing
-resourceful
-resources
-resourcing
resuming
reunion

rheumatic

-rookery -ies
routinely

rubella
ruinous
-rurally
ruthlessly

* * * * *

recuperate
removable /
removeable
remuneration
repudiate
repudiating
reunion

rheumatism

-Romania / Roumania /
Rumania

rudimentary

In these words you can hear oo as in smooth or ue as in newt

S

*

*chute slope for things to slide down

school ed
scoop ed
scoot
screw ed

*shoe footwear
[shod]
*shoo ed scare away
-shook
*shoot fire / hit with bullet / move very fast / new growth from plant
[shot]
-should
shrewd

skew ed

sleuth ed
slew
sluice

smooth ed

snoop ed
snooze d

soon
-soot
soothe d
*sou coin of low value
soup

spook ed
spool ed
spoon ed
spruce

stew ed
-stood
stool
*stoop ed bend down
*stoup basin for holy water
strew ed
[strewn]

*sue d take legal action / plead
suit
-sure

swoop ed

* *

saloon
salute

schoolboy
schoolgirl
schooling
schooner
scooter
scuba

seclude
-secure d
seduce d
sewage
*sewer big waste pipe

shoeing
shooting
-shouldn't

skewer ed

smoothie
smoothly

snooker ed
snoozing

sooner
soothing
soufflé
soupçon

spoonful
-sputnik

steward
strudel
Stuart
student
stupid
stupor

subdue d
Sudan
*suer person who seeks justice or marriage
sueing / suing
suet
-sugar ed
suitcase
suited
suitor
super
superb
supreme
-surely
sushi

* * *

pseudonym

saluting

schoolchildren
schoolmaster
schoolmistress es
schoolteacher
screwdriver
scrutinise d
        ze
scrutiny

secluded
secluding
-securing
seducing

solution
souvenir

spurious

stewardess es
studio s
studious
stupefy -ies
stupefied
stupendous

subduing
Sudanese
suicide
suitable
suitably
superbly
supersede
superstar
superstore
supervise d

* * * * * *

scrutinising
        zing

-security -ies

stupidity -ies

suicidal ly
suitability
superannuation
superconductor
superego
superficial ly
superfluous
superhuman
superimpose d
superimposing
superintendent
superior
superlative
supermarket
supermini
supermodel
supernatural ly
superpower
superseding
supersonic ally
superstition
superstitious
supervising
supervision
supervisor
supervisory
supremacy

T

*

***threw** hurled
***through** by way
of / because of

***to** towards
 tomb
***too** also
-**took**
 tool ed
 toot
 tooth ed
-**tour** ed

***troop** ed move as
a group
***troupe** group of
entertainers
 truce
 true d
 truth

 tube d
 tune d

***two** 2

* *

taboo ed
tattoo ed

throughout

today
to-do
tombstone
tonight
toolbar
toolbox es
toolkit
toothbrush es
toothcomb
toothpaste
toothpick
toucan
toupee
-**tourist**
toward
towards

trousseau
truant
truly
truthful ly

***tuba** wind instrument
***tuber** underground
stem or root
tubing
Tudor
Tuesday
tulip
tumour
tumult
***tuna** fish
***tuner** person who
tunes
tunic
tuning
tutor ed
tutu

twofold
two-thirds

* * *

together
tomorrow
-**tourism**
-**tournament**

truancy
truism
truthfully

tubular
tuition

* * * * *

tubercular
tuberculin
tuberculosis
tumultuous
Tunisia
tutorial

In these words you can hear oo as in smooth   or ue as in newt

U

*

*ewe female sheep
*ewes more than one
ewe

*use employ
used

*yew tree
*yews yew trees

*you person / people

◀ for H . . .
see page 215

for Y . . . ▶
see page 224

* *

-euro s
-Europe

Ukraine

*undo reverse an action
[undid]
[undone]
*undue beyond normal
limits
union
unique
unit
unite

-**urine**

usage
useful ly
useless
user
using
usual ly
usurp ed

* * *

eucharist
-eureka!

Uganda

unicorn
uniform ed
unify -ies
unified
union
unionist
unison
unitary
united
unity
universe

-**Uranus**
-**urethane**
-**urinary**
-**urinate**
-**Uruguay**

usable
usefully
usefulness
usually

utensil
uterus es [uteri]
utile
utilise d
ze

* * * * *

eucalyptus
euphemism
euphonium
euphoria
-European
euthanasia

ubiquitous

ukelele
Ukrainian

unanimity
unanimous ly
unicellular
unicycle
unification
uniformity
unilateral ly
unionist
unitary
universal ly
university -ies

-**uranium**
-**urinary**

utilisation
zation
utilising
zing
utility -ies
utopia

V

*

view ed

* *

viewer
viewpoint

* * *

* * * *

voluminous

W

*

*few not many

*hew ed cut down

*hoop large ring or band

*hue colour

*whew / phew relief!

* *

-**woman** [women]
-**wooden**
-**woodland**
-**woodwork**
-**woollen**
-**woolly**
-**wouldn't**
wounded

* * *

whoever
whooping-cough

-**woodcutter**
-**woodpecker**

* * * *

In these words you can hear **oo** as in smooth   or **ue** as in newt   **223**

W

*
who which person
or people
who'd
who'll
whom
whoop ed　shout
joyfully
who's who is
whose belonging to
whom or what

-**wolf** [wolves]
-**wolfed**
womb
*-**wood** timber / area
with many trees
woof weft
-woof! bark of dog
-**wool**
*-**would** was willing to /
used to / was going to
wound

Y

*
ewe female sheep
ewes more than one ewe

yew tree
yews yew trees

you person / people
addressed
you'd
you'll you will
-your belonging to you
-you're you are
-**yours**
youth
you've

yule Christmas time

* *
-euro s
-Europe

-**yourself**
-**yourselves**
youthful ly

for U . . .
see page 223

* * *
eucharist
-eureka!

youthfully
youthfulness

* * * * *
eucalyptus
euphemism
euphonium
euphoria
-European
euthanasia

Yugoslavia

Z

*
zoo
zoom ed

* *

* * *

* * * * **
zoological ly
zoology

In these words you can hear **oo** as in **smooth**　or **ue** as in **newt**

A

*	**	***	* * * * **
aft	aardvark	advancement	adagio
		advancing	advantaging
ah	advance d	advantage	
		advantaged	Antarctica
*alms gifts to the poor	afar		
	after	aftermath	arbitrarily
		afternoon	arbitrary
*arc curve	aghast	afterwards	arbitrating
arch es			arbitration
arched	ajar	answering	arbitrator
are		Antarctic	archaeological /
*aren't are not	alarm ed		archeological
*ark (Noah's)	almond	apartheid	archaeologist /
arm ed		apartment	archeologist
*arms more than one arm / weapons of war	amen		archaeology /
		arbitrate	archeology
	answer ed	arbutus	archipelago s / es
art		archaic	architecture
	apart	archbishop	Argentina
ask ed		archery	arguable
	*arbor shaft	architect	arguably
*aunt relative	*arbour garden or part shaded by trees	arduous	argumentative
		arguing	armadillo s
	arcade	argument	arterial
	archer	armada	artesian
	archive	armament	articulate
	arctic	armature	articulating
	ardent	armistice	articulation
	ardour	armoury -ies	artificial ly
	argon	arsenal	artillery
	argue d	arsenic	artistically
	armchair	artefact / artifact	
	armful	artery -ies	
	armour ed	artesian	
	armpit	artfully	
	army -ies	arthritis	
	arson	arthropod	
	artful ly	artichoke	
	artist	article	
	artwork	artifact / artefact	
		artisan	
	asking	artistic ally	
		artistry	
	Auntie / Aunty		

for H . . .
see page 230 ▷

In these words you can hear the vowel sound **ar** as in **shark**

B

*

*baa lamb's cry
*balm ointment
*bar red prevent /
  barrier / rod
barb ed
*bard poet
barge d
*bark ed sound like
  that of a dog / outer
  covering of a tree
*barm yeasty froth
barn
*barque boat
*barred prevented /
  fixed with bars
*bask ed enjoy
*Basque person living
  near the Pyrenees
bath ed

blah
blast

bra
branch es
branched
brass es

* *

*balmy -ier, -iest sweet-
  smelling / mad
banal
barbel
barber
bargain ed
barging
barking
barley
barman [barmen]
*barmy / balmy mad
barndoor
barney
barring
barter ed
basket
basking
bastard
bathroom
*bazaar Eastern
  market

behalf

*bizarre peculiar

bombard

branches
brassy -ier, -iest

* * *

Bahamas
banana
Barbados
barbaric ally
barbecue d
barnacle
barwoman [barwomen]
basketball

bombardment
Botswana

brassier
bravado

* * * * *

barbarian
barbarically
barbecuing

In these words you can hear the vowel sound **ar** as in **shark**

C

*

calf [calves]
calm ed
*calve d produce a calf
can't
car
card
carp ed
cart
*carve d cut
cask
*cast throw / mould /
decide parts in a
play / squint
[cast]
*caste social class

*chance lucky event /
risk
chanced
chant
*chants does chant /
more than one chant
char red
*chard leaf vegetable
*charred scorched
charge d
charm ed
chart

clasp ed
class es
classed
clerk

craft

czar / tsar

* *

calmly
carafe
carbon
carcass es / carcase s
cardboard
cargo es
carmine
carpet
carton
cartoon
cartridge
cartwheel
carving
*caster / castor
powdered sugar /
swivelling wheel
casting
castle
castling
*castor oil
catarrh

chancing
chandler
charade
charcoal
charging
charming
charring
charter ed
*chorale hymn tune

cigar

classmate
classroom
classy -ier, -iest

command
contrast
*corral enclosure
for cattle and
horses

craftsman [craftsmen]
crafty -ier, -iest

khaki

Koran / Qur'an

* * *

cacao
carbonate
cardiac
cardigan
cardinal
carnation
carnival
carnivore
carpenter
carpentry
cartilage
cartoonist
castaway

chancellor
chapati
chargeable
charlatan

commander
commandment
compartment

craftier
craftiest

karate

koala

* * * * *

carbohydrate
carbonation
carboniferous
carburetter /
carburettor
carcinogenic
carcinoma
carnivorous

D

*

daft
dal / dhal
dance d
dark
darn ed
dart

*draft rough plan /
selected group
*draught current of
air / depth of ship
in water / piece in
game
draughts

**

dancer
dancing
darken ed
darker
darkly
darkness
darling
data

demand
depart

disarm ed
discard
discharge d

drama
drastic ally
draughty -ier, -iest

***

demanded
demanding
department
departure

disaster
disastrous
discharging
dishearten ed

drastically

****

disarmament

drastically

E

*

for H . . .
see page 230

for I . . .
see page 230

**

embark ed

enchant
enhance d
enlarge d
entrance d

***

embargo es
embargoed

enchanting
enhancing
enlarging
entrancing

escarpment

example

****

In these words you can hear the vowel sound ar as in shark

F

*

far
farce
farm ed
fast

flask

France

* *

facade / façade
far-fetched
farmer
farmhouse
farming
farmland
farmyard
*farther greater
distance
farthest
fasten ed
faster
fastest
*father male parent
fathered

* * *

faraway
farcical
fastener
fatherly

*fiancé man engaged
to be married
*fiancée woman
engaged to be
married
finale

pharmacist
pharmacy -ies

* * * * *

father-in-law

pharmaceutical

G

*

garb
gasp ed

glance d
glass es

gnarled

gouache

*graft cause to grow
together / hard work
grant
graph ed
*graphed made a
graph
grasp ed
grass es
grassed

guard

* *

gala
garage d
garbage
garden ed
gardener
gardening
gargle d
gargling
garland
garlic
garment
garnet
garter ed

Ghana
ghastly -ier, -iest

giraffe

glancing
glasses
glassy -ier, -iest

gouache

granted
grasping
grassland
grassroots / grass-roots
grassy -ier, -iest
gratis

guitar

* * *

garaging
gardener
gardening

Ghanaian

grasshopper

guardian
guitarist

gymkhana

* * * *

Guatemala

H

*

half [halves]
halve d
hard
hark ed
harm ed
harp ed
harsh
*hart male deer

*heart organ that
pumps blood /
centre / inmost
feelings
hearth

* *

halal
half-time / halftime
halfway
halving
harbour ed
hardboard
hard-boiled
harden ed
harder
hardest
hardly
hardship
hardware
hardwood
hardy -ier,-iest
harem
harmful ly
harmless
harness es
harnessed
harpoon ed
harvest

heartbeat
heartbreak
heartburn
hearty -ier,-iest

hijab

hurrah!

* * *

harlequin
harmfully
harmonic ally
harmonise d
    ze
harmony -ies
harpsichord
harvester
Hawaii
Hawaiian
heartbroken

* * * * *

harmonica
harmonically
harmonious
harmonisation
    zation
harmonising
    zing
harmonium

I

*

◁ for E . . .
see page 228

* *

impart

Iran
Iraq

Islam

* * *

impartial ly

incarnate

Iraqi

* * * *

impartially
impassable

J

*

jar red

◁ for dr . . .
see page 228

* *

giraffe

jargon
jarring

jihad

* * *

gymkhana

* * * *

In these words you can hear the vowel sound **ar** as in **shark**

K

*	**	***	****
	khaki	karate	
	Koran / Qur'an	koala	

for C . . .
see page 227

L

*	**	***	****
lance d	lager	lasagne	
larch es	lancing	laughable	
lard	larder		
large	largely	legato	
lark ed	larger	lethargic	
last	large-scale		
laugh ed	largest		
	largo		
	larkspur		
	*larva [larvae] insect grub		
	lasted		
	lastly		
	lather ed		
	latte		
	laughter		
	*lava melted rock from volcano		
	llama		

M

*
ma mother
ma'am
mar spoil
marred
March month
march es advance with
regular steps / music
for marching
marched
mark ed
mars spoils
Mars planet
marsh es
mask ed
mass es
mast

* *
macho
madame
mama
marble d
marbling
marching
margin
marker
market ed
marking
marquee very big tent
marquess British
nobleman
marquis nobleman
marring
marshal officer /
arrange in order
marshalled
marshy -ier, -iest
marten animal
martial warlike
martin bird
martyr ed
marvel led
Marxist
massage d
master ed

mirage

morale
moustache d

* * *
macabre
mafia
Malawi
Mardi Gras
margarine
marginal ly
markedly
marketed
marketing
marketplace
marmalade
marmoset
marshalling
marshmallow
martini
martyrdom
marvelling
marvellous
Marxisn
marzipan
massaging
masterful ly
masterly
masterpiece
mastery

* * * *
marginally
marsupial
masterfully

N

*
gnarled

nan / naan

* *
nasty -ier, -iest
Nazi

* * *
narcissus es [narcissi]
narcotic
nastier
nastiest
Nazism

* * * *

In these words you can hear the vowel sound **ar** as in **shark**

P

*

*pa father
*pah scornful
exclamation
palm ed
*par what is normal
parch es
parched
park ed
part
pass es
*passed went by
*past time that has
passed / beyond
path

plant

prance d

psalm

* *

papa
parcel led
parchment
pardon ed
parka
parking
parlour
parsley
parsnip
parson
partake
[partook]
[partaken]
partial led
partly
partner ed
partridge
part-time
party -ies
passing
passport
password
pasta
pastime
pasture d
pathway

pianist
piano s

planted
planter
planting
plaster ed

prancing

* * *

Pakistan
parcelling
Parkinson's
parliament
partaken
partaking
partialling
partially
particle
partisan
partition ed
partnership
passers-by
Passover
pasteurise d
ze
pastoral ly
pasturing

pharmacist
pharmacy -ies

pianist
piano s
piranha

plantation

ptarmigan

pyjamas

* * * * *

Pakistani
parliamentary
participant
participate
participating
participation
participle
pasteurising
zing
pastorally

pharmaceutical

pianoforte
pistachio s

> In this word the 'ar' is neutral.
>
> particular ly

Q

*

qualm

* *

Qur'an / Koran

R

*

raft
ranch es
rasp ed

* *

rafter
rascal ly
raspberry
rather

regard
remark ed
retard

* * *

rascally
raspberry -ies

regarded
regarding
regardless
retarded

* * * *

rechargeable
remarkable
remarkably

In these words you can hear the vowel sound **ar** as in **shark**

233

S

*	**	***	***** *
psalm	charade	charlatan	**sarcastically**
			sardonically
scar red	cigar	**safari**	
scarf -ves		Sahara	**scenario** s
schwa	**saga**	**salami**	
	salmon	**sarcasm**	**Somalia**
shaft	**sample** d	**sarcastic** ally	
shark	**sampler**	**sardonic**	
sharp	**sampling**		
	sardine	**sharpening**	
slant	**sari**	**sharpshooter**	
smart	**scarlet**	**sonata**	
	scarring	**soprano** s	
snarl ed			
	sergeant	**staccato**	
*spa resort with		**starvation**	
mineral spring	**sharpen** ed		
*spar pole /	**sharpening**	**sultana**	
practise boxing	**sharply**	**surpassing**	
spark ed	**sharpness**		
sparred			
sparse	**slalom**		
	slander ed		
staff ed			
stance	**smartly**		
star red			
starch es	**sparkle** d		
starched	**sparkler**		
stark	**sparkling**		
start	**sparring**		
starve d	**spartan**		
suave	**starboard**		
	starchy -ier, -iest		
	stardom		
	starfish		
	starlight		
	starling		
	starring		
	starry		
	started		
	starter		
	starters		
	starting		
	startle d		
	startling		
	start-up / **start-up**		
	starving		
	stratum [strata]		
	surpass es		
	surpassed		

In these words you can hear the vowel sound **ar** as in **shark**

T

*
tar red
tart
task

trance

tsar / czar

* *
target ed
tarmac
tarnish es
tarnished
tarring
tartan

* * *
ptarmigan

targeted
targeting
tarpaulin

tiara

tomato es

tripartite

* * * *

V

*
vase
vast

* *
vantage
varnish es
varnished
vastly
vastness

* * *
vibrato

* * * *

Y

*
yard
yarn ed

* *
yardage
yardstick

* * *

* * * *

Z

*
czar / tsar

* *

* * *
Zimbabwe

* * * *

In these words you can hear the vowel sound **ar** as in shark

A

*

*air atmosphere /
manner / feeling /
tune
aired

*-err ed make a mistake

*heir next owner

for H . . .
see page 238 ▷

* *

affair

**aircraft
airfield
airline
airmail
airport
airtight
airway
airy** -ier, -iest

aware

Eire

heiress es
heirloom

* * *

**aerial
aerobic
aerodrome
aerofoil
aeroplane
aerosol
aerospace**

*airier more airy
airliner

*area field / space

awareness

* * * * * * *

**aerobatic
aerobatics
aerodynamic** ally
**aerodynamics
aeronautic
aeronautical
aeronautics**

air-condition ed
air-conditioning

aquarium s [aquaria]

B

*

*bare uncover (ed)
*bared uncovered

*bear animal
*bear carry
 [bore]
 [born / borne]

*-bird feathered animal

*blare d sound loudly
*-blur red go fuzzy
 d
*-bur bur oak
*-burr / bur prickly
 seedcase / rough edge
*-burred prickly / rough

* *

**barefoot
barely**
*baring uncovering

bearer
*bearing carrying
beware

*blaring sounding
 loudly
*-blurring going fuzzy

*-burring removing the
 burrs

* * *

barium

bewaring

* * * *

Bulgaria

C

*

cairn
*care attention /
 worry / look after
*cared looked after

chair ed

*-cur worthless dog
*-curd soft, fatty
 substance

*-Kurd Kurdish person

* *

**carefree
careful** ly
**careless
carer
caring**

**chairlift
chairman** [chairmen]

compare d

* * *

canary -ies
**carefully
carelessly
caretaker**

**chairperson
chairwoman**
[chairwomen]

**comparing
contrary**

-Kurdistan

* * * *

In these words you can hear the vowel sound air as in bear

D

*
dare d

* *
dairy -ies
daring

declare d
despair ed

* * *
declaring

* * * *

E

*
**air atmosphere /
manner / feeling / tune
aired

**-err ed make a mistake

**heir next owner

* *
aircraft
airfield
airline
airmail
airport
airtight
airway
airy -ier, -iest

éclair

Eire

heiress es
heirloom

* * *
aerial
aerobic
aerodrome
aerofoil
aeroplane
aerosol
aerospace

**airier more airy
airliner

**area field / space

* * * * * * *
aerobatic
aerobatics
aerodynamic ally
aerodynamics
aeronautic
aeronautical
aeronautics

aquarium

for H . . .
see page 238 ▷

for I . . .
see page 239 ▷

In these words you can hear the vowel sound air as in bear

F

*	* *	* * *	* * * *
*fair just / funfair / market / fine weather / light in colour	*faerie / faery fairy / fairyland	fairytale	
*fairs more than one fair	fairground		
*fare charge for ride / food / get on	fairly		
*fared did fare	fairness		
*fares more than one fare / gets on	*fairy -ies magical tiny person		
	farewell		
	faring		
*flair natural skill	flaring		
*flare burst into flame / get wider at the bottom	forbear		
flared	[forbore]		
	[forborne]		
*-fur coat of animal	*-furry -ier, -iest feeling like fur		
*-furred coated with fur	pharoah		
*-furs coats of animals			
*-furze gorse			

G

*	* *	* * *	* * * *
glare d	garish		gregarious
	glaring		

H

*	* *	* * *	* * * *
*hair thread-like growth	hairbrush es	haircutting	hilarious
*haired having hair	haircut	hairdresser	
*hare animal	hairdo	hairdryer / hairdrier	Hungarian
*hared ran like a hare	hairline	hairstyling	
	hairpin		
*heir next owner	hairspray		
*-her she / belonging to her	hairstyle		
*Herr [Herren] German for 'Mr'	hairy -ier, -iest		
	haring		
	heiress es		
	heirloom		
	*-heron large bird		
	*Herren title for German men		

238

In these words you can hear the vowel sound *air* as in bear

I

*

* *

impair ed

* * *

* * * * *

invariably

for E . . .
see page 237

L

*

lair

* *

* * *

* * * *

M

*

*mare female horse
*mayor head of town
or city

*-myrrh fragrant oil
or gum

* *

mayoress es

* * *

* * * *

malaria

P

*

*pair set of two / get
or put together in twos
paired
*pare d trim / peel

*pear fruit
*-per for each

prayer

*-purr ed sound of
happy cat

* *

*pairing making pairs
parent
*paring trimming /
peeling

pharaoh

pierrot

prairie
prepare d

*-purring sounding like
a happy cat

* * *

parenthood

pierrot

preparing

* * * *

In these words you can hear the vowel sound air as in bear

R

*	**	***	****
rare	**rarely**	**rarity** -ies	
	rarer		
	rarest	**repairing**	
	repair ed		

S

*	**	***	****
scarce	**scarcely**	**scarcity** -ies	
scare d	**scarecrow**		
	scaring	**shareholder**	
share d	**scary** -ier, -iest		
		sparingly	
snare d	**shareware**		
***spare** extra / give /	**sharing**		
keep from giving			
***spared** did spare	**snaring**		
*-**spur** projecting part /			
urge on	**sparing**		
*-**spurred** urged on	**squaring**		
square d	**staircase**		
	staring		
***stair** step or steps			
***stare** d look fixedly			
*-**stir** red move around			
swear			
[swore]			
[sworn]			

In these words you can hear the vowel sound air as in **bear**

T

*	**	***	****
*tare weed / weight of empty vehicle or container	**tearing**	**thereafter** **thereupon**	
	thereby **therefore** **therein** **thereof** **therewith**		
*tear rip [tore] [torn]			
*their belonging to them			
*theirs something belonging to them			
*there to/in that place / also used with 'is', 'are', 'was', 'were' and other forms of 'to be'			
there'd			
there'll			
*there's there is / there has			
*they're they are			

V

*	**	***	**** **
	vary -ies	**variant**	**variability**
	varied	**various**	**variable**
		varying	**variation**
			vicarious ly

W

*	**	***	****
*ware products for sale / pottery	**warehouse**	**whereabouts**	
	wary -ier,-iest	**whereupon**	
		wherever	
*wear carry on body / get worse with use [wore] [worn]	**wearing**		
	werewolf [werewolves]		
*-were form of verb 'to be'	**whereas**		
	whereby		
	wherefore		
	wherein		
*where to/in which place			

In these words you can hear the vowel sound *air* as in *bear*

241

A

*

*-**air** atmosphere /
manner / feeling /
tune
-**aired**

*-err ed make a mistake

*-heir next owner

for H . . .
see page 247 ▷

* *

absurd

adjourn ed

-**affair**
affirm ed

-**aircraft**
-**airfield**
-**airline**
-**airmail**
-**airport**
-**airtight**
-**airway**
-**airy** -ier, -iest

alert

assert
astern

avert

-**aware**

-Eire

-heiress es
-heirloom

* * *

-**aerial**
-**aerobic**
-**aerodrome**
-**aerofoil**
-**aeroplane**
-**aerosol**
-**aerospace**

*-**airier** more airy
-**airliner**

allergic
alternate

*-**area** field / space

assertion
assertive

attorney

-**awareness**

* * * * * * *

absurdity -ies
adverbial ly
adversity -ies
advertisement

-**aerobatic**
-**aerobatics**
-**aerodynamic** ally
-**aerodynamics**
-**aeronautic**
-**aeronautical**
-**aeronautics**

affirmative ly

-**air-condition** ed
-**air-conditioning**

alternative ly

-**aquarium** s [aquaria]

assertiveness

In these words you can hear the vowel sound **er** as in **bird**

B

*	**	***	****
*-**bare** uncover(ed)	-**barefoot**	-**barium**	-**Bulgaria**
*-**bared** uncovered	-**barely**		
	*-**baring** uncovering	-**bewaring**	
*-**bear** animal			
*-**bear** carry	-**bearer**	**burglary** -ies	
[bore]	*-**bearing** carrying	**burgundy** -ies	
[born / borne]	-**beware**	**bursary** -ies	
***berth** bunk / place			
for ship at quay	**birdie**		
berthed	**birdseed**		
	birthday		
birch es	**birthplace**		
birched			
***bird** feathered	*-**blaring** sounding		
animal	loudly		
***birth** delivery of	***blurring** going fuzzy		
child / origin	**blurry** -ier, -iest		
*-**blare** d sound loudly	**burden** ed		
***blur** red go fuzzy	***burger** sandwich		
blurt	***burgher** citizen		
	burglar		
***bur** bur oak	**burka / burqa**		
burn ed	**burlap**		
[burnt]	**burly** -ier, -iest		
***burr / bur** prickly	**Burma**		
seedcase / rough edge	**burner**		
***burred** prickly / rough	**burning**		
burst	***burring** removing the		
[burst]	burrs		
	bursar		

> **Here 'er' is neutral, like the 'er' in 'perhaps'.**
>
> Bermuda

C

*

-cairn
*-care attention / worry / look after
*-cared looked after

-chair ed
chirp ed
church es
churn ed

cirque

*cur worthless dog
*curb ed restrain
*curd soft, fatty substance
curl ed
curse d
curt
curve d

*kerb edge of pavement

kirk

*Kurd Kurdish person

* *

-carefree
-careful ly
-careless
-carer
-caring

certain

-chairlift
-chairman [chairmen]
churchyard

circle d
circling
circuit
circus es

clergy

*colonel army officer
-compare d
concern ed
confer red
confirm ed
conserve d
converge d
converse d
convert
courteous

curdle d
curdling
curfew
curling
curly -ier, -iest
cursed
cursing
cursor
curtail ed
curtain ed
curtsey s / curtsy -ies
curtseyed / curtsied
curving
curvy -ier, -iest

*kernel seed in nut

* * *

-canary -ies
-carefully
-carelessly
-caretaker

certainly
certainty -ies
certify -ies
certified

-chairperson
-chairwoman
-[chairwomen]

circular
circulate
circumscribe d
circumstance

clergyman [clergymen]

commercial ly
-comparing
concerning
conferring
conserving
-contrary
convergent
converging
conversely
conversing
conversion
courteous
courtesy -ies

curlier
curliest
curvature

Kurdistan

* * * * *

circuitous
circulating
circulation
circulatory
circumcision
circumference
circumnavigate
circumscribing
circumstances
circumstantial

commercially
conservatism
conservative
conservatory -ies
convertible

Here the 'er' is neutral.
certificate

---

for Qu . . .
see page 251

In these words you can hear the vowel sound er as in bird

D

*

-**dare** d

dearth

dirge
dirt

* *

-**dairy** -ies
-**daring**

-**declare** d
defer red
*desert leave
deserve d
-**despair** ed
*dessert sweet dish
deter red

dirty -ies
dirtied
dirty -ier, -iest
discern ed
disperse d
disturb ed
diverge d
diverse
divert

* * *

-**declaring**
deferring
deserted
deserter
deserving
detergent
determine d
deterring

dirtier
dirtiest
dispersing
dispersion
disservice
disturbance
diverging
diverted

* * * * * *

determination
determining

discernible
diversification
diversify -ies
diversified
diversity

E

*

*-**air** atmosphere /
manner / feeling / tune
-**aired**

earl
***earn** ed get money
by working
earth ed

***err** ed make a mistake

*-**heir** next owner

irk ed

urge d
***urn** vase / vessel

for H . . .
see page 247 ▷

for I . . .
see page 247 ▷

* *

-aircraft
-airfield
-airline
-airmail
-airport
-airtight
-airway
-airy -ier, -iest

early -ier, -iest
earnest
earnings
earthquake
earthworm
earthy -ier, -iest

-**éclair**

-**Eire**

emerge d

exert

-heiress es
-heirloom

irksome

urban
urchin
urgent
urging

* * *

-aerial
-aerobic
-aerodrome
-aerofoil
-aeroplane
-aerosol
-aerospace

*-**airier** more airy
-airliner

*-**area** field / space

earlier
earliest
earnestness
earthenware

emergence
emerging

encircle d
encircling

eternal ly

excursion
exertion
external ly

urgency
urgently

* * * * * * *

-aerobatic
-aerobatics
-aerodynamic ally
-aerodynamics
-aeronautic
-aeronautical
-aeronautics

emergency -ies

ergonomics

eternally
eternity

exterminate
exterminating
extermination
externally

In these words you can hear the vowel sound **er** as in **bird**

F

*

*-**fair** just / funfair /
market / fine weather /
light in colour
*-**fairs** more than one
fair
*-**fare** charge for ride /
food / get on
*-**fared** did fare
*-**fares** more than one
fare / gets on

fern

*-**fir** tree
firm ed
*-**firs** more than one fir
first

*-**flair** natural skill
*-**flare** burst into
flame / get wider at
the bottom
-**flared**
flirt

*-**fur** coat of animal
furl ed
*-**furred** coated with fur
*-**furs** coats of animals
*-**furze** gorse

* *

*-**faerie / faery** fairy /
fairyland
-**fairground**
-**fairly**
-**fairness**
*-**fairy** -ies magical
tiny person
-**farewell**
-**faring**

ferment
fertile
fervour

firmly
firstly

-**flaring**

-**forbear**
[forbore]
[forborne]

furnace
furnish es
furnished
furring
*-**furry** -ier, -iest like fur
further ed
furtive

-pharaoh

* * *

-**fairytale**

fertilise d
ze

fleur-de-lis
flirtation

furniture
furthermore

* * * * *

fermentation
fertilisation
zation
fertiliser
zer
fertilising
zing
fertility

fraternity -ies

for th . . .
see page 253

G

*

germ

girl
girth

-**glare** d

jerk ed

* *

gerbil
German

gherkin

girder
girdle d
girlfriend
girlie / girly

-**glaring**

gurgle d
gurgling

jerkin
*-**jersey** woollen jumper
*-**Jersey** Channel Island

journal
journey ed

* * *

Germany
germicide
germinate

journalist

* * * * * *

germicidal
germinating
germination

-**gregarious**

journalism
journalistic ally

246

In these words you can hear the vowel sound **er** as in **bird**

*

*-**hair** thread-like
growth
*-**haired** having hair
*-**hare** animal
*-**hared** ran like a hare

***heard** did hear
***hearse** funeral car
*-**heir** next owner
***her** she / belonging
to her
herb
***herd** group of
animals
*-**Herr** [Herren] German
for 'Mr'
***hers** her property
***hertz** measure of
frequency in cycles
per second

hurl ed
hurt
[hurt]
***hurts** does hurt

* *

-**hairbrush** es
-**haircut**
-**hairdo**
-**hairline**
-**hairpin**
-**hairspray**
-**hairstyle**
-**hairy** -ier, -iest
-**haring**

-**heiress** es
-**heirloom**
herbal
herdsman [herdsmen]
hermit
*-**heron** large bird
*-**Herren** title for
German men

hurdle d
hurdling
hurtful ly
hurtle d
hurtling

* * *

-**haircutting**
-**hairdresser**
-**hairdryer / hairdrier**
-**hairstyling**

herbaceous
herbivore

hurtfully

* * * *

-**hilarious**

-**Hungarian**

Here 'er' is neutral, like the 'er' in 'perhaps'.

herself

I

*

irk ed

* *

immerse d
-**impair** ed

incur red
inert
infer red
infirm
insert
inter red
invert

irksome

* * *

immersion
imperfect

incurring
inertia
inferring
insertion
internal ly
interpret ed
interring
inversion

* * * * *

impermeable
impersonal
impersonate
impersonating
impersonation
impertinent
impervious

infirmary -ies
interminable
internally
interpolate
interpolating
interpretation
interpreted
interpreter
interpreting
-**invariably**

for E . . .
see page 245

J

*
germ

jerk ed

* *
gerbil
German

jerkin
*jersey woollen
jumper
*Jersey Channel
Island

journal
journey ed

* * *
Germany
germicide
germinate

journalist

* * * * * *
germicidal
germinating
germination

journalism
journalistic ally

K

*
*-cared looked after

*curd soft, fatty
substance

kerb ed

kirk

knurl ed

*Kurd Kurdish person

* *
*colonel army officer

*kernel seed in nut

* * *

* * * *

◁ for C . . .
see page 244

for Qu . . .
see page 251 ▷

L

*
-lair

learn ed
[learnt]

lurch es
lurched
lurk ed

* *
learned
learner
learning

* * *

* * * *

In these words you can hear the vowel sound **er** as in **bird**

M

*

*-**mare** female horse
*-**mayor** head of town
 or city

merge d

mirth

***myrrh** fragrant oil
or gum

* *

-**mayoress** es

merchant
mercy -ies
merger
merging
mermaid

murder ed
murky -ier, -iest
murmur ed

* * *

maternal ly

mercenary -ies
merchandise
merciful ly
merciless
***mercury** liquid metal
***Mercury** planet

murderer
***murderess** es female
 murderer
***murderous** capable of
killing
murmuring

* * * *

-**malaria**
maternally
maternity

mercenary -ies
mercifully
mercurial

N

*

knurl ed

nerve

nurse d

* *

nervous
nervy -ier, -iest

nursing
nurture

* * *

nasturtium

nervously
nervousness

nursery -ies

* * * *

O

*

* *

observe d

occur red

* * *

alternate

observance
observant
observer
observing

occurring

* * * * *

alternative

observable
observatory -ies

In these words you can hear the vowel sound er as in bird

P

*

*-**pair** set of two / get
or put together in twos
-**paired**
*-**pare**d trim / peel

*-**pear** fruit
*-**pearl** jewel
*-**per** for each
perches
perched
permed
pert

-**prayer**

purged
*-**purl** knitting stitch
*-**purr**ed sound of
happy cat
purse

* *

*-**pairing** making pairs
-**parent**
*-**paring** trimming /
peeling

perfect
perfumed
perky-ier, -iest
permit
Persia
Persian
person
perspex
perverse
pervert

-**pharaoh**

-**pierrot**

-**prairie**
preferred
-**prepare**d
preserved

purchased
purple
purpose
*-**purring** sounding like
a happy cat

* * *

-**parenthood**

percolate
perfectly
perforate
perfuming
permanent
permeable
permeate
pernicious
perpetrate
persecute
persevered
personally
personnel
pertinent
perversion

-**pierrot**

preferring
-**preparing**
preserving

purchaser
purchasing
purposefully

* * * * *

percolating
percolator
perforating
perforation
permanently
permeable
perpendicular
perpetuity
persecuting
persecution
persevering
personality-ies
personally
perspiration

preservative
proverbially

purposefully

In these words 'er' and 'ur' are pronounced as neutral sounds, like the 'er' in 'persist'.

P*ER*SISTENT WORDS

perceive d	perfect ionist	permission	persistence	persuasive
percent	perform ed	permit ted	persistent ly	pervade
percentage	performance	permitting	personification	pervading
perceptible	performer	pernicious	personify -ies	pervasive
perception	performing	peroxide	personified	purport
perceptive	perhaps	perpetual ly	personal (?)	pursuant
perceptual ly	perimeter	perplex es	perspective	pursue d
percussion	peripheral ly	perplexed	perspire d	pursuer
percussive	periphery -ies	perplexing	perspiring	pursuit
perfection	permissible	persist	persuade	
			persuasion	

for pre . . .
see page 82

In these words you can hear the vowel sound **er** as in **bird**

Q

*	**	***	****
quirk	quirky -ier, -iest		

R

*	**	***	***** *
-rare	-rarely	-rarity -ies	returnable
	-rarer		reverberate
	-rarest	recurring	reverberating
		recursion	reversible
	recur red	referral	
	refer red	referring	
	rehearse d	rehearsal	
	-repair ed	rehearsing	
	research es	-repairing	
	researched	researcher	
	reserve d	reserving	
	return ed	returning	
	reverse d	reversal	
	revert	reversing	

In these words you can hear the vowel sound **er** as in **bird**

S

*

cirque

-**scarce**
-**scare** d
scourge d
scurf

search es
searched
*__serf__ slave
*__serge__ woollen cloth
serve d

-**share** d
shirk ed
shirt

Sir

skirt

slur red

smirk ed

-**snare** d

*-**spare** extra / give /
keep from giving
*-**spared** did spare
sperm
*__spur__ projecting part /
urge on
spurn ed
*__spurred__ urged on
spurs
spurt

-**square** d
squirm ed
squirt

*-**stair** step or steps
*-**stare** d look fixedly
stern
*__stir__ red move around

surd
*__surf__ foaming sea
surfed
*__surge__ d rush forward

-**swear**
[swore]
[sworn]
swerve d
swirl ed

252

* *

certain

circle d
circling
circuit
circus es

-**scarcely**
-**scarecrow**
-**scaring**
-**scary** -ier, -iest
scurvy

searching
searchlight
sermon
serpent
servant
server
service d
serviette
servile
serving

-**shareware**
-**sharing**
sherbet

sirloin

skirmish es
skirmished

-**snaring**

-**sparing**
spurring

-**squaring**

-**staircase**
-**staring**
sterling
stirring
sturdy -ier, -iest

submerge d
surface d
surfboard
surfer
surfing
surgeon
surging
surly -ier, -iest
surname
*__surplice__ church gown
*__surplus__ es excess
survey

* * *

certainly
certainty -ies
certify -ies
certified

circular
circulate
circumscribe d
circumstance

-**scarcity** -ies

Serbia
servicing
serviette

-**shareholder**

-**sparingly**

submerging
suburban
surgery -ies
surgical ly

* * * * *

circuitous
circulating
circulation
circulatory
circumcision
circumference
circumnavigate
circumscribing
circumstances
circumstantial

serviceable

superfluous
surgically

Here 'er' is neutral, like the 'er' in 'perhaps'.

S**UR**PRISING WORDS

surmount
surpass es
surpassed
surpassing
surprise d
surprising
surprisingly
surrender ed

surround
surroundings
surveillance
surveying
surveyor
survival
survive d
survivor

In these words you can hear the vowel sound **er** as in **bird**

T

*

*-**tare** weed / weight
or empty vehicle or
container

*-**tear** rip
[tore]
[torn]
term ed
*-**tern** bird
terse

*-**their** belonging
to them
*-**theirs** something
belonging to them
*-**there** to/in that
place / also used with
'is', 'are', 'was', 'were'
and other forms of
'to be'
-**there'd**
-**there'll**
*-**there's** there is /
there has
therm
*-**they're** they are
third
thirst

turf ed
Turk
*-**turn** ed change
direction
turps

twirl ed

* *

-**tearing**

-**thereby**
-**therefore**
-**therein**
-**thereof**
-**therewith**
thermal ly
thermos
thirdly
thirsty -ier, -iest
thirteen th
thirty -ies
Thursday

*-**turban** head-covering
*-**turbine** engine
turbot
*-**Turkey** country
*-**turkey** bird
Turkish
turmoil
turner
turning
turnip
turnout
turnpike
turnstile
turquoise
turtle

* * *

terminal ly
terminate
terminus es [termini]
ternary
tertiary

-**thereafter**
-**thereupon**
thermally
thermostat
thirtieth

turbojet
turbulence
turbulent
turmeric
turnover
turpentine

* * * * *

terminally
terminating
termination
terminology -ies

tubercular
tuberculin
tuberculosis

> Here 'er' is neutral, like the 'er' in 'perhaps'.
>
> thermometer

U

*	**	***	****
earl	early -ier, -iest	earlier	ergonomics
*earn ed get money	earnest	earliest	
by working	earnings	earnestness	
earth ed	earthquake	earthenware	
	earthworm		
err ed	earthy -ier, -iest	**urgency**	
		urgently	
irk ed	irksome		
urge d	**urban**		
***urn** vase / vessel	**urchin**		
	urgent		
	urging		

V

*	**	***	***** *
verb	-**vary** -ies	-**variant**	-**variability**
verge d	-**varied**	-**various**	-**variable**
verse d		-**varying**	-**variation**
verve	**verbal** ly		
	verdict	**verbally**	**versatility**
	verger	**vermilion**	**vertically**
	verging	**vernier**	
	vermin	**versatile**	-**vicarious** ly
	version	**vertebra** s / -ae	**virtually**
	versus	**vertebral**	**virtuosity**
	vertex [vertices]	**vertebrate**	**virtuoso** s
		vertical ly	
	virgin	**vertices**	
	virtual ly		
	virtue	**virginal**	
		virtually	
		virtuous	

In these words you can hear the vowel sound **er** as in **bird**

W

*

*-ware products for
sale / pottery

*-wear carry on body /
get worse with use
[wore]
[worn]
*were form of verb
'to be'
weren't

*-where to/in which
place
*whirl ed spin around
*whirr / whir sound
*whirred did whirr
*whorl turn of spiral
*whorled shaped in
a spiral

*word unit of meaning
work ed
*world the earth
worm ed
worse
worst
worth

* *

-warehouse
-wary -ier, -iest

-wearing
werewolf [werewolves]

-whereas
-whereby
-wherefore
-wherein
whirlpool
whirlwind
whirring

workbench
workbook
worker
workforce
workhouse
wording
working
workload
workman [workmen]
workout
workplace
workroom
worksheet
workshop
worktop
worldly -ier, -iest
worldwide
worsen ed
worship ped
worthless
worthwhile
worthy -ies

* * *

-wherabouts
-whereupon
-wherever

workable
working-class
workmanlike
workmanship
workstation
workwoman
[workwomen]
worldlier
worldliest
worshipper
worshipping

* * * *

workaholic

Y

*

-year
yearn ed

* *

yearning

* * *

* * * *

In these words you can hear the vowel sound **er** as in **bird**

A

*

*all every one

*aught anything at all

*awe fear and wonder
*awed made to feel
 awe
*awl boring tool

*oar rowing blade

*-odd unusual

*or marks choice
*ore mineral

*ought should

**

aboard
abroad
absorb ed

accord

adore d
adorn ed

afford

almost
alright
also
*altar holy table
*alter ed change
although
always

appal led
applaud
applause

ashore
assault
assure d

auburn
auction ed
audit
*auger tool
*augur suggest for
 the future
*August month
*august impressive
aura s / -ae
*aural ly by the ear
austere
author
autumn

award
awesome / awsome
*awful ly dreadful
awkward

*-offal less valuable meat

*orally by the mouth
orbit ed
orchard
orchid
ordeal
order ed
organ
orgy -ies
ornate
orphan ed

***

abortion
absorber
absorbing
absorption

accordance
according

adoring
adsorption

albeit
almighty
already
alternate

appalling

assorted
assortment
assurance
assuring

audible
audience
auditor
auditory
*aurally by the ear
aurora
Austria
authentic ally
authorise d
 ze
autism
autistic ally
autograph ed

awfully

*orally by the mouth
oration
orbital
orbited
orbiting
orchestra
orchestral
orchestrate
ordeal
ordering
orderly -ies
ordinal
ordinary
organic ally
organise d
 ze
organist
orgasm
☛

**** *****

accordingly
accordion

adorable

affordable

alteration
alternating
alternative ly
alternator
altogether

auditorium s [auditoria]
auditory
authentically
authorising
 zing
authority -ies
autistically
autobiographical ly
autobiography -ies
autocracy -ies
autocratic ally
automatic ally
automation
automobile
autonomic
autonomous
auxiliary -ies

orchestrating
orchestration
ordinarily
ordinary
organically
organisation al
 zation al
organiser
 zer
organising
 zing
organism
oriental
orientate
orientation
ornithologist
ornithology
orthographic ally
orthography -ies

for H . . .
see page 261 ▷

In these words you can hear the vowel sound **or** as in **horse**

A

for H . . .
see page 261 ▷

* * *
orient
ornament
orthodox

B

*

****bald** lacking hair
balk / baulk ed
****ball** round object /
dance
****balled** made into a
ball
baulk / balk ed
****bawl** yell
****bawled** did yell

****boar** male pig
****board** plank / daily
meals / committee
****boor** rough fellow
****bore** drill / drilled
hole / carried / fail to
interest / tide-wave
****bored** drilled /
lacking an interest
****born** delivered at birth
****borne** carried
bought

brawl ed
brawn
broad
brought

* *

ballpoint
ballroom
balsa
balti
Baltic
basalt
bauxite

because
befall
[befell]
[befallen]
before
besought

****boarder** person who
pays for food and bed
boarding
borax
****border** edge / frontier
bordered
boredom
boring
bourgeois

brawny -ier, -iest
broadcast
[broadcast]
broadly
broadside

* * *

befallen
beforehand

borderline

bourgeoisie

broadcaster
broadcasting

* * * *

borealis

In these words you can hear the vowel sound **or** as in **horse**

257

C

*

call ed
*caught got / trapped
*caulk ed fill gaps with fibre and tar
*cause bring about / reason
caused
*caw harsh bird cry
*cawed did caw
*caws does caw

chalk ed
*chord notes sounded together / string / term in geometry
chore

*clause words in sentence / part of written agreement
claw ed
*claws curved nails or limbs

*coarse rough
*cord string
*core central part / take out the core from
*cored did core
*cores more than one core
*cork bark of cork tree
corked
corm
corn
corned
*corps group
corpse
*course track / direction / part of meal / of course
coursed
*court enclosed area / friends of sovereign / seek favour

crawl ed

for Qu . . .
see page 266 ▷

* *

callback
calling
cauldron
causal ly
causing
caustic ally
caution ed
cautious

chlorate
chloric
chloride
chlorine
*choral for or by a choir
choroid
chortle d
chorus es
chorused

conform ed
cordial ly
cordless
corgi
corkscrew ed
corner ed
cornet
cornfield
cornflakes
*cornflour starch made from maize
*cornflower flowering plant
corporal
corporate
corpus es [corpora]
cortex es [cortices]
courgette
coursework
courting
courtroom
courtship
courtyard

crawling

*-coral substance formed from bones of sea creatures

* * *

causally
causation
caustically
cautiously

chlorinate
chloroplast

conformist
cordial ly
corduroy
cormorant
cornea
corneal
cornerstone

*cornflower flowering plant
corpora
corporal ly
corporate
courtier

* * * * *

causality
caustically

chlorinating
chlorination

conformity
coordinate
coordinating
coordination
coordinator
cordially
corporally
corporation

In these words you can hear the vowel sound **or** as in **horse**

D

*

daub ed
daunt
dawn ed

door

*draw pull / sketch
[drew]
[drawn]
*drawer sliding
container
drawl ed

dwarf ed

* *

daughter
daunting
dauntless
dawdle d
dawdling

deform ed
deport

distort
distraught
divorce d

doorbell
doorknob
doormat
doorstep
doorway
dormant
dormouse [dormice]
dorsal

drawback
drawbridge
drawing

* * *

discordant
disorder ed
distortion
divorcee
divorcing

dormitory -ies

* * * *

daughter-in-law

deformity -ies
deplorable

disorganised
ze

dormitory -ies

E

*

for I . . .
see page 262 ▷

* *

endorse d
enforce d
*ensure d make certain
enthral led
escort

exalt
exhaust
explore d
export

*inshore near the shore
*insure d protect against
loss

* * *

endorsing
enforcement
enforcing
enormous
*ensuring making
certain
enthralling

exalted
exhausted
exhaustion
explorer
exploring

*insuring protecting
against loss

* * * * * * *

enormously

euphoria

exorbitant
extraordinarily
extraordinary

In these words you can hear the vowel sound **or** as in **horse**

259

F

*

fall
[fell]
[fallen]
false
fault
*faun goat-god
*fawn young deer /
colour / try to win
favour
*fawned did fawn

fiord / fjord

flaunt
*flaw ed fault
*floor ed levelled area

*-fond showing love
*for in place of /
to belong to / because
force d
ford
*fore front / leading
position
forge d
fork ed
form ed
*fort fortress
*forth forward
*fought contested
*four 4
*fourth 4th

fraud
fraught

for th . . .
see page 268 ▷

**

falcon
fallen
falling
fallout
falsehood
falter ed
faulty -ier, -iest

fiord / fjord

flawless
flora
floral
fluoride
fluorine

*forbear hold back
[forbore]
[forborne]
forceful ly **forc**
forceps
forcing
forearm
*forebear / forbear
ancestor
forecast
[forecast]
foreground
forehand
foreleg
foreman [foremen]
foremost
forename
foresee
[foresaw]
[foreseen]
foresight
foreskin
forestall ed
foretell
[foretold]
forewarn ed
*foreword preface
forfeit
forging
forgo / forego
[forwent / forewent]
[forgone / foregone]
forlorn
formal ly
format ted
former
forming
*forte loud / strength
fortnight
fortress es
fortune
*forty 40

***

falsify -ies
falsified
falsity

fluorescence
fluorescent

forcefully
forcible
forcibly
forecaster
forefather
forefinger
forerunner
forever
forgery
formalise d
ze
*formally officially
formation
formative
formatted
formatting
*formerly previously
formula s [formulae]
formulate
forthcoming
fortieth
fortify -ies
fortitude
fortunate

fraudulent

* * * * **

fluorescence
fluorescent
fluoridation /
fluoridisation
zation

foreseeable
forget-me-not
formality -ies
formidable
formulating
formulation
forsythia s
fortification
fortuitous ly
fortunately

Here the 'or' is neutral, like 'or' in 'forget'.

F*OR*GOTTEN WORDS

forbid	forget-me-not
[forbade / forbad]	forgetting
[forbidden]	forgive
forbidding	[forgave]
forensic	[forgiven]
forgave	forgiveness
forget ting	forgiving
[forgot]	forsake
[forgotten]	[forsook]
forgetful ly	[forsaken]
forgetfulness	forsaking

260

In these words you can hear the vowel sound **or** as in **horse**

F

for th . . .
see page 268 ▷

**
forum
***forward** s onward
fourteen th

Fräulein

G

*
***gall** cheek / bitterness/
sore / swelling
***Gaul** ancient region
of Europe
gaunt
gauze

***gnaw** keep biting
***gnawed** did gnaw

gore d
gorge d
gorse

jaunt
jawed

*-**nod** ded move head
down and up
***nor** and not

**
galling
galore
gaudy -ier, -iest
gauntlet

Georgian

glory -ies
gloried

gorgeous
gorging
goring

jaunty -ier, -iest
jawing

Jordan

***
Gibraltar

glorify -ies
glorified
glorious

****
Jordanian

H

*
***hall** large room /
passage
halt
***haul** drag /
amount gained
hauled
haunch es
haunt
***haw** hawthorn berry
hawk ed

***hoar** white
***hoard** store
***hoarse** rough and
husky
***horde** gang / tribe
horn ed
***horse** animal

***whore** prostitute
***whored** used prostitutes

**
halter
haughty -ier, -iest
haulage
haunches
haunted
hawthorn

hoarding
hormone
hornblende
hornet
horseback
horsehair
horseman [horsemen]
horsepower
horseshoe

whoring

***
haughtily

horsemanship
horsepower
horsewoman
[horsewomen]

****
historian

horticultural
horticulture

In these words you can hear the vowel sound or as in horse

I

*

* *
*ensure d   make certain

ignore d

implore d
import

indoors
indorse / endorse d
inform ed
*inshore   near the shore
instal led / install ed
*insure d   protect
against loss

◁ for E . . .
see page 259

* * *
*ensuring   making certain

immortal ly
importance
important

indorsing / endorsing
informal ly
informant
informer
installing
instalment /
installment
insurance
*insuring   protecting
against loss

* * * * *

immortality
immortally

inaugural
inauguration
incorporate d
incorporation
informally
informative

J

*
jaunt
jaw ed

◁ for dr . . .
see page 259

* *
jaunty -ier, -iest
jawing

Jordan

* * *

* * * *
Jordanian

K

*

◁ for C . . .
see page 258

for Qu . . .
see page 266 ▷

* *
Koran / Qur'an

* * *

* * * *

> **Here the 'or' is neutral, like 'or' in 'forget'.**
> Korea   Korean

In these words you can hear the vowel sound **or** as in **horse**

L

*
laud praise highly
launch es
launched
law state regulations
lawn

lord ruler
Lord God / titled peer
lore inherited tradition

* *
launcher
launder ed
launderette
laundry -ies
laurel
lawful ly
lawyer

lordship

* * *
laudable
launderette
laureate
lawfully

* * * * *
laborious ly

M

*
mall public walk /
walk lined with shops
malt
-maul ed handle
roughly / heavy mallet
mauve

-moll gangster's girl
moor open land /
fasten to land or
to buoy
more additional /
a larger amount
morn morning
Morse
mourn show sadness
at loss or death
mourned

* *
Malta

moorland
morning before
midday
morpheme
morphine

morsel
mortal ly
mortar
mortgage d
mortice d /
mortise d
mourner
mournful ly
mourning showing
sadness at loss or
death

* * *
Majorca
marauder
marauding

Minorca
misfortune

moreover
mortally
mortgaging
mournfully

* * * *
memorial

mortality

N

*
gnaw keep biting
gnawed did gnaw

-knot ted tied fastening /
hard part of wood / sea
mile (per hour)

naught / nought zero

-nod ded move head
down and up
nor and not
norm
north
-not used in denial,
negation, refusal
nought / naught zero

* *
-knotty -ier, iest full of
knots

naughty -ier, -iest
badly behaved

normal ly
Norman
north-east
northern
northward /
northwards
north-west
Norway

* * *
naughtier
naughtiest
naughtiness
nausea
nauseous
nautical ly

normalise d
ze
normally
northeaster
northerner
northernmost
northwester
Norwegian

* * * * *
nautically

normalising
zing
normalisation
zation
normality
notorious

In these words you can hear the vowel sound or as in **horse**

263

O

*	**	***	**** *****
*all every one	almost	albeit	alteration
	alright	almighty	alternating
*aught anything at all	also	already	alternative ly
	*altar holy table	alternate	alternator
*awe fear and wonder	*alter ed change		altogether
*awed made to feel awe	although	audible	
*awl boring tool	always	audience	auditorium s [auditoria]
		auditor	auditory
*oar rowing blade	auburn	auditory	authentically
	auction ed	*aurally by the ear	authorising
*-odd unusual	audit	aurora	zing
	*auger tool	Austria	authority -ies
*or marks choice	*augur suggest for the	authentic ally	autobiographical ly
orb	future	authorise d	autobiography -ies
*ore mineral	*August month	ze	autocracy -ies
	*august impressive	autograph ed	autocratic ally
*ought should	aura s / -ae		automatic ally
	*aurally by the ear	awfully	automation
	austere		automobile
	author	*orally by the mouth	autonomic
	autumn	oration	autonomous
		orbital	auxiliary -ies
	awesome / awsome	orbited	
	*awfully dreadful	orbiting	orchestrating
	awkward	orchestra	orchestration
		orchestral	ordinarily
	*-offal less valuable	orchestrate	ordinary
	meat	ordeal	organically
		ordering	organisation al
	*orally by the mouth	orderly -ies	zation al
	orbit ed	ordinal	organiser
	orchard	ordinary	zer
	orchid	organic ally	organising
	ordeal	organise d	zing
	order ed	ze	organism
	organ	organist	oriental
	orgy -ies	orgasm	orientate
	ornate	orient	orientation
	orphan ed	ornament al	ornamental
		orphanage	ornithologist
		orthodox	ornithology
			orthodoxy -ies
			orthographic ally
			orthography -ies

for H . . .
see page 261

In these words you can hear the vowel sound or as in horse

P

*

paunch es
*pause brief gap /
  hesitate
paused
*paw foot of animal
*pawed examined by
  paw
pawn
*pawned left in return
  for loan
*paws feet of animal

*-pod ded form pods /
  casing
*-pond pool
*poor badly off
porch es
*pore tiny hole /
  study closely
*pored studied
  closely
*pores tiny holes
pork
port
*pour flow out
*poured did pour

prawn

* *

palfrey
palsy
pausing
pawpaw

perform ed

poorly
poring
porous
porpoise
portal
porter
porthole
portion
portrait
portray ed
pouring

purport

* * *

performance
performer
performing

plausible

porcelain
porcupine
portable
portcullis es
portico
portrayal
Portugal
Portuguese

precaution
proportion

* * * * * *

pictorial ly

pornographic ally
pornography
portfolio

proportional ly
proportionate ly

Q

*
quart
***quarts** more than
one quart
***quartz** mineral

**
quarter
quartet
quartile

***
quarterly

****
quartermaster

R

*
***raw** untreated /
sore / chilly

***roar** loud noise
roared
***-rot** ted decay

wrath
***wrought** made to fit

**
raucous

recall ed
record
recourse
reform ed
report
resort
resource d
restore d
retort
reward

roaring

***
recorded
recorder
recording
reformer
reported
reporter
resourceful
resources
resourcing
restoring

******
reorganisation
zation
reorganise d
ze
reorganising
zing

In these words you can hear the vowel sound or as in horse

S

*

salt
*sauce tasty liquid /
rude talk
*saw looked at /
cutting tool
*sawed did saw
[sawn]

scald
scorch es
scorched
score d
scorn ed
scrawl ed

shawl
*shore coast
shored
shorn
short
shorts

small

snore d

*soar fly high
*soared flew high
*-sod turf
*sore painful
*sort group
*sought looked for
*source origin

spawn ed
spore
sport
sprawl ed

squawk ed

*stalk stem / hunt /
walk stiffly
stalked
stall ed
staunch es
staunched
*-stock ed supply
store d
*stork bird
storm
straw

*sure certain

swarm ed
*sword weapon
swore
sworn

* *

salty -ier, -iest
saucepan
saucer
saucy -ier, -iest
sauna
saunter ed
sawdust

scorer
scoring
scornful ly
scorpion

shoring
shortage
shorten ed
shortening
shorter
shortest
shortfall
shorthand
shortly
short-term

señor es

signor i

slaughter ed

smaller
smallest
smallpox
small-scale

snoring
snorkel

sportsman [sportsmen]
sporty -ier, -iest

stalker
*stalking hunting /
walking stiffly
stalling
stalwart
*-stocking ed leg covering
storage
storehouse
*storey floor
storing
stormy -ier, -iest
*story -ies tale
strawberry -ies

support
surely

swarthy -ier, -iest

* * *

saucily

scornfully
scorpion

shortcoming
shortening

signora s

sonorous

sorcerer
sorcery

sportswoman
[sportswomen]

strawberry -ies

supported
supporter
supporting

* * * * *

storyteller

subordinate
subordinating

In these words you can hear the vowel sound or as in horse

267

T

*	* *	* * *	* * * *
***talk** speak	**talking**	**talkative**	**tutorial**
talked	**taller**		
tall	**tallest**	**thesaurus** es [thesauri]	
***taught** instructed	**tawny** -ier, -iest	**thoughtfully**	
taunt			
***taut** tight	**thorax** es / -ces	**tornado** es	
	thoughtful ly	**torpedo** es	
thaw ed		**tortilla**	
thorn	**Torah**	**torturing**	
thought	**torment**		
thwart	**torsion**	**traumata**	
	torso s	**traumatic**	
***tor** hill	**tortoise**		
torch es	**torture** d		
torched	**Tory** -ies		
***tore** did tear	**toward**		
torn	**towards**		
***torque** turning			
force / necklace	**transform** ed		
*-**tot** young child /	**transport**		
small amount / add	**trauma** s [traumata]		

V

*	* *	* * *	* * * *
vase			**Victorian**
***vault** gymnastic leap /			**victorious**
underground room /			
arched roof			
*-**volt** unit of electrical			
force			

U

*	* *	* * *	* * * * *
	unborn	**undaunted**	euphoria
		unlawful ly	
			unfortunate ly
			unlawfully
			unorthodox

268   In these words you can hear the vowel sound **or** as in **horse**

W

*

*hoar white
*hoard store
*horde gang / tribe

*-rotted decay

*walked go in steps
walled
waltz es
waltzed
*war conflict
*ward part of
hospital / person
under legal protection
warmed
warmth
*warn caution
warned
warp ed
*warred waged war
wart

wharf [wharves]
*whore prostitute
*whored used
prostitutes

*-wok cooking pan
*wore was dressed in
*worn carried on the
body / worse for wear

wrath
*wrought made to fit

* *

walker
walking
wallflower
walnut
walrus es
warble d
warbler
warbling
warden
wardrobe
warfare
warhead
warlike
warmer
warmly
warning
warpath
warring
warship
wartime
water ed

whoring

withdraw
[withdrew]
[withdrawn]
withdrawal
withdrawn

* * *

wallflower
wallpaper ed
waterfall
waterfowl
waterproof ed
watershed
watertight
waterway
watery

withdrawal

* * * *

walkie-talkie
watercolour

Y

*

yawn ed

*yore ancient times
*your belonging to
you
*you're you are
yours

* *

Yorkshire
yourself
yourselves

* * *

* * * *

euphoria

In these words you can hear the vowel sound or as in horse

269

A

*	* *	* * *	* * * *
	ahoy!	**adjoining**	**avoidable**
	annoy ed	**annoyance**	
	anoint	**annoying**	
	appoint	**appointment**	
	avoid	**avoidance**	
		avoided	

B

*	* *	* * *	* * * *
boil ed	**boiler**	**boisterous**	
***boy** lad	**boiling**		
	boycott	**buoyancy**	
broil ed	**boyfriend**		
	boyhood		
***buoy** marker			
buoyed	**buoyant**		

C

*	* *	* * *	* * * *
choice	**cloister** ed		
coil ed	**coinage**		
***coin** money			
coined			
coy			
*quoin cornerstone			

for Qu . . .
see page 274 ▷

270   In these words you can hear the vowel sound oi as in oyster

D

*

* *

deploy ed
destroy ed
devoid

disloyal ly

doily -ies / **doyley** s

* * *

deployment
destroyer

disloyally
disloyalty

* * * *

disloyally
disloyalty

E

*

* *

embroil ed
employ ed

enjoy ed

exploit

* * *

embroider ed
employee
employer
employment

enjoying
enjoyment

* * * *

embroidery

enjoyable

F

*

foil ed

* *

foyer

Fraülein

* * *

Freudian

* * * *

271

In these words you can hear the vowel sound oi as in oyster

G

*

**

***

****

*groin part where
legs join body
*groyne low structure
built out into water

H

*

**

***

****

hoist

J

*

**

***

****

join ed
joint
joist
joy

joiner
joining
jointly
joyful ly
joyous

joinery
joyfully

In these words you can hear the vowel sound oi as in oyster

L

*
loin
loyal ly

* *
loyal ly
loyalist
loyalty -ies

* * *
loyalist
loyally
loyalty -ies

* * * *

M

*
moist

* *
moisture

* * *
moisturise d
       ze

* * * *
moisturiser
      zer
moisturising
      zing

N

*
noise

* *
noisy -ier, -iest

* * *
noisier
noisiest
noisily

* * * *

O

*
oil ed

for H . . .
see page 272

* *
oilfield
oilseed
oilstone
oily -ier, -iest
ointment

oyster

* * *

* * * *

In these words you can hear the vowel sound **oi** as in **oyster** **273**

P

*

ploy

point
poise d

* *

poignant
pointed
pointer
pointing
pointless
poison ed

* * *

pointedly
poisoner
poisonous

* * * *

Q

*
*coin money

*quoin cornerstone
quoit

* *

* * *

* * * *

R

*

royal ly

* *

recoil ed
rejoice d
rejoin ed

royal ly
royalty -ies

* * *

rejoicing

royally
royalty -ies

* * * *

274   In these words you can hear the vowel sound oi as in oyster

S

*

soiled

spoiled
[spoilt]

**

savoy

soya

***

sequoia

****

T

*

toiled
toyed

**

toilet

***

****

V

*

voiced
void

**

voicing
voyaged

***

voice-over
voyaging

****

In these words you can hear the vowel sound oi as in oyster

275

A

*	**	***	* * * * **
	abound	accountant	accountability
	about		accountable
		allowance	accountancy
	account		
		announcement	allowable
	allow	announcer	
	*allowed permitted	announcing	
	*aloud loud enough		
	to be heard	arousal	
		arousing	
	amount		
		astounded	
	announce d	astounding	
	around		
	arouse d		
	astound		

B

*	**	***	* * * *
blouse	bouncing	boundary -ies	bountifully
	bouncy -ier, -iest	bountiful ly	
*bough branch	boundary -ies		
bounce d	boundless		
bound	bounty -ies		
bout	bowel		
*bow bend / front	bower		
of ship			
bowel	brownie		
	browsing		
brow			
brown ed			
*brows more than			
one brow			
*browse d nibble /			
dip into books			

In these words you can hear the vowel sound ou as in owl

C

*

chow

cloud
clout
clown ed

couch es
couched
count
cow ed
cower ed

crouch es
crouched
crowd
crown ed

* *

cacao

chowder

cloudless
cloudy -ier, -iest

confound
*council group for
directing affairs
*counsel advice
counselled
countdown
counted
counter
countess es
counting
countless
county -ies
*coward person who
lacks courage
cowboy
cower ed
*cowered did cower
cowshed
cowslip

crowded

* * *

*councillor member of
a council
counselling
*counsellor person
who gives advice
countenance d
counteract
counterfeit
counterfoil
counterpart
counterpoint
countersink
[countersunk]
cowardice
cowardly

* * * * *

countenancing
counter-attack
counterexample

D

*

doubt
***dour** unsmiling
***douse / dowse** put
into water / put out
doused / dowsed
dowel led
***dower** property of
bride or widow
down ed
***dowse** d use divining
rod

drought
drown ed

* *

denounce d
devour ed
devout

discount
dismount

doubtful ly
doubtless
***dousing / dowsing**
putting into water /
putting out
dowdy -ier, -iest
dowel led
dowelling
downcast
downfall
downhill
downland
download
downright
downstairs
downstream
downturn
downward
downwards
dowry -ies
dowser
***dowsing** using
divining rod

drowsy -ier, -iest

* * *

denouncing

doubtfully
dowelling

E

*

* *

empower ed

endow ed

* * *

empower ed

encounter ed

* * * *

In these words you can hear the vowel sound ou as in owl

F

*

flounce d
*flour ground grain
*flower ed blossom

*foul dirty
fouled
found
*fowl bird

Frau [Frauen]
frown ed

for th . . .
see page 283

* *

flouncing
flounder ed
*flower ed blossom
flowerpot

*fouler dirtier
*founded established
founder
*foundered sank /
collapsed
foundry -ies
fountain
*fowler bird hunter

Frauen

* * *

flowerpot

foundation

* * * *

G

*

gouge d
gown

grouch es
grouched
ground
grouse [grouse]
groused
growl ed

* *

glower ed

gouging

grouching
grouchy -ier, -iest
grounding
groundless
groundsel
groundwork
grousing

* * *

* * * *

H

*

hound
*hour 60 minutes
house d
how
how'd
howl ed

*our belonging to us

* *

hourglass es
hourly
housefly -ies
household
houseplant
housewife [housewives]
housework
housing

* * *

householder
housekeeper
housekeeping
houseparent
however

* * * *

In these words you can hear the vowel sound ou as in owl

J

*   * *   * * *   * * * *

joust
jowl

◁ *for dr . . .*
see page 278

L

*   * *   * * *   * * * *

***Laos** country   **louder**   **loudspeaker**
                   loudest
loud   **loudly**
lounge d   **lounging**
***louse** insect   **lousy** -ier, -iest
lout

M

*   * *   * * *   * * * *

mound   **miaow / meow**   **mountaineer**   **mountaineering**
mount   **mountainous**
mouse [mice]   **mountain**   **mountainside**
mouth   **mounted**   **mountaintop**
mouthed   **mousy** -ier, -iest
                  mouthful
                  mouthing
                  mouthpiece

In these words you can hear the vowel sound **ou** as in **owl**

N

*	**	***	****
noun		nowadays	
now			

O

*	**	***	****
*hour 60 minutes	hourglass es	outbidden	

ounce	ourselves	outbidding
*our belonging to	outbid	outgoing
us	[outbid]	outlining
ours	[outbidden]	outlying
out	outboard	outnumber ed
	outbox es	outpatient
owl	outbreak	outrageous
	outburst	outshining
	outcome	outsider
	outcrop	outspoken
	outcry -ies	outstanding
	outdo	outwardly
	[outdid]	outwitted
	[outdone]	outwitting
	outdoor	
	outdoors	
	outer	
	outfit	
	outflow	
	outgrow	
	[outgrew]	
	[outgrown]	
	outing	
	outlaw ed	
	outlay	
	outlet	
	outline d	
	outlook	
	outpost	
	output	
	outrage d	
	outright	
	outrun	
	[outran]	
	[outrun]	
	outset	
	outshine	
	[outshone]	
	outside	
	outskirts	
	outstretch ed	
	outward	
	outwit ted	
	outwith	

for H . . .
see page 279

In these words you can hear the vowel sound ou as in owl

281

P

*

plough ed

pouch es
pouched
pounce d
pound
pout
power ed

proud
prow
prowl ed

* *

ploughman
[ploughmen]
ploughshare

pouncing
powder ed
power ed
powerful ly
powerless

profound
pronounce d
proudly
prowess

* * *

powerful ly
powerless

pronouncement
pronouncing

* * * *

powerfully

R

*

round
***rouse** d   awaken /
become more active
rout
row
***rows**   quarrels

* *

rebound
recount
renown ed

rounded
rounders
rounding
roundup
rousing
router
rowdy -ier, -iest

* * *

roundabout

* * * *

In these words you can hear the vowel sound ou as in owl

S

*

scour ed
scout
scowl ed
scrounge d

shout
shower ed
shroud

slouch es
slouched

snout

sound
sour ed
south
sow

spouse
spout
sprout

stout

* *

Saudi
sauerkraut

scoundrel
scourer
scouring
scrounging

shouted
shouting
shower ed
showery

sounded
sounder
sounding
soundly
soundproof ed
soundtrack
sourdough
southbound
south-east
southward /
southwards
south-west

surmount
surround

* * *

showery

south-eastern
southwester /
sou'wester
south-western

surrounded
surrounding
surroundings

* * * *

T

*

thou

tout
towel led
tower ed
town

trounce d
trout
trowel led

* *

thousand
thousandth

tousle d
towel led
towelling
tower ed
towering
townhouse
township

trauma s [traumata]
trouncing
trousers
trowel led
trowelling

* * *

towelling
towering

traumata
traumatic
trowelling

* * * *

In these words you can hear the vowel sound **ou** as in owl **283**

V

*

vouch es
vouched
vow ed
vowel

* *

voucher
***vouchers** more than
 one voucher
***vouches** does vouch
vowel

* * *

* * * *

W

*

wound
wow

* *

* * *

* * * *

Y

*

yowl ed

* *

yowling

* * *

* * * *

In these words you can hear the vowel sound ou as in owl

Developing the ACE dictionary

The need for a new approach

There is justifiable concern about standards of reading and writing throughout the English-speaking world. Careful researchers such as Thorstad (1991), Upward (1992) and Spencer (2001, 2007) have repeatedly shown that the nature of English spelling is one of the reasons why children and young people in European countries with regular spelling systems perform much better than those in the United Kingdom. Both word recognition (especially for longer words) and spelling are affected. Moreover, Italian children can usually spell any word they can read, but British children can typically spell fewer than half of the words they can decode.

My own research (Moseley, 1996) has demonstrated that poor spellers will often use a restricted vocabulary in their writing, preferring short words that have one letter representing one sound, avoiding common words that are hard to spell and trying to play safe by repeating familiar words. Writing tasks are not enjoyed by many pupils and may become limited in quantity, range and frequency.

No amount of studying spelling patterns and learning spellings will do much to improve the situation if daily opportunities for meaningful writing are not provided across the curriculum. At the same time, there must be modelling, shared learning, encouragement and feedback regarding all aspects of writing, including spelling.

Beech (2004) found that 8-year-olds and 10-year-olds reported using a dictionary only once a week on average. He noted that such infrequent use would bring little benefit, but also showed that about a third of the children were slow and inaccurate. The younger children were much more likely to use a dictionary to check spellings than to find meanings and there was a strong relationship between speed of locating words, word recognition and spelling ability.

All this points to the need for a reference source that is quick and easy to access, structured to draw attention to spelling patterns, and rewarding to use whenever writing is undertaken. Shenton (2007) saw the ACE dictionary as addressing the user-unfriendly paradox that 'in order to access information within a source, the user must often apply knowledge that he or she does not yet possess'.

With a conventional dictionary children often do not possess the knowledge required to find the right page, let alone to find a specific word. The ACE Dictionary's Index was designed to direct the user to the right page, and finding the right word makes use of skills that even beginner readers possess. If the word is unfamiliar it is located by using both *analytic and synthetic phonics*, the reversible processes so strongly advocated in *Letters and Sounds* (DES, 2007).

For the field trials throughout the UK and in Ireland, a hundred copies of a pre-publication ACE dictionary were produced. It was important to demonstrate that all users could cope with the ACE page format and would not be put off by the number of words provided. Improvement suggestions were acted on for the first edition in 1985, including those concerning regional differences in pronunciation.

As a part of the field trials an A4 class set was provided to a Year 1 class in Whitley Bay as well as a half-size A5 version. The class coped very well with both versions and even sent a specially composed acrostic to the author. Timed trials showed that they were faster in finding words with the A5 version, indicating that small print presents no problems when scanning down columns.

How the words were chosen

Both British and American sources have been used in compiling the *ACE Spelling Dictionary*. Many words have been added in response to suggestions from users of the dictionary and this feedback process continues.

One major vocabulary source was the *American Heritage Word Frequency Book* (Carroll *et al*, 1971). This contains no fewer than 86,741 word types (words and word forms) from books used in schools by children in the age range 8 to 14. The complete range of school subjects was covered. Unless they were judged to be unfamiliar to British users, all words (but not all word forms) in the first 23,000 word types of the American heritage list were included in the *ACE Spelling Dictionary*.

In order to meet the needs of British students, lists supplied by subject teachers for all areas of the curriculum have been included, as has the subject-specific vocabulary from National Curriculum documents. Particular care has been taken to cover scientific, technical, mathematical and ICT vocabulary. The *Evans Technical Dictionary* (1982) and a list of mathematical terms published by the Scottish Qualifications Authority (2000) are among the sources used.

For the third edition, more than 3000 words were taken from the British National Corpus, from collections of children's writing at www.kidpub.com, from frequency counts of newspaper articles published on the internet and from various lists of new words added to well-known dictionaries.

A list of the major vocabulary sources is given at the end of the book.

Action research with ACE

A survey of research on ways of improving spelling (Moseley, 1994) suggests that those which combine a variety of powerful features are the most successful. It is also important to see spelling as an integral part of writing. Work by the author in which a weekly piece of creative writing was produced at home with the help of the *ACE Spelling Dictionary* showed that dyslexic learners could make very rapid progress in only five weeks when provided with individual targets and feedback. A similar approach was taken by Hancock (1992), working with a mixed-ability group of Year 6 children. The children used the ACE dictionary for checking their work and also chose six words to learn per week. Hancock reported an improvement in the overall quality of written work (as judged 'blind' by an independent evaluator), a 50 per cent reduction in spelling error rate and an improvement in written vocabulary. One boy with a spelling problem and a negative attitude towards spelling 'was extremely enthusiastic to succeed ... and ... his small and frequent achievements ... did much to boost his confidence and self-esteem'.

In an earlier classroom study (Moseley, 1989) it was those with weak spelling and reading who made the most progress. The pupils used the *ACE Spelling Dictionary* to proofread all written work, while the teacher was able to use one-to-one conferencing time for discussion of the content and structure of the writing. Spelling improved at an average rate of 1.7 months per month, while the seven poorest spellers progressed at more than twice this speed. These gains were accompanied by significant improvements in the quantity and quality of writing as well as rapid improvement in word recognition.

ACE Spelling Activities (Moseley and Singleton, 1993) grew out of earlier work with dyslexics in which learning activities were linked with the ACE Dictionary. Moseley (1994) reported that in classroom trials in which the learning strategies included at the end of the ACE dictionary were used, sixty-five pupils aged 8–11 improved in their spelling by nineteen months in only five months. The intervention was based on the daily learning at home of four to six words from the graded spelling lists provided. Both verbal and visual strategies proved effective, but two very important components were pronouncing the words in a different way, according to the spelling; and saying the letter names before writing each letter string.

One teacher and her pupils wrote to the author about her imaginative use of dictation passages, followed by an ACE checking activity limited to ten words. The pupils wrote with evident confidence and enjoyment, saying that 'over thirty children have bought their own dictionaries'. One reassured the author about the use of the 'smooth newt' sound clue by saying, 'My friend and I found a newt we brought it bake and built an aquarium for the newt, its a female. At the moment its hibernating.'

It is hoped that the *ACE Spelling Dictionary* will continue to encourage teachers and helpers to devise new ways of using it to suit all pupils, with individual strengths and weaknesses and with different approaches to learning.

How to look, listen and learn with ACE

Looking up words in order to spell them correctly is only one way of using the *ACE Spelling Dictionary*. Other ways of using it can be just as valuable and can help to increase your speed of word recognition as well as your knowledge about words. You can do this by timing yourself as you look for words of a certain type. You might like to work with someone and take turns in looking up words. The words can be chosen by topic, by use, by length, by stress pattern, by sound, by features of spelling or by grammatical function. It can also be fun to think of combinations of these – for example, to find as many long words as possible that can be used to express enjoyment of food, grouping them according to the stressed syllable.

Some of the activities at the end of this book demonstrate specific ways of using the dictionary. Many more ideas for actively exploring it will be thought of by those who use it. What is provided here is a detailed account of some of the rules that have been followed, especially those that relate to alphabetical order and to the inclusion of different forms of the same word. You do not need to understand all of these before you start to use the dictionary, but you may need to refer to them at times and they may suggest some useful activities.

Alphabetical grouping of words

Within each section words are grouped by initial letter, taken in alphabetical order. A letter is omitted if there are no words beginning with it in that particular section.

Within each column of words there are smaller sets, each beginning with the same two letters. This makes the columns easier to scan, and cuts down search time. It does not take long to learn that 'sc' is near the top of a set of words beginning with 'S', that 'sm' is about halfway through and that 'sw' is near the end.

Some words are entered in more than one place. This happens when the first sound in the word does not uniquely determine what the first letter is. For example, words beginning with a silent letter (like 'knife' and 'gnome') are entered under 'N' according to the initial sound as well as under the appropriate silent letter. Words like 'ceiling' and 'chassis' are entered under both 'S' and 'C'. Words like 'kangaroo' and 'karate' are entered under 'C' and under 'K'. Lighter print is used for double-entered words when they begin with a different letter from the rest of the words in a column.

In certain cases, cross-reference pointers are used instead of double or multiple entries. A cross-reference is always provided from 'K' to 'C' within the same section, instead of repeating a long list of 'C' words under 'K'. Dropped 'h's, confusion between initial 'e' and 'i' and between 'f' and 'th' as well as uncertainty about the spelling of words beginning with 'qu' are also taken care of by the use of cross-reference pointers.

Meanings

In cases where two words sound the same (or nearly the same) but have different meanings, you need to check that you have found the right word. All such words have an asterisk (*) against them and their meanings are given alongside. These words are called homonyms (words with the same sound but with different meanings). Some of them are also homographs (words with the same spelling but with different meanings).

If the meaning or meanings do not fit the word you are looking for, all you have to do is to try another similar-sounding word with an asterisk against it. That will be in the section you are looking at, but sometimes at the top or bottom of the list.

Plurals

If the plural form of a noun is not shown, it is safe to assume that you simply add an 's'. So, if you find 'journey', you will be able to spell 'journeys'.

All 'es' and '-ies' plurals are shown; for example 'box es' and 'baby -ies'. Where, as in 'baby -ies', there is a dash before the ending, part of the word has to be removed before the plural ending is added. The most common pattern is for a final 'y' to be removed before adding '-ies'. Plurals of Latin or Greek words and any unusual plurals such as 'calves' are printed in square brackets; for example, [criteria], [phenomena] and [calves].

Present participles

These are given for the more common words and in all cases where a final consonant is doubled before 'ing' is added (e.g. 'swim' and 'swimming').

When the present participle form (ending in 'ing') is not given, you can be sure that the spelling falls into one of two patterns:

a) for words not ending in 'e', add 'ing'
b) for words ending in 'e', remove the 'e' before adding 'ing'.

Past tenses

The past tense form is given for the more common words and whenever a final consonant is doubled before 'ed' is added (e.g. 'skid' and 'skidded').

In all words where the final 'ed' has the sound 't' (as in 'ticked') the past tense marker is given alongside: 'tick ed'. The past tense marker is also given for long vowel words ending in 'e': 'phone d'.

All irregular past tense forms are given in full. They are entered in the appropriate sections, but are also included, printed in square brackets, immediately below the corresponding present tense form. Two examples are the following:

bring   **buy**
[brought]   [bought]

Comparatives and superlatives

These are given in full for the more common words and whenever a final consonant is doubled (as in 'bigger' and 'biggest'). Where a final 'y' is changed to '-ier' or to '-iest' this is also always shown (e.g. 'saucy -ier, -iest'). If you cannot find a particular word with the ending 'er' or 'est', you can be sure that the spelling falls into one of the two following patterns:

a) for words not ending in 'e', add 'er' or 'est'
b) for words ending in 'e', remove the 'e' before adding 'er' or 'est'.

Dialects

The vowel sound sections are based on 'received' pronunciation (RP), but regional accents have been provided for. Trials were carried out throughout the British Isles, and wherever major shifts in the pronunciation of vowels required it, words were entered in more than one section. Wherever a dash appears in front of a word it means that for some speakers that word is pronounced with the same vowel sound as the other words in the section.

In the /a/ section words pronounced in RP with an /ar/ sound have a dash in front of them. These words are pronounced with an /a/ in Scotland, and in most cases in the north of England. In the /o/ section the words with a dash in front of them belong there only for Scottish speakers. In the short vowel /u/ and /oo/ section, two RP sounds have been put together, with a dash before the /oo/ sound words. In the north of England there may be no difference in pronunciation between the two groups. In the section containing words with the long /oo/ sound, the words with a dash before them belong there only for Scots. In parts of the Midlands and in Merseyside the sounds /air/ and /er/ are pronounced in the same way. The /air/ words are therefore entered in the /er/ section as well, a feature which also makes sense for some of the words as pronounced in Scotland.

A major feature of Scottish speech is the rolled **r** following a vowel. The RP /ar/, /air/, /er/ and /or/ sounds are therefore pronounced differently in Scotland. There are cross-reference pointers in the appropriate ACE sections, but these will not be needed if Scots always refer to the third part of the dictionary for words with vowels followed by an 'r'. This applies to all of the short vowels, and for the long vowels /ae/ and /oe/. It does not, however, apply to the long vowels /ee/, /ie/ and /ue/.

The following table is provided for the benefit of Scottish users:

Words with	Section	Examples
SHORT /a/ followed by 'r'	/ar/	shark, article
SHORT /e/ followed by 'r'	/er/	early, nervous
SHORT /i/ followed by 'r'	/er/	bird, firmly
SHORT /o/ followed by 'r'	/or/	horse, warning
SHORT /u/ followed by 'r'	/er/	hurt, worm
LONG /ae/ followed by 'r'	/air/	rare, airport
LONG /ee/ followed by 'r'	/ee/	clear, steer
LONG /ie/ followed by 'r'	/ie/	wire, tyre
LONG /oe/ followed by 'r'	/or/	hoarse, bored
LONG /ue//oo/ followed by 'r'	/ue//oo/	pure, poor

Strategies for improving spelling

Dealing with difficult and much-needed words

The following activities and strategies are suitable for use either by students working on their own – maybe with a helper – or in a classroom context. The techniques used in the activities can also be applied to other difficult words. Both content and techniques can be personalised.

We provide two spelling banks: 60 common tricky words and 660 other high frequency words used by young writers. The sixty common tricky words account for about 30 per cent of all misspellings made by children in Years 3–6 (Moseley, 1997). It is especially important that these are correctly written from the outset so that misspellings do not have to be unlearned. For this reason a reference card is recommended, to be used both while writing and when proofreading.

Three additional lists of frequently used words are provided for the regular study and learning of spellings. While the word list in *Letters and Sounds* (DES, 2007) is based on the vocabulary of reading schemes (Masterson *et al.*, 2003), these three lists are derived from combined samples of the words that children use. Taken together, the two ACE spelling banks account for between 40 per cent and 60 per cent of the words found in children's writing at ages 9–11.

Words you need to know

Some of the words you need to use a lot are not easy to spell. Once you can cope with those you will feel much more confident about spelling. To save you the trouble of looking up these words every time you need them, here is a *Master list of tricky words*. You will know some of these already, so the first thing to do is to shorten the list to the ones you really need.

Master list of tricky words

an	of	all	it's	off
saw	too	two	was	a lot
came	come	hour	into	kept
knew	know	said	then	they
want	went	were	when	again
could	heard	might	right	still
that's	their	there	tried	until
where	always	bought	caught	friend
houses	inside	myself	opened	people
played	police	school	turned	another
decided	outside	running	started	stopped
thought	through	because	suddenly	sometimes

What to do

1 Put a tick next to each word in the list that you know very well (or take a test, twenty at a time).

2 Get a piece of card that will fit into your *ACE Spelling Dictionary* or your jotter.

3 Copy out your own list of tricky words, in two columns. Leave a space or draw a box beside each word so you can write tally marks to show how many times you have recognised it. You can add some words of your own if you want to.

4 Ask a helper who is good at spelling to check your card when it is ready for use.

5 Get to know your tricky words. Take four words at a time and make up some sentences which include them. Write out your sentences. When you get to a tricky word, find it on your card so you spell it correctly. Take a good look and spell out the letters before and as you write. When you have finished, proofread all your sentences, using the Master list and the *ACE Spelling Dictionary*.

6 Get your card out every time you do some writing. Whenever a tricky word comes along, check it on your card before you write it down. Every time you do this, put a tally mark next to the word. You can cross off tricky words when you no longer need to check them on your card, but you should not do that until you have at least ten tally marks against a word.

7 Use your card to proofread work produced by you or by other writers.

8 Make a new card about every three months until you have narrowed down your list of tricky words to one or two. Eventually you will have no words at all on your list.

9 Try to learn your tricky words four at a time, always using letter names and at least one other method such as a memory aid (see pp. 295–296 for other effective methods).

Memory aids for tricky words

	LONG MEMORY AID	SHORT MEMORY AID
a lot	'A lot' is not one word.	two words (1) + (3)
again	Two wins: a gain and a gain **again**.	that pain **again**!
all	Ball, call, fall, hall, tall, wall – they **all** have 'all'.	We **all fall** down!
always	This is **always** one word with one 'l', all the time.	al(l) …
an	An egg, an anything beginning with **A E I O U**.	an A- an E- an I- an O- an U-
another	**A N O**ther was dropped from the team.	one word (2 + 5 = 7)
because	Big elephants can always understand small elephants.	be (2) + cause (5) = 7
bought	Beware of untamed great hungry tigers!	_ ough _
came	We **came** to have a game (magic E).	came (magic E)
caught	Her naughty daughter caught a cold.	caught: did catch
come	Come home and have some tea.	Come home for tea!
could	**Could/should/would** Old uncles love dancing?	I would if I could.
decided	The CID decided not to take sides.	decide on a decider
friend	Friday and at the weekend I'll see my friends.	fri-end
heard	Did hear, by ear.	_ ear _
hour	Our train leaves in an **hour** (60 minutes).	How long? An hour.
houses	How do you spell **houses**? There's no W and no Z!	a h ou se for sale
inside	You can hide **inside** or outside.	one word (2 + 4 = 6)
into	Run **into** the room and jump onto the chair.	one word (2 + 2 = 4)
it's	**It's** short for 'it is' and the ' stands for the letter **I**.	it is
kept	We **kept** on thinking about 11 **Sept**.	The keeper **kept** goal.
knew	(silent **K**) – understood?	k-n as in 'knobbly knee'
know	(silent **K**) – understand?	k-n as in 'knobbly knee'
might	I **might** get it right!	_igh_
myself	myself yourself himself herself	one word (2 + 4 = 6)
of	'O-F' is a one-off – one **of** a kind.	Of sounds like ov.
off	On and off, **off** is confused with **of**.	one F is not on
opened	The **ED** ending is needed in opened and closed.	open (4) + ed (2) = 6
outside	You can hide inside or **outside**.	one word (3 + 4 = 7)
people	People eat omelettes: people love eggs.	popular pe o ple
played	Yesterday I played with words ending in **ED**.	pl ay ed
police	Be nice and polite to the police.	Police notice: ICE!
right	I go home by going first left and then **right**.	I might get it r igh t.
running	Doubled consonant before **ING** in words like running.	run, running
said	A-I makes an /e/ sound in said, again and against.	A one-off (AI) again.

saw	I saw that **was** is **saw** spelt backwards.	See what I **saw** – a seesaw!
school	School is where you learn cool spellings.	sch (3) + ool (3) = 6
sometimes	**Sometimes** is one word for more than one time.	one word (4 + 5 = 9)
started	We start with **ST** and finish with **ED** (7 letters).	start (5) + ed (2) = 7
still	Many words end with **LL** after a short vowel.	Is Bill still ill?
stopped	Doubled consonant before **ED** in words like stop**p**ed.	stop, stopped
suddenly	I suddenly forgot the middle part of sud **den** ly.	sudden (6) + ly (2) = 8
that's	**That's** short for 'that is' and the ' stands for the letter i.	That's short for 'that is'.
their	The dog we own is ours, not yours; **their** dog is theirs.	There is **their** heir!
then	But **then**, **the** walls of our **den** are very thin!	**Then** and then and then.
there	There → to or in that place. There is/are/was/were/etc.	**There** is their heir!
they	The tricky bit may well be the **EY**.	They did not obey.
thought	We th**ought** of un**tam**ed **great hungry tigers**!	O U Great Hungry Tiger!
through	It's a **rough** path, but we **ought** to get **through**.	Through a tough exam.
too	**Too** many o's to put in a two-letter word.	My toe is **too** big **too**.
tried	Try to learn this pattern: no **Y**, but **I** + **ED** in **tried**.	I try, she tries, he tried.
turned	U R able to add **ED** to **turn**.	turn (4) + ed (2) = 6
until	One **l** as in **nil**: unlike fill, hill, kill, pill, till, will.	_ _ til
want	After a /w/ sound you often want **A** instead of **O**.	What do you want?
was	**Wasn't Annie stunning?**	'Was' has an **A** and an **S**.
went	**Twenty** of us **went** into the big tent.	WE NT: we **went** in.
were	Why is w**ere** spelt like wh**ere**?	were: in the past
when	**Wh**en do question words start with **WH-**?	**When** they start with **W**.
where	**Where** were you when I took your place? Here.	Where? Here.

More much-needed words

Learn to spell these words so that you get them right when you write.

Lists 1, 2 and 3 (pp. 302–304), each containing 220 useful words, have been prepared from samples of children's speech and writing. Short regular words in which letter errors rarely occur are not included in the three lists. These spelling bank lists are graded, but do not include the sixty common words that are most often misspelt. Those are in the *Master list of tricky words* on page 293 and are best learned by using a reference card in the course of writing, as explained.

Using the lists at home

If you are using the lists to work on your spelling at home, the first thing to do is plan your own programme. Consult your T/H about this. You will need to have realistic targets that enable you to make steady progress without having too much to do. A lot will depend on how quickly you need to achieve results, and you should bear in mind any other activities you are committed to on a regular basis.

You will also need to find out which words you should concentrate on. It is not intended that you should always start with List 1. Use the test that follows to decide where to start.

Using the lists in school (for the T/H)

If these lists are used in school, one could be covered in one term, at the rate of twenty words a week. That allows for some repeated learning of words misspelt in weekly tests. Lists 1, 2 and 3 are suitable for NC Levels 2, 3 and 4–5 respectively, and for Scottish Levels A, B and C. Those who need an accelerated spelling programme can work on the lists for a whole year.

Note that it is not intended that the same list should be given to all members of a class. The following test can be used to decide which list should be used by which students.

Spelling test

Your T/H says each word, repeats it in a phrase or sentence, pauses briefly and then says the word again. You should not write it down until you hear it for the third time.

1 SHIP ... The passengers boarded the ship ... SHIP

2 FOOTBALL ... My football strip ... FOOTBALL

3 READING ... What are you reading? ... READING

4 TELL ... Tell me a story ... TELL

5 SEVEN ... Seven puppies in a basket ... SEVEN

6 SPOKE ... I spoke slowly to Gran on the phone ... SPOKE

7 SLOWLY ... We walked very slowly ... SLOWLY

8 NEAR ... We live near the park ... NEAR

9 PERSON ... Who is that person crossing the road? ... PERSON

10 ANYTHING ... Have you anything to report? ... ANYTHING

11 PRETTY ... The garden was looking very pretty ... PRETTY

12 BEFORE ... Tidy your room before you go out ... BEFORE

13 OWNER ... Who is the owner of this car? ... OWNER

14 MUSIC ... I listen to music on my MP3 player ... MUSIC

15 HAPPENED ... What happened in the playground? ... HAPPENED

16 FOLLOWED ... The stray dog followed me ... FOLLOWED

17 SUGAR ... Sugar in your tea ... SUGAR

18 MOUNTAIN ... The top of the mountain ... MOUNTAIN

19 USUAL ... I woke up at seven, as usual ... USUAL

20 INTERESTING ... An interesting story ... INTERESTING

When you have written down all the words, your T/H should check them. From your score, find out which list of words is right for you.

Score 0–4: Work with List 1: average word length 4 letters.
Score 5–14: Work with List 2: average word length 5 letters.
Score 15–20: Work with List 3: average word length 6 letters.

The 220 words in each list have been grouped into subsets of four words, on the basis of a topic or language pattern. There are five word sets across the page, which is normally enough for a week's work. Nouns, verbs, adjectives and adverbs have been grouped together, with some miscellaneous sets at the end. This has been done to help you to think of meaningful links between words and to use the words in sentences.

Note that words with an asterisk (*) against them may need special attention. These are ones for which it is hard or impossible to find a rhyming word with the same spelling pattern. You may be able to think of a non-rhyming word with the same letter string (e.g. watch/match) or find some other way of remembering the letters.

The word subsets are not arranged in order of difficulty.

Individual personalised lists

You can follow your own individual programme, so that you do not study words that you can already spell. You may like to begin with the shorter words in each list.

You will need to set your own target of how many words to learn over a certain period. Here are some suggestions for how a programme of learning could be drawn up. Adapt them to suit your situation. Remember to ask your T/H for advice about this.

Every fortnight choose 20, 40 or 60 words to learn from one of the lists, aiming to master at least 100, 200 or 300 words in a 12-week term. Underline the words and then write them down in sets of 4. If possible, there should be some meaningful link between the words in a set as this makes the words and their spellings easier to remember. You can choose words that will fit into the same sentence, that are linked by topic or that have the same spelling pattern. If you cannot find enough words you need to learn in the list, words may be taken from other sources.

With individually chosen lists, appropriate individual tests are needed. These are best organised by using a helper or helpers. In class, you and another student may test each other in turn.

Another kind of individual list, for use in correcting drafts (NC Level 3, Scottish level C and above) is described on pages 300–301.

How to learn

If you look at words in a list and get your T/H to test you, you may find you do not remember the spellings very well. A more active approach will lead to better results. You should Study – Copy – Check – Highlight and then Learn.

Study – spell the word aloud using helpful groups of letter strings
Copy – you are only allowed one glance per syllable
Check – letter by letter or in strings of up to four letters
Highlight – mark the tricky parts you need to remember
Learn – by one or more of the methods below.

Try the different methods of learning suggested below and decide which works best for you.

a) Pronounce the words in a different way, according to the spelling.

b) Trace over or write the word, saying the letter names before you write each letter string.

c) Shut your eyes and say or spell the word as you 'write' it in large letters with your finger.

d) With eyes shut see the word in your mind, count the letters in groups and then check.

e) Study the word so well that you can spell it backwards.

f) Study the word, say a tongue-twister or count to 10, then spell the word.

g) Think of a memory link or mnemonic for the whole word or just for the tricky part (e.g. On **Fri**day and at the week**end** I'll see my friends. **Find** really **in**teresting **fri**ends.).

h) IF there is a suffix, look for a common pattern such as an -es plural, an -ed tense ending, consonant doubling or y changing to -ies or -ied.

i) Use the *ACE Spelling Dictionary* to find a word that rhymes with the one you are learning and is spelt in the same way; think of a rhyme and then check the spelling, or simply look through the one- and two-syllable columns in a single vowel section. Remember that words in the lists that are marked * do not have suitable rhymes.

j) Find another word you already know that has the same spelling pattern (e.g. ton**gue**, ar**gue**).

k) Learn the tricky part (or parts) first, before trying the whole word.

Repeat – say, write and spell really rapidly, like a r-a-pp-e-r

Test – look, say, cover, write, check.

At the end of a learning session, write down a sentence containing the words you have studied. This should help you to spell those words correctly later on when you are writing.

Daily routine

Every day you will study two, four or six words from your list (or a different number, depending on your own programme). It is helpful if the words are related in some way. Enter the date and the words to be learned in a jotter.

<u>Steps to success</u>

1st word – learn (using chosen method)
self-test – look – say – cover – write – check

2nd word – learn
self-test – look – say – cover – write – check
double-check – look at both words – say – cover – write – check
Continue if both words are correct; otherwise practise and try again.

3rd word – learn
self-test – look – say – cover – write – check

4th word – learn
self-test – look – say – cover – write – check
double-check – look at both words – say – cover – write – check
Continue if both words are correct; otherwise practise and try again.

Final test – all four words should be written correctly when dictated in a random order

If you do not pass the final test, you should try to learn the words again, perhaps by a different method. On the other hand it may be better to reduce the number of words.

When you succeed in the final test, your T/H should initial the list in your jotter and record the learning method(s) you used (from the a) to k) list).

If you find it easy to learn the number of words you study each day, you might like to increase the number by one or two.

Note that if you are trying to learn six words you can double-check with groups of two or three words.

Weekly test

Once a week a test session should be held. In class this can be set up in pairs, so that each learner both gives and receives a test on the words chosen for that week. Words spelt correctly should be given a tick on their personal list. Those not spelt correctly should be studied again the following week. They should be spaced out over the week, not tackled on a single day along with the new words for that day.

Spelling correctly and correcting mistakes

If you use the STUDY – COPY – CHECK – HIGHLIGHT – LEARN approach, you will probably make fewer mistakes with words you have recently studied. You cannot expect that you will never again have to think about those words. Indeed, every time you realise that you have used a word that is on your list or seems to fit a familiar pattern, you score a success. All you have to do then is to check the spelling. If it is correct, that is excellent.

Good spellers are aware of common patterns between families of words. The more often you look up words in the *ACE Spelling Dictionary*, the more you will notice these patterns. Looking for word families based on Lists 1–3 will introduce you to thousands of words. Learning method i) (looking up rhyming words) is one of the best ways of 'getting to know' more word families. This method also encourages you to use a wider vocabulary when you write.

Most people miss spelling mistakes when they proofread a piece of work. You can improve in doing this if you make a personal alphabetical list of the words you want to learn from Lists 1, 2 and 3. It is sensible to include some interesting words from the same families and any hard-to-spell words you have previously attempted. If you arrange the list in syllable columns, as in the *ACE Spelling Dictionary*, it will be easier to scan. Read through the list before you check a draft; this will make it much more likely that you will recognise the words in the piece.

Your list might look like this:

*	**	*** (+)
aren't	against	ambulance
board	allow	arrival
break	answer	beautiful
brought	answered	disappeared
clothes	believe	February
course	buried	hospital
guard	curtain	idea
it's	harbour	investigate
knocked	haunted	parliament
let's	later	remembered
passed	people	suitable
past	present	unfortunately
piece	quickly	vegetables
race	really	
spare	swimming	
they're	themselves	
threw	without	
you're		

It is a good idea to check a draft at least three times, each time concentrating on a limited range of words. First, look for any words of three or more syllables that need to be checked. Then go through the passage again, looking for two-syllable words that might present problems. Finally, concentrate on one-syllable words, taking care not to skim over words such as 'its', 'they' and 'was'. These are so common that it is easy for your eye to pass over them without really noticing them.

The more often you identify and correct spelling mistakes, the better your spelling will become. You can give full attention to what you are writing if you know how to put things right.

List 1

father	*baby	dog	bus	money
dad	babies	hair	car	gold
mother	boy	way	road	bank
mum	girl	park	street	shop
look	ask	come	be	*are
looked	asked	*coming	been	will
find	call	came	*being	could
found	called	went	stay	couldn't
one	some	bad	*front	*his
*two	left	good	ready	*her
three	all	better	nice	our
four	more	best	happy	your
garden	door	tea	book	king
farm	room	water	story	queen
wood	window	time	bed	lady
sea	fire	things	night	man
go	*was	woke	see	catch
goes	*wasn't	help	saw	make
*going	would	told	*put	made
gone	wouldn't	sleep	seen	eat
black	big	next	my	away
blue	little	last	*this	around
red	new	long	that	back
white	old	round	other	home
*children	*morning	*Christmas	*woman	*people
sister	*afternoon	tree	teacher	name
brother	week	day	school	hand
*aunt	year	dinner	work	*eyes
do	*has	give	dance	*watch
don't	*have	gave	walk	*watching
did	*having	take	walking	start
didn't	had	took	walked	started
when	how	first	no	by
just	so	*once	yes	for
now	down	out	*very	with
then	here	over	well	without
giant	he	him	*who	please
*castle	she	himself	*someone	me
ghost	we	you	which	*that's
house	they	them	*something	much
play	named	like	upon	or
playing	think	married	about	but
played	say	live	*from	*because
fell	*said	*lived	after	while

List 2

*aeroplane
air
plane
*world

tell
spoke
shouted
hear

*these
those
any
many

wife
*husband
*person
*group

hope
hoped
hoping
getting

*young
*beautiful
*pretty
dear

*machine
wheel
hole
light

seemed
*imagine
guess
*understand

quickly
slowly
early
later

mountain
side
ice
winter

buy
wear
used
grown

*animals
bird
snake
*horse

listen
listened
*answer
*answered

high
*higher
smaller
short

*family
table
chair
*kitchen

pick
picked
pull
*pulled

whole
closed
past
seven

dragon
head
*heart
blood

die
died
jumped
killed

already
behind
ever
o'clock

piece
*picture
place
*village

before
why
whether
*whenever

present
balloon
*colour
*music

read
reading
mean
meant

*every
its
sure
true

*sugar
*breakfast
meat
*course

drop
dropped
break
*breaking

tired
*lonely
dark
*careful

ears
nose
mouth
*voice

sitting
waiting
*happen
*happened

*even
*also
*really
enough

*numbers
*nothing
*thousands
*difference

*I'd
*I'll
*I'm
*I've

*clothes
*body
*shoes
foot

point
write
writing
written

wide
*straight
near
real

boat
ship
shape
*owner

try
trying
cry
cried

dead
broken
dry
strange

*word
*idea
*notice
*language

meet
brought
passed
followed

nearly
*usually
*finally
together

few
half
*anyone
*anything

*you'd
*you'll
*you're
*you've

prince
princess
life
love

hold
*build
built
*covered

*usual
*different
*interesting
*coloured

*football
field
line
*corner

*finish
*finished
leave
fly

*nearby
*maybe
quite
alright

*radio
station
*minutes
*sentence

should
*does
*doesn't
done

onto
across
along
against

*no-one
*everyone
*everything
whose

*what
*what's
*let's
*themselves

List 3

mouse	*squirrel	creatures	fish	*chocolate
mice	goat	*butterfly	*rabbit	coffee
*puppy	*wolf	*dinosaur	*potato	flour
*puppies	*elephant	*monster	*potatoes	*apron
wash	*allow	swim	*arrived	threw
washing	*allowed	swimming	*offered	throw
washed	wished	rain	received	blew
dressed	*cannot	raining	grabbed	blow
*basket	lawn	shirt	*drawer	crash
*bowl	flowers	skirt	shelf	surprise
*board	patch	sheet	shelves	fright
brush	*vegetables	*curtain	stairs	*skeleton
fishing	believe	approach	lie	drag
float	*wondering	*recognised	lying	dragged
floated	*realised	remember	lay	*bury
drowned	*investigate	*remembered	laid	*buried
shock	*uncle	*February	*harbour	pony
*ambulance	*cousin	*months	beach	*ponies
*hospital	*grandfather	*holiday	*island	saddle
*oxygen	*neighbours	*Saturday	cave	stables
*climb	push	hopped	*whisper	*burst
tied	*pushed	hopping	*whispered	guard
falling	knocked	pretended	*whistle	*chase
slipped	smashed	hurt	screamed	*disappeared
pencil	*alphabet	*camera	*parliament	noise
*rubber	*calendar	*film	*palace	*policeman
*ruler	fractions	*submarine	*television	*uniform
*scissors	*graph	*magazine	*programme	*court
*dangerous	frightening	*favourite	*curious	lazy
*terrible	*poisonous	*orange	spare	dirty
massive	frightened	*purple	*quiet	*impossible
*enormous	scared	*visible	haunted	funny
*telephone	*visitor	*system	switch	flame
*message	*Germany	defence	*contact	volcano
rhyme	*London	*exhibition	*explosion	thunder
*tongue	*countries	*manager	bridge	*lightning
*motor	*excellent	*British	dining	*downstairs
racing	*wonderful	*Chinese	*hungry	*upstairs
tight	*fantastic	*Japanese	fried	*somewhere
*physical	*exciting	*Egyptian	*frozen	*everywhere
*bicycle	*hello	he'd	*aren't	*anyway
bike	*everybody	he'll	we'd	*somehow
race	*quietly	*he's	we'll	*anybody
track	*sixth	*they're	*we're	*somebody

Searching for patterns

The *ACE Spelling Dictionary* is an ideal resource for investigating aspects of language related to spelling and word recognition. Government strategy documents encourage the use of enquiry and investigation on the part of learners, recognising that we often remember what we have found out better than what we have been told.

A valuable analysis of spelling in GCSE English scripts is provided in *Improving Writing at Key Stages 3 and 4* (QCA, 1999). This draws attention to the persistence of homonym errors, phonetically plausible errors, omission of sounds and letters, problems with word endings and problems with word division. All of these areas can usefully be made the focus of an ACE investigation.

Here are some suggestions for investigating a range of spelling and other linguistic patterns, as well as exceptions to those patterns.

1 Spend five minutes looking for one-syllable words which have **es** added to the base word. Does this only happen after certain final consonant spellings?

2 Taking one vowel section at a time, count the vowel spellings in one or more columns and arrange them from the most to the least common.

3 **When you add ing to words ending with e, you knock off the e.** This does not apply if the ending is a double vowel (e.g. /ee/ as in 'see', /ie/ as in 'tie', /ue/ as in 'sue'). See how many words that fit this pattern you can find in ten minutes.

4 Find out what happens when you need the past tense form of long vowel words ending in **e**. The e is already there, so what is the consonant you add to the base word? This consonant can represent two different phonemes: what are they?

5 See how many three-syllable words you can find where a final **y** changes to **ie**. Group these under the endings: ies, ied and ier/iest. Spend ten minutes on this.

6 Take five minutes to find words of one and two syllables which have a plural ending in **ves** (e.g. 'loaves'). **Let's say it's safe to use the ves spelling if you hear the sounds /v/ /z/ at the end.**

7 **With words like 'wit'** (i.e. words having a single-letter short vowel and a single final consonant) **you double the final consonant when you add endings such as ed, ing, er, est, y, ier and iest.** That means you get: slow-witted, outwitting, witty, wittier, wittiest. See how many one-syllable words that fit this pattern you can find in ten minutes. Are there any exceptions?

8 **In a two-syllable word, double the final consonant only if the stress is on the last syllable,** so 'begin' + ing is 'beginning' but 'open' + ing is 'opening'). Find ten words like 'beginning' with doubled consonants and ten like 'opening' where the stress is on the first syllable.

9 Find ten words like 'itch' (one syllable, with a single-letter short vowel and **tch** right after the vowel). Find ten more one-syllable words with a letter between the short vowel and the /ch/ sound, such as: belch, inch, lunch.
Find twenty words ending in **ch** from any of the long vowel sections.
What pattern do you notice? Are there any exceptions apart from 'rich', 'much' and 'such'?
Can you explain in a simple way when to use **tch**?
Carry out similar searches in order to establish when to use **dge** rather than **ge** and when to use **ck** rather than **k**.

10 Think about the spelling 'rule': **i** before **e** except after **c**. What is the ratio of hits to misses if this rule is applied to words in the long vowel /ee/ section? Can the rule be improved?

11 How many words of four or more syllables in which the last syllable contains a neutral vowel sound can you find in five minutes?

12 Make a list of homonym pairs from the /or/ section where spelling confusion is likely.

13 Full of ... ? truthful → truthfully   helpful → helpfully   grateful → gratefully.
Find five more words listed in the *ACE Spelling Dictionary* that fit the **ful** → **fully** pattern.

14 Look for word roots, prefixes, suffixes and spelling patterns; e.g. sign, signature, signal; form, deform, inform, formal, information. This extends vocabulary and provides support for spelling.

15 Find homonym pairs both of which can function as nouns, adjectives or adverbs. Then find some homonyms in which the words have different grammatical functions.

All of the investigations suggested above can be modified to suit the needs of the individuals or groups and it will often be found that a new investigation can be devised to address a particular query or problem.

Photocopiable activity sheets that reinforce and extend many of the pattern activities in this section can be found in *ACE Spelling Activities* (Moseley and Singleton, 1993).

Meeting National Curriculum objectives

An extensive range of activities and games for developing phonic skills and recognising and spelling words with 'tricky' parts is provided in *Letters and Sounds* (DES, 2007).

Where focused intervention is needed, it should be based on careful assessment. The detailed assessment statements for the six phases of *Letters and Sounds* provide a well-structured general framework. The present author has developed a complementary diagnostic assessment tool, the *Word Recognition and Phonic Skills Test* (Moseley, 2008). This yields objective measures of key aspects of word recognition normally acquired up to the age of 9. It provides a reliable profile of the stage reached in word recognition, of knowledge of higher frequency, lower frequency, regular and irregular words, of consonant and vowel spellings and of the tendency to omit elements. The manual also includes suggestions for teaching based on individual profiles of strengths and weaknesses. These are designed to provide a firm foundation for further word-level work in reading and writing. The diagnostic information can also be used to inform the choice of pattern investigation activities using, for example, *Letters and Sounds* and the *ACE Spelling Dictionary*.

Using the *ACE Spelling Dictionary* will help you to:

- show awareness of rhyme and alliteration
- recognise rhythm in spoken words
- apply the skills of segmenting words into their constituent phonemes
- learn variously from simultaneous visual, auditory and kinaesthetic activities which are designed to secure essential phonic knowledge and skills
- recognise and use alternative ways of spelling the graphemes already taught
- learn which words take which spellings
- spell common words correctly
- read and spell less common alternative graphemes including trigraphs
- identify the constituent parts of two- and three-syllable words to support the application of phonic knowledge and skills
- use knowledge of common inflections in spelling, such as plurals and -ly, -er
- read and spell phonically decodable two-syllable and three-syllable words
- read high and medium frequency words independently and automatically
- spell with increasing accuracy and confidence, drawing on word recognition and knowledge of word structure, and spelling patterns, including common inflections and use of double letters
- increase knowledge of word families, roots, derivations, morphology and regular spelling patterns
- use independent spelling strategies
- identify misspelt words in own writing; keep individual spelling logs; learn to spell them
- apply knowledge of spelling skills and strategies with increasing independence

- review and revise spelling strategies for dealing with words in familiar and unfamiliar contexts, or when imaginative and ambitious choices are made, or under time or other constraints

- spell most words correctly including some complex polysyllabic words and unfamiliar words

- spell correctly throughout a substantial text including ambitious or complex polysyllabic words

- apply skills in editing and proofreading in a range of different texts and contexts, reviewing and revising writing as it progresses

- identify some of the ways in which spoken English varies in different regions and settings

- investigate spoken English from a range of regions and settings and explain how it varies.

It's easier to get into good spelling habits early on than to correct poor spelling later.

References

Beech, J.R. (2004) Using a dictionary: its influence on children's reading, spelling, and phonology. *Reading Psychology*, 25, 19–36.

Department for Education and Skills (2007) *Letters and Sounds: Principles and Practice of High Quality Phonics*. London, Department for Education and Skills.

Hancock, R. (1992) *An appraisal of the Aurally Coded English Spelling Dictionary*. BEd. project, University of Sunderland.

Masterson, J., M. Stuart, M. Dixon, and S. Lovejoy (2003) *Children's Printed Word Database*. Economic and Social Research Council project (R00023406). At: http://www.essex.ac.uk/psychology/cpwd/

Moseley, D.V. (1989) Utilisation d'un dictionnaire à codage oral pour l'orthographe et la reconnaissance des mots: une étude en milieu scolaire. *Glossa*, 14, 14–19.

Moseley, D.V. (1994) From theory to practice: errors and trials. In G.D.A. Brown, and N.C. Ellis, (eds.) *Handbook of Spelling: Theory, Process and Intervention*. London, Wiley.

Moseley, D.V. (1996) How poor spelling affects children's written expression. *Topic*, 16, Item 8. Slough, NFER, 1–6.

Moseley, D.V. (1997) The assessment of spelling and related aspects of written expression. In J. Beech and C. Singleton (eds.) *Psychological Assessment of Reading and Spelling*. London, Routledge.

Moseley, D. (2008) *Word Recognition and Phonic Skills Test* (WraPS 3). London, Hodder Education.

Moseley, D. and G. Singleton (1993) *ACE Spelling Activities*. Cambridge, LDA.

Primary National Strategy (2007) *Letters and Sounds* (pack). London, Department for Education and Skills.

Qualifications and Curriculum Authority (1999) *Improving Writing at Key Stages 3 and 4*. London, QCA.

Shenton, A.K. (2007) The paradoxical world of young people's information behaviour. *School Libraries Worldwide*, 13 (2), 1–17.

Spencer, K.A. (2001) Differential effects of orthographic transparency on dyslexia: word reading difficulty for common English words. *Dyslexia*, 7, 217–228.

Spencer, K.A. (2007) Predicting children's word-spelling difficulty for common English words from measures of orthographic transparency, phonemic and graphemic length and word frequency. *British Journal of Psychology*, 98, 305–338.

Thorstad, G. (1991) The effect of orthography on the acquisition of literacy skills. *British Journal of Psychology*, 82, 527–537.

Upward, C. (1992) Is traditionl english spelng mor dificlt than jermn? *Journal of Research in Reading*, 15, 82–94.

Major vocabulary sources

[author(s) unknown] (1982) *Evans Technical Dictionary*. London, Evans.

Carroll, J.B., P. Davies and B. Richman (1971) *The American Heritage Word Frequency Book*. Boston, Houghton Mifflin.

Leech, G., P. Rayson and A. Wilson (2001) *Word Frequencies in Written and Spoken English: based on the British National Corpus*. London, Longman.

Scottish Qualifications Authority (2000) *Standard Grade Arrangements in Mathematics*. Glasgow, Scottish Qualifications Authority.